Islam and The West: A Dialog

First Edition
1419 AH / 1998 CE

Islam and the West: A Dialog

Edited by

Imad-ad-Dean Ahmad

and

Ahmed Yousef

United Association for Studies and Research

American Muslim Foundation

ISLAMIC ROUNDTABLES #1

© Copyrights 1419 AH / 1998 AC
by United Association for Studies and Research (UASR)

ISBN 1-882669-17-7

Published jointly by:

United Association for Studies and Research (UASR)
P.O. Box 1210, Springfield, VA 22003-1210
Tel.: (703) 750-9011 Fax: (703) 750-9010
E-mail: uasr@aol.com

and the
American Muslim Foundation (AMF)
1212 New York Avenue, NW, Washington, DC 20005-6102
Tel.: (202) 789-2262 Fax: (202)789-2550
E-mail: amc@amermuslim.org
Website: http://www.amermuslim.org

Printed in the United States of America by International Graphics
10710 Tucker Street, Beltsville, Maryland 20705-2223 USA
Tel.: (301) 595-5999 Fax: (301) 595-5888 E-mail: igfx@aol.com

Acknowledgement

In addition to thanking all the participants, especially the presenters, the editors are pleased to express their gratitude to Ali R. Abuza'kuk for his production assistance, to Dr. Robert Crane, Dr. Anisa Abdelfattah and Ahmad AbulJobain for their assistance in proofreading, and to acknowledge the efforts of Intisar Rabb and the other transcribers. We are especially grateful to Abdurahman Alamoudi and the American Muslim Foundation for sponsoring the publication of this volume.

Contents

Forward

In the name of God, the Beneficent, the Merciful,

For more than ten years the United Association for Studies and Research (UASR) has tried to correct the imbalanced perception in the West of Islam and Islamic political movements, and to overcome the arrogance with which the discussion of Islamic politics and the Muslim right to self-governance in Muslim countries has been approached by Western policy-makers and popular Media. In fulfillment of this mission the UASR, under the direction of Dr. Ahmed Yousef, initiated the roundtable discussions that are the backdrop for the dialogs presented in this book.

UASR has hosted some of America's most important Western scholars, bringing them together with Muslim scholars, intellectuals, and activists. The result is this work. Though the effort has been humble and the discussions mostly congenial, relying on those Western and Muslim scholars whom we might call "moderates," the importance of the dialog is in its very existence. So important it is to us, that the American Muslim Foundation (AMF) has made it a labor of love to assist in its publication. The AMF was founded to serve the Muslim community by serving as a catalyst and resource for inter-organizational and cross-cultural cooperation.

With time, we hope that the most hard-core extremist fringe of Islamists and anti-Islamists will find themselves seated together at the UASR, engaged in discussions geared toward cooperation between the East and the West, and based on identified common interests, with recognition and respect for each others unique qualities and cultures. The dialog presented in this volume represents the groundwork for this coming epoch in East/West relations.

Abdurahman Alamoudi, President
The American Muslim Foundation,
Washington, D.C.
Safar, 1419 AH
June 1998 CE

Preface

In the name of God, the Beneficent, the Merciful,

For many years there has been a call from both Muslims and Westerners for a dialog between the two. Scholars like John Esposito have powerfully made the case that we need such a dialog, but until now little real dialog has taken place. Conferences too often consist of panels of Western experts on Islam and representatives of the establishment oof Muslim countries. No non-Muslims, however objective and open-minded, can replace the Islamic engagé in providing insight into the Islamic revival. Nor can any establishment Muslim, however sincere in faith, substitute for the critics of his establishment in explaining the Islamist cause.

The United Association for Studies and Research (UASR) series is remarkable in its truly roundtable format, which allows Muslim intellectuals and activists who identify themselves with the Islamic resurgence to speak to the Western experts on an equal level. This constitutes a dialog in the true sense. Such a format allows the experts to add a new dimension to their understanding while at the same time giving the Muslims a more intimate perspective on the problems of communication with the West and insights nto ow those problems may be overcome.

We desire that the benefits of these conversations extend beyond the room in which they were held and to provide a record to which all engaged in the study of the Islamic revival aand its political dimension may refer. We are pleased that UASR and the American Muslim Foundation (AMF) have undertaken the publication of the edited proceedings of these roundtables and grateful to the Minaret of Freedom Institute (MFI) for sponsoring the editorial costs. Our objective is to make the contents and the style of the roundtables available to policymakers, scholars, journalists, and the general public.

Having moderated all but two of the discussions presented in this volume, I am particularly pleased that this first volume in what shall, *in shâ Allah,* be a series, is devoted to an exchange of perspectives between Muslims—both American and from the Muslim world—and non-MuslimWesterners. (We plan to focus the next volume in the series on regional assessments of the Muslim world.) The fundamental problem confronted by the Islamic revival in the West is the failure of Muslims to articulate their desires, standards, and concepts to Westerners in a language they can understand. Conversely, too few Muslims have had the opportunity to hear the frank informed views of knowledgeable Western scholars in a setting comfortable to themselves. By engaging first-class Western experts on Islam in a direct dialog and publishing those results in a format at once accessible and scholarly, we open the door to a fruitful and constructive relationship between Muslims and Westerners in general.

The reader who explores these pages will walk away with the realization that neither the Muslim world nor the West is monolithic. Our presenters are all Americans, but they range from conservative to liberal, from diplomats to policymakers, from the academic community to the intelligence community and to the media. One presenter is an analyst from an institute situated at the U.S. Army War College while another is a fellow with the U.S. Institute for Peace. Muslim participants include an Islamic Salvation Front (FIS) parliamentarian, Muslim journalists, presidents of Islamic think tanks, and directors of Muslim advocacy groups. Most of the participants are both Muslims and Americans. Brief biographies of all the participants will be found in the list at the end of this volume.

The format for all discussions was the same: an opening presentation by the featured speaker followed by a frank discussion with the featured speaker at the hub. I served as moderator for all the discussions in this volume except for those featuring Robert Neumann (moderated by Osman Shinaishin) and Joyce Davis (moderated by Ahmad AbulJobain). The procedure for editing discussions for this volume was the same in all cases except one. The editors worked collaboratively with the presenters to revise the presenter's typescript or the transcripts of the formal presentations into a final typescript. The editors worked directly from the taped transcript to edit the main discussion. Wherever the final text selected for inclusion has not been reviewed by the quoted participants, we have used brackets and/or ellipsis marks to indicate all but minor changes. The goal was to make the text as readable as possible while remaining faithful to the style and sentiments of the participants.

The one exception to the above procedure is the roundtable with Stephen Pelletiere. Due to the presenter's affiliation with the intelligence community we agreed not to tape the discussion. Instead, the points he covered have been taken from his previously published text "A Theory of Fundamentalism: An Inquiry into the Origin and Development of the Movement," (Carlisle Barracks, PA: Strategic Studies Institute, 1995) which we have adapted and abridged to cover the subject of the roundtable. Since no transcript of the open discussion was possible, a series of comments and questions put to Dr. Pelletiere in writing along with his responses have been appended to the text here in the same format as the discussions which follow the other presentations.

Despite the range of perspectives covered in this volume, there are certain themes that keep returning as a subtext, occasionally emerging at the center of the discussions. Among them: the relationship of politics and religion; the positive and negatives aspects of the Enlightenment; the degree to which "Western" or "Islamic" values may actually be universal values; the multifarious definitions of democracy and how they conflict with each other; the fact that conflicts *within* the West or the Muslim world may actually be more significant than conflicts *between* them; the problems posed by the systemic tendency of politicians to sacrifice the long-term best interests of their people and country to short-term expediency; the suggestion that the real conflict in the future may be not between the Western and Islamic cultures but between secular culture and religious culture of whatever denomination. Not a few of these issues have significance beyond the scope of the immediate subject matter of Islam and the West. I believe that readers who carefully explore the dialog that follows will be well rewarded.

The present format is one of frank, direct, face-to-face dialog among participants with both a wide range of views and a solid knowledge of the subject matter. We believe this format brings out the distinctions and shadings of thought within both the Western and the Muslim camps more clearly and reliably than can be found in any previous single volume. We want Westerners to understand the Islamic movement and Muslims to understand the West. We also want the inclusion of American Muslims in the discussion to be a reminder of the intersection of the two cultures. If we have succeeded even partially in these goals, all praise belongs to God. If we have fallen short, the responsibility is ours. We ask God to judge us by our intentions and forgive us our faults.

Imad-ad-Dean Ahmad

Minaret of Freedom Institute

Bethesda, Maryland

May, 1998

Introduction

Islam vs. the West:
an Illusory Collision Course

Islam officially interacted with Christianity for the first time in the 7th century. The prophet Muhammad directed his disciples to the Negus of Abyssinia, where they sought refuge from Mecca's pagan despots. More than a millennium later, in an ironic twist of fate, Muslims again flee from tyranny to the West. Yet much has happened in between. Muhammad's certainty that his followers would be safe in foreign lands is not shared by modern-day Islamists.

The root of their suspicions goes back to the Crusades; yet contemporary cynicism is borne of more recent times. As the Ottoman Empire began its slump into disintegration, Europe's Industrial Revolution was underway. Western influences began encroaching on the Muslim world, sparking renewed civilizational debate. During the 18th and 19th centuries, the absence of mass media precluded diffusion of such discourse outside intellectual circles. Colonial expansion, however, ensued, enraging regional peoples and reawakening their Islamic identities. The mosque, as much as the pen, now expressed the citizenry's disaffection.

Islamists became vocal detractors of Western hegemony by the 1920s, spurred on by France and Britain's brazen division of Middle Eastern states as part of their war booty. They charged the West with political iniquity and moral bankruptcy. Muslim intellectuals initially concentrated on the latter, though a number of them equally defended Western progressiveness. Over subsequent decades, those to whom the public turned were the critics: Muhammad Iqbal, Abul a'ala al-Mawdudi, Malik Bennabi, Ali Shariati, Muhammad Qutb, and Sayyid Qutb.

The advent of Marxism, and its proliferation in the Third World, concerned such figures the most. Communism, and its ardently atheist philosophy, is anathema to Muslim culture; and Islamists viewed it as an ideological invasion. In fact, it posed a greater threat to the Muslim world than other forms of Westernization. Initially, Islamists begrudgingly joined forces with the socialist camp; for example, the Muslim Brotherhood with Gamal Abel Nasser in Egypt and their equivalent with the National Liberation Front (FLN) in Algeria. Yet once the Arabs routed the colonialists, secular nationalists embarked on a purging campaign. Islamists fled to countries that had no Communist influence such as Saudi Arabia.

Those that stayed suffered torture, incarceration and, frequently, death, battling pro-Soviet regimes–ideologically and in the streets–throughout Iraq, Algeria, Egypt, Syria, and Yemen preoccupied the Islamists. Theirs was a difficult task. Communist revolutionary thought appealed to large segments of the populace, particularly the youth. Post-colonial emotion ran high; and many people, while cognizant of their Muslim identity, found comfort in the socialists' egalitarian rhetoric. The most enduring Muslim-Communist conflict took place in Afghanistan, ending only recently with Soviet withdrawal.

Although by the late 1950s Islamic groups actively confronted Communists, they had already come to learn that the West would not be an ally. Israel's unilateral declaration of independence in 1948 marked a turning point in how Islamists viewed the United States and Western Europe. The latter nations' pro-Israeli stance meant that the West was no longer a purely intellectual opponent; it had become a political foe as well.

Leaders of Muslim-majority countries adopted a two-tiered approach. On one hand, they condemned Israel, boycotting companies that dealt with the Jewish State. On the other, they cultivated economic and political ties with the West. Arab Gulf countries in particular had no quarrel with the West and fostered relations based solely on common interests. All parties ignored the Israeli dimension; and, therefore, no serious ideological conflict arose other than a slew of unheeded UN resolutions. The situation enraged Islamists who felt their respective leaders tacitly accepted Israel's colonization of Palestinian territory while succumbing to Western hegemony.

The 1979 Iranian Revolution, and the West's subsequent response, fortified Islamist resolve at a time when the West could have won the upper hand. Muslim groups welcomed Iran's "Islamic" revolution; yet they were soon disillusioned. Ayatollah Khomeini wanted regional agents, not partners. Thus, while Islamists distanced themselves operationally, they continued to voice sympathy for Iran because the West seemed to wage war against the faith and not the politics. Islamists believed America's overt support for Saddam Hussein during the Iran-Iraq war proved that the West had embarked on a modern-day crusade to secularize the region.

Adding fuel to the fire, Islamists saw Western silence in the face of regional tyranny as de facto approval of secular autocratic rule. Islamists do not see the West's cordial relationship with potentates as a necessary part of pursuing interests with whomever is in power. To them, the West simply opposes any Muslim movement's ascendance to positions of national authority.

Tensions mounted during the Gulf War. Although thirty-odd countries entered into an uncomfortable alliance to counter Saddam Hussein's invasion of Kuwait, many Muslims resented the West's involvement. Images of Baghdad under fire and the incineration of a retreating convoy compounded the anger. Islamists were, and are, convinced that the American-led coalition intentionally set out to destroy Iraq's infrastructure by targeting communications facilities, manufacturing plants, and factories. Pundits reasoned that the liberation of Kuwait was a minor issue. The real aim was re-establishing Israel's regional military superiority.

As recent bombings in Saudi Arabia indicate, the presence of American armed forces in the Arabian Gulf has hardened perceptions of a new colonial era; but this time the aim is not to "civilize" natives, but to "protect" them. Islamists see American soldiers protecting monarchs and absolute rulers while ignoring public calls for political participation; so they conclude that the United States does not support democratic freedom. Moreover, while Western powers criticize Muslim groups for their methods, the same yardstick is not applied to state-sanctioned torture and imprisonment.

As a result, ties between the West and Islamic groups continue to deteriorate. For example, in 1991, Hamas, the Palestinians' Islamic Resistance Movement, met with several Western officials, including diplomats from the United States, Britain, Italy, and Germany. The dialogue seemed to progress positively until the United States abruptly ended all contact and officially included the group in its 1992 annual report on global terrorism. A Hamas statement in response typified Islamist views of American policy:

> "[The decision] defies logic, and [undermines] the individual's and the people's right to express their ideological and political outlook freely.... The majority of the Palestinian population has expressed its profuse opposition to the current [peace] negotiations. Does this mean that the American move has placed our people in the 'terrorist' category?"

Thus, since the common cause of diminishing the Communist threat has been accomplished, Islamists feel that Western sights have been set on their faith (despite American assertions to the contrary). The groundwork for Samuel Huntington's prophecy of a civilizational clash seems to be in progress. The rationale is that culture, not ideology, will determine the course of future conflict. The West will face a new nemesis in the form of a Confucian-Islamic connection challenging "Western interests, values and power."

Huntington and like-minded theorists presume that Eastern, particularly Islamic, culture are diametrically opposed to the West by nature. The hypothesis leaves no room for placing even partial responsibility on America and its European allies for existing friction. Yet irrespective of where the blame lies, reality dictates that the Muslim-Western relationship requires reevaluation in order to avoid conflict. In the absence of balloting, Islamic groups of differing platforms have seized power via revolution (Iran) or military coups (Sudan). Some have taken the electoral route and were denied victory (Algeria) or pressured to step down (Turkey) by their military; others patiently participate in superficial elections (Jordan, Kuwait,), while others ascend to power peacefully for the long-term (Malaysia). Dealing with inevitable Islamist roles in government necessitates cultivating a balanced relationship.

Two factors preface conflict resolution: establishment of a clear language of discourse and identification of common ground. Western policy-makers and Islamist ideologues must first identify shared principles, clarifying semantic differences that cause misunderstanding. Areas of agreement in this instance are broad.

Both civilizations share common roots in the Abrahamic traditions—Islam, Judaism and Christianity. The essence of each culture, therefore, shares similar values (family, justice and piety). Geographic boundaries as much as tradition have contributed to varying interpretations of faith. All, for example, cherish human rights—freedom, equality, and the sanctity of property. Yet while the West has a relatively libertarian view, Muslims are conservative.

In the spheres of pluralism and multiculturalism, however, there are fewer areas of disagreement. Both Muslim and Western societies are comprised of many ethnic groups, further subdivided by region and language. The American "melting pot" has long been an intrinsic part of the Muslim world, where cosmopolitan cities have flourished for centuries. Diversity, therefore, is a universal value. Groups in the United States—Anglo-Saxon, African-American, Hispanic, Asian and Native American—have all contributed to that nation's prosperity. Despite the existence of racism, Americans have been able to bring people together recognizing their achievements not their race. Muslim society is at least as inclusive, regardless of ideology. Minorities have long participated in regional politics:

- Boutros-Boutros Ghali, a Christian, served as Egypt's Deputy Prime Minister for Foreign Affairs prior to leading the United Nations

- Leopold Senghor, a Christian, once led Senegal, a Muslim majority nation

- Julius Nyerere, a Christian, once governed Tanzania, another predominantly Muslim country

- Christian presidents rule Ethiopia and Eritrea, both majority Muslim states

- Tariq Aziz, Iraq's Foreign Minister, is a Christian.

Unlike the West, tolerance of minorities is part and parcel of Muslim society. Islamists do not seek its negation; they merely want a role in their respective political systems. Sudan's government, for example, is accused of being an Islamic fundamentalist state; yet its vice president is Christian. When Islamists came to power, they did not purge the administration of minorities. Islamist priorities, therefore, are not totalitarian but progressive, based on enlightened national interests, many of which are shared by the West. Edward Mortimer, foreign affairs editor at the London-based *Financial Times* wrote in *Foreign Affairs* (Summer 1993, p. 38):

> If Islamic parties do come to power, European governments should not adopt an attitude of a priori hostility towards them. The fact that these parties wish to reduce or even eradicate what they see as corrupting Western moral or cultural influences within their own societies does not mean there will be an inevitable conflict of interest between them and Europe. On the contrary, it will be in the interest of such governments to forge close economic ties with Europe, since if the European market was closed to

them they would find themselves presiding over an economic crisis even more acute than the one which brought them to power. In fact, they will find they share with Europe an interest in maintaining confidence, stimulating growth and providing employment at home.

The pursuit of interests, therefore need not be a zero-sum game, whereby one party advances at the expense of the other. Islamists in the Middle East, for example, share America's concern regarding the guaranteed flow of oil and safe waterways. As Mortimer notes, Islamists need the funds that oil sales bring to fuel development plans while the West requires a guaranteed supply to sustain its infrastructure.

The same principle applies to trade routes, particularly safe shipping lanes. The Suez Canal, the Strait of Bab al-Mandab, the Strait of Hormuz, the Bosphorous, the Dardanelles and the Strait of Gibraltar all flow in or near Muslim countries. Islamists are aware that ensuring the safe passage of goods through these routes is a necessity.

Economic concerns, however, do not represent the main sticking points. Western objections revolve predominantly around human rights, addressed above, and Israel. The United Nations' "global village" has frequently denounced Israeli obstinacy and called for the Jewish State to abide by international law. Europe inches towards a relatively balanced role. Yet America has made a habit of blind support for both Labor and Likud, particularly during election years.

Intransigence, however, threatens to topple the fragile peace process. Islamists recognize the stability peace brings, and have offered a truce based on Israel's unequivocal renunciation of irredentist policies (settlements, military occupation) and its willingness not to interfere with Palestinian democracy. The alternative, i.e., the current status of instability and potential war, is not in any party's interests.

Israel and Palestine offer a microcosmic view of Islamic-Western relations. In order for the latter to reap the fruits of economic stability, democracy, however defined, must take its course in the Muslim world. The West's tacit approval of abrogating election results when in favor of Islamists (Algeria) or authoritarian crackdowns on all Muslim parties (Egypt, et al.) merely polarizes the situation.

Despite Western fears, Islamic groups have abided by electoral results when free and fair elections have occurred. Even when Islamists obtain clear majorities, as in Turkey, they have proven pliable to avoid friction. The new Islamist president acquiesced when his secular partners insisted on retaining the military and foreign affairs portfolios, among others. Therefore, in order to avoid violent bids for power, the West must nurture freedom in the Muslim world. Shaw Dallal, an international lawyer and adjunct professor of international relations at Utica College, writes in *The Link* (Feb.-March 1993, p. 8): "[A new policy by the Clinton Administration] should be a policy that would...be free from domestic self-serving pressures and influences. Above all, it should be a policy free from the influence of unwarranted fears and imagined enemies, and should be motivated by a valid U.S. national interest."

Western powers claim they are not opposed to Islam, merely its "terrorist" manifestation, but then define any Islamist or Muslim political opposition group as terrorist. The term "terrorism" is applied both to those who engage in arbitrary violence as well as those who demand political inclusion and, once denied, rebel. The West does not differentiate between the two; and neither does it recognize that all Islamists are not, by their nature, opposed to the West. *Los Angeles Times* correspondent Kim Murphy notes (4/6/93):

> [W]hile many see the Muslim world emerging as the next frontier of conflict after the Cold War, it is not so much because Muslims represent a military or terrorist threat but because they present an even more basic challenge: a growing social and political force that questions some of the West's conceptions of reality—

about the nature of progress, the relationship between God and humankind, the role of technology and modernization and morality in human lives. A new generation of Islamists, many of them educated in the West, are ready to turn democratic concepts against repressive regimes throughout the Middle East

Islamism, once a dormant and easily contained force, has been gaining momentum since the 1980s. Communism's collapse and democratic reform in countries outside what Edward Djerejian has called the Arc of Crisis have emboldened Islamic movements; and they are actively demanding that they be given an opportunity to share in power. Moderate Islamist calls for reform, an end to violence, and improved relations with all parties concerned are genuine. The 1989 Nationalist-Religious Dialogue held in Cairo and the subsequent Nationalist-Islamist Conference held in Beirut during 1994 are only two of the many forums established to accomplish civil reconciliation.

Despite a predominant lack of Western sensitivity to Muslim society's needs, Islamists in America and Europe are gradually being heard. Their goal is to convince the West that even-handed policies and promoting pluralism will foster mutual benefit. The steps are small; yet they may lead to better understanding between two great cultures into the 21st century–a century that will see Islamic civilization contribute positively to world progress as it did half a millennium ago.

Ahmed Yousef

United Associates for Studies and Research

Springfield, VA

May, 1998

Islamic Movements
and Western Interests:
Strategic Imperatives

Graham Fuller: It's a great pleasure for me to be here to talk to you. I talk to many Western audiences about Islamic questions, which is interesting, but fairly predictable by now. I'm much more interested in being able to talk here with Muslims who are very interested in the role of Islam and politics.

I lived many years in the Muslim world. I have tremendous respect and appreciation for Islamic culture, and I've been exceptionally interested in this question of problems between the West and the Islamic world. I have written a book with a colleague of mine called *A Sense of Siege: The Geopolitics of Islam and the West* (Boulder: Westview, 1995). Christ versus Mohammed is just not the issue. The issue is very much more complicated, and we tried to break it down into many component parts. First of all, what are Muslim grievances, all of them: historical, psychological, problems from Colonialism, problems from Imperialism, problems of Western military power, problems of Western intervention in the Arab world, economic issues–any issue, whatsoever, perceived from the Islamic side? And what are Western grievances? Psychological hang-ups and problems, military issues, economic, oil–all of these things. We sought to break the problems down, in effect, into more manageable elements and, hopefully, elements that can be dealt with by both cultures.

I don't like the famous Samuel Huntington article about "Clash of Civilizations." Although he's talking about some real issues, I don't see that these are two civilizations that are destined to clash. I think the problem is, frankly, more complicated than just "culture."

Let me first talk about Western concerns about Islamic movements, in general. In the West, in general, but especially in the United States, we have some kind of near obsession today about Islamic political movements, and you know the origins of this. Basically, for Americans–I won't say for Europeans, because their historical experience is different–our attention to Islam and maybe obsession with this issue came with the Iranian Revolution. And I've wondered why was this the case? First of all, because it was a complete surprise. No one in America really predicted that this was going to happen. Even how it could happen was a surprise. Political Islam as a force was completely unknown in the United States at this time. Then there was the trial of four Americans, the hostage crisis, and Imam Khomeini. Now, I think what really upset Americans in Khomeini's language was not that he said Americans were stupid. All countries are stupid from time to time and Americans know that we can be stupid in our policies from time to time. But Khomeini said, "You are evil." That, I think, was what really upset Americans, because that's something different. American culture is intensely secular in one way, and also quite religious on the personal level and in other ways. It's a very interesting mixture. Americans were unprepared for the return of religion into politics in the Middle East, but we now see religion in politics increasingly in the United States, also.

Lastly, I think, from the American point of view–from everyone's point of view–the world is changing and it is difficult for the United States to adapt itself to new conditions, new values after the end of the Cold War–new relationships of power. Yes, the United States is the sole super power, but what does that really mean these days? How willing are you to get involved, and for what? What matters? What doesn't matter? I think we are becoming more sensitive in this country to the ideas of respect for distant cultures–because we are a multi-cultural society–but this comes slowly.

Let me now talk about Western interests in particular, and especially American interests, and how I see these evolving in the Muslim world. First, I think from the Western point of view, when Imperialism began to spread around the world there was no particular focus on Islam or Islamic culture, or any particular local culture. As you know, in the 17th, 18th, even 19th centuries, European nations were in intense rivalry with each other for control of the world. And, indeed, by the end of the Colonial period, most of the Third World was dominated by Western powers. But the competition was not anti-Islam, per se–it was a competition over territory. This time, too, was one of the dramatic moments where Western technology clearly had become superior to technology of other great civilizations, such as China or the Muslim world. The gap at that point was very great and there was, naturally, a feeling of great superiority on the part of Westerners towards not just Islamic culture, but Third World culture in general–including the great civilizations of India and China.

The next general stage of the Western interest was that of controlling key resources and the struggle for resources overseas and, obviously, in the Middle East oil was near the top. In an era of Colonialism it was assumed natural that the West should physically control those resources in order to guarantee that they would be always available. Otherwise there was no apparent authority in those states that could assure that the resources would flow for Western modernization and industrialization. At the same time, too, I think the West began to recognize the emergence of the nation state in the Middle East and become more interested in it, but they wanted states that would be friendly towards the West. We went through the whole period of the nationalization of oil, which was a tremendous shock for Western power, because this was the first time that the West had to accept the idea that the Islamic countries would themselves control these resources. Nasser nationalized the Suez Canal and you had nationalization of oil in Iran, Iraq, and many other countries in the Middle East. So the way the West viewed the control of the region began to change. Westerners gradually began to give up some sense of control, but that took many years and several *coup d'etats*, as you know, supported by the West.

After World War II, the West, especially the United States, did not look at the interests of the specific countries so much, but saw them through the eyes of the Cold War. Anything to keep the Russians out was the main goal. We realized politics is more complicated than that, but the Cold War was the dominant concern, and that had a great impact on how people thought of the problem. Obviously, American unfamiliarity with the Middle East, the influence of the Jewish community in the United States, and Israel's support of the West through the Cold War period also affected the balance of Western thinking on these problems. And today, we face issues of the new International Order. What kind of a new International Order will there be? Who will be friends and allies of the United States? What kind of allies does the West want to have? Do we need allies? If so, what kind? How much control of the international situation do we need or want, and how much can America afford to have? This is just a quick sketch of the evolution of American thinking on these issues.

Now let me mention today what I think, specifically, are the main problems that the West has in looking at the Muslim world and understanding it. These are very complex and I won't get into them all, because we can do that in the discussion period. First, the United States has believed that modernization is the wave of the future and that the American experience is, perhaps, the most important model and, perhaps, sometimes the only model. This idea, I think, was quite deeply implanted in American thinking for a long time. We need to look at these issues tonight: What is modernization and how it will affect countries of the Third World and, particularly, the Muslim world? There is a tendency in American political thinking to view Islamic movements, by those who are not especially informed about it, as simply a Muslim desire to escape modernism and to avoid it. And I think you know that this is not the case, at all. It is, perhaps, true of some groups, but I think, on the whole, most of the Islamist groups are not interested in escaping modernization.

Then, there is the problem of imbalance of power. The United States, simply by its existence, is a dominant force in much of the world and very much in the Middle East, as well, simply because of its power, its wealth, the power of the media, the power of international television, all kinds of cultural impacts–food, clothing, arts, films, amusements, all of these things coming out of the United States represent very great power. This power is not necessarily sought–it has simply emerged from American culture and the market place.

American military power clearly is sought, but the imbalance of power between the United States and the rest of the world makes other countries of the world uncomfortable. We are coming to realize this now. But what can you do, realistically, about it, because that imbalance will always exist? How do we cope with this problem? We believe, in the United States, in the expansion of democracy and human rights and free market systems–and we do believe in these things–but there is a double standard. Most American policy-makers in private will certainly admit that this double standard exists. But I would suggest that double standards are not completely abnormal. All countries will be gentler with friends than they are with enemies. We, in our human daily lives, are gentler with people who are close to us– even while we hold our principles–than we are, perhaps, with people who are further away. But problems of double standards are angering to the rest of the world, and cause people to challenge whether Americans really believe in these values at all. My answer is, yes, we do believe in the values, we simply don't apply them uniformly.

Let me put a few more points on the table so that we can get into a discussion. Basically, the United States still feels it necessary to maintain the kind of military power that will be able to handle any major confrontation to Western interests. But what kind of military power is needed is the subject of daily debate–as you know–and what interests we are defending is also a subject of daily debate. At this point, you can find Americans who are not really sure that anything is worth defending overseas. When we talk about oil, for example, I am something of a radical because I'm not sure that oil is what the problem is all about. I wonder whether oil has ever been truly threatened in the Middle East from the Western point of view. Every bad guy–from the American point of view–in the Middle East, has always sold oil. Qadhdhafy loves United States oil companies and always sells oil. Saddam Hussein has always sold oil. Khomeini, in Iran, always sold oil. The one state that did actually begin to threaten the U.S. oil supply was our close ally, Saudi Arabia, in 1973. Then we had Iran-Iraq war and this was the nightmare of oil planners. Here you had two big oil countries, Iran and Iraq, destroying each other's oil wells, sinking the ships–oil tankers–in the Persian Gulf. This was the ultimate threat to oil, yet still oil flowed; so I'm not convinced that the flow of oil is actually the problem for American policy-makers, even though we talk about it a great deal. I don't think that oil has seriously been threatened and, frankly, I doubt that it will be seriously threatened in the future, either. Then some will say, "Okay it's not that anyone will stop the oil, but if there's war or unrest or you have a radical government, oil markets can be very severely shaken affecting international economic markets and financial markets." There's some truth to this, but I don't know whether heavily armed defense policy will avoid these problems.

There is a real concern about protecting our Gulf allies, but I believe the biggest threats to our Gulf allies in the region are mainly internal. Saddam Hussein, unfortunately, has done more to support hardliners in American thinking than anyone else, because he did what was almost unthinkable. To be honest, if you had asked me in 1991, before Saddam invaded Kuwait, "Would Saddam Hussein invade Kuwait?" I would've said, "No. Yes, he'll go up to the border and brandish weapons, and maybe take a few military posts along the border, but that's all that ever happens in the Middle East. Nobody actually seizes countries in the Middle East." Saudi Arabia never really has been threatened by military force, but with Saddam, actually was close to being threatened militarily for the first time in modern history. I think this has lent strength to Pentagon planners to say, "Look, it's happened before–why won't it happen again?" The answer is, yes, maybe it conceivably could happen again. But, basically, I think the major threat to regimes is internal, from dissatisfaction of populations within their own countries.

Political movements–left or right–are more likely to severely change the political situation in the Middle East than external invasion. So, even here, there is an argument among policy-makers and security specialists about what the true nature of the threat is. In my view if Saddam had taken control of Kuwait, he would have become much wealthier, more powerful, and in a position yet to expand his own power further. And I would argue, without any apologies, that Saddam Hussein is the worst ruler that the history of the modern Middle East has seen. I understand why there has been sympathy for him among many Muslims. Given the frustration and the anger at the West for so long, when somebody is willing to stand up and challenge the West, there is a kind of admiration for this strength. But I hardly feel this man represents the best that the future of the Middle East can offer.

Let me just offer to you now, in closing what I would see as some of the key dilemmas of Islamist movements in the Middle East. If you were a Western group, I would tell you that Islamic politics are on the rise. I would tell you that we will see more Islamist governments in more Middle Eastern countries in the future–I don't know where, for sure, but certainly Algeria, maybe Egypt, and probably some others in the Muslim world, still uncertain. I would tell a Western group that this growth of Islam comes from many different factors, but certainly from countries that suffer from economic hardships, social hardships, illegitimate governments, oppressive governments, from states where there are no other political alternatives, from states where the West, in particular, has perhaps been dominant in the past or is seen to be oppressing those states today; and if those local governments are allied with the West, they are losing legitimacy. Those are the conditions that typically lend strength to Islamist movement. But Islamist movements are broad and very diverse. I've talked with Islamists in many different countries–in Turkey, in Central Asia, in the Arab world there is a broad variety. Let me tell you, as a person who is sympathetic towards the Islamist experiment, what I think are some of the difficulties the Islamist movements face. Overall, if the Islamists are not committed to democratization–then they are going to be running into serious long-term problems in the region.

In this discussion we right away get into the very complex problem of whether Western values are universal values or simply Western values? Democracy is one Western value–and when I say Western, I'm not saying we invented the idea, but it happens that democratic institutions first became established in the West. This does not mean that it has to be a patented Western idea. I democracy is a universal value, simply because most people in the world want to have a voice in the way they are governed. It's that simple–most people in the world want to have a voice over the way they are governed. Secondly, Jefferson and Madison and others who drew up the Constitution were imbued with Christian ideas.   The basic belief among Christians is that God created man, but God gave man free will and man is capable of evil. Therefore, if man is capable of evil, then evil can creep into the political system. And, therefore, you cannot trust any man in politics, in government–you must have mechanisms for limiting power, because abuse is probable.   Not possible, but probable.   And that's why we have all these complex systems of government.   I think this is a very sound view of human nature. Basically, most Islamist movements–if they are going to survive and have a voice in the future–will probably have to recognize the idea of the role of democracy.   But what kind of democracy–how do we implement it? There are different ways to do this, but I would insist on the basic idea of democracy.

Muslims and Christians share the big dilemma of the Enlightenment. I would argue that the roots of what is best and worst in the West today stem from the Enlightenment. There are a few key ideas here that I think are very important to think about. One of them is the idea that most knowledge of the world is gained by observation and inquiry. In England and France in the 17th Century, people were saying, "Look, we don't accept anybody's a priori vision of what they think is happening in the world; you must prove it. If water is an element, then let's prove that water is an element. If water boils at a certain degree and freezes at a certain degree, we learn from this experimentation and observation. And we learn about the heavens, not from Christian teaching–which maybe a thousand years ago said the sun goes around the earth, but from direct observation." They said, "Whatever the teachings may have been, we see that the observation is different."   This line of thinking fundamentally meant challenge to authority–even to religious authority, when religion presumed to tell you about astronomy or about engineering, or about science. People said, "I'm sorry–you may be respected in moral areas, but we don't accept your views on how to build a bridge, or what the source of disease is, or what the planetary structures are out there. We don't accept that." But this kind of thinking is very dangerous, because essentially, authority becomes regularly challenged by everyone. It is very difficult for any kind of authority to continue to exist when people say, "Well, wait a minute–let's look at it."

This development has been revolutionary. We in the West have challenged almost all authority. Then, where is the source of authority and moral authority today in the Western world? It is very difficult to decide what this source of moral authority will be. The Enlightenment was inevitable; we have to challenge authority; we have to think on our own. You cannot ask students to simply accept everything the mullah says is true because the mullah says it's true. But where do we decide that we will listen to moral authority and where do we not? This is a dilemma for Christians, for Jews, for Muslims, for Buddhists, and for everybody else in the world. We're going to have to work on this question together, as to the source of moral authority and how we decide. There are no easy answers here, but I'm happy to see that Americans are now more and more beginning to struggle with this dilemma.

My view of American society is that we have attained superb accomplishments here, but perhaps we have pushed these Western ideas of freedom and individualism to the limit. We insist, appropriately, that one must think for oneself on most things. An employee is derelict if he doesn't tell his boss when something is wrong: "I'm sorry, but, you know, your recommendation on how to run these machines isn't working, and the machine is going to blow up or burn out." This is the essence of Western thinking, to challenge authority when you have some knowledge, whether or not the person is senior to you.

You have to challenge arbitrary authority in the modern world. But with the challenge to all authority, secular and religious, a crisis about the sources of values emerged. One of the reasons you once found conservatives and liberals saying, "No religion in school!" was historic abuse of religion by the Catholic Church. I think now we find liberals and conservatives saying, "Look, let's not teach religion in schools anymore, but let us certainly teach about religion, lots of courses in which we examine, 'What do Christians believe?' 'Where did they get their ideas?' 'What is the main basis of Christian thought?' 'What do Jews believe?' 'Where is the origin of their thinking?' 'What do Muslims believe?' 'What is the origin of their thinking?'" I think this way at least we will begin to focus again on some of these moral issues that concern all of us in raising our children or examining the media, TV, Hollywood, etc.

I think we are coming into a new era where the United States is going to have to think in fresh terms about how American goals can co-exist with goals in other countries and, particularly, in the Muslim world. How can we be more sensitive to goals of other countries, and still pursue our interest? There are a few things that Americans will find unacceptable, such as terrorism and radicalism–whether its Muslim or Communist or Nationalist, but we also have to recognize that some of these radical movements have roots in past actions of the West in these regions. Not all of the seeds are Western, but many. I think we are beginning to appreciate that fact more now, but we are still uncomfortable with these changes that are coming.

I please ask you to be very frank in your responses.

DISCUSSION

Abdurrahman Alamoudi: [What is the Western attitude to the Islamist political agenda?]

Fuller: I don't yet see a real Islamist political program. The Qur'an does not talk about foreign policy or investment policy for foreign countries, or educational policy on technical education or all sorts of complex issues. I'm not saying that some inspiration or some ideas may not come from the Qur'an–of course it can. But Islamists cannot simply point to the Qur'an as the answer. It needs interpretations. What are those interpretations?

Muhammad al-Asi: What about the Zionist factor?

Fuller: There's no question that Zionism for the Arab world has been a great challenge, but I don't think that Zionism is the only challenge in the Middle East. If Israel were to disappear tomorrow, the Arab world and the Muslim world would have very big problems requiring solutions. But, I do not want to underestimate or belittle the tremendous challenge that the creation of Israel posed to the Palestinians, especially, and to newly born Arab states, creating a tense military and security environment in the early years. But not all the problems come from Zionism.

al-Asi: Whether there are more Zionists in the Clinton administration than there were in the Bush administration, whether there were more arguments in public between Bush and some of the elements of the Zionist interest–the United States foreign policy is unmistakably not accommodationist towards political Islamic expression anywhere in the Muslim world.

Fuller: Your view is that Zionism is opposed to the development of any form of political Islam?

al-Asi: Oh, absolutely. There's no doubt, I think, in anyone's mind.

Fuller: That's probably basically true, largely out of fear that it will be radical and, as you know, the United States in principle, is also generally uncomfortable with radicalism, of any type, and the feeling that this will lead to another Iran or another Sudan, if you will. The problem is real for busy policymakers. I may say "Look, political Islam is going to have more power in the future and we have to reach some accommodation with it." They say, "Can you guarantee it will be democratic? Can you guarantee that they will not be dedicated to policies that are anti-American?" I say, "No, I cannot guarantee those things." Let me put it very bluntly: between pro-American dictators and anti-American dictators any politician will say, "I'll take the pro-American dictator." But I don't think we're opposed to Islam in principle, and I would ask you why you think it's true.

al-Asi: The whole obsession of Zionism in America is that any Muslim order anywhere will affect Palestine.

Fuller: Yes, but I think you're slightly exaggerating this. Israelis tend to think more openly on these questions than much of the American Jewish community here. Israeli thinkers, on this issue are desperate to have some good relations with Islam–especially non-Arab Islam–to prove that they are not prejudiced on the question of Islam. This is their desire, anyway. I'm not saying that they're accomplishing it. So you find tremendous efforts by Israelis to get along with Turks, with Azerbaijanis, with Uzbeks, with Malaysians, etc.

Unidentified Questioner: [Asks about the perception in Washington that Israel is an ally against Islamic "fundamentalism."]

Fuller: I don't think that very many people in Washington seriously think that Israel is an ally against Islamic "fundamentalism." I think the strategic role of Israel to the United States is now less than it has been at any time for a long period. One reads in *The Washington Post*, that the American Jewish community now is losing interest in sending money to Israel, that they don't feel as much need to do this today as they did. So, you can see, even here, the issue is changing. I find even AIPAC people now talking about getting money to help the Palestinians because they now see that this is in the Israeli national interest to have Palestinian stability. I'm not saying that Israel is doing this from altruistic, friendly reasons; it's for reasons of state interest. And I think the interest in Israel is now not the only criterion by which Americans think about the Middle East or Islam.

Imad-ad-Dean Ahmad: You've mentioned some changes in attitudes that are due to changing situations. Israel, itself, now sees as its national interest the pursuit of the so-called peace process, and therefore, Israel itself wants to see some level of aid to come in to the Palestinians to come in that will guarantee moving ahead with the peace plan. I can now criticize Israel in the press, but cannot criticize the "peace process"–that will not be published. What we're seeing then is not a decrease in the influence of the Zionists, but a change in their objectives. I think that we have to concede that this is a big factor in the problems between the West and the Muslim world. Politicians may not really be sympathetic with Israel, but they will vote and speak as they think is necessary to stay in office.

Fuller: Okay, but I would hope that you're not falling into the trap that says that, because Israel now wants the peace process, therefore, the peace process is bad for the Muslim world. I would argue that the peace process is extremely valuable and important for the Muslim world. I would argue that Israel's greatest damage to the Arab world on a de facto basis–except for the personal damage to Palestinians–was to facilitate the emergence of Arab dictatorships and the security mentality in Arab states and strengthen their position. I would argue that the peace process is a chance to open up the region politically in ways that could not be done before as long as the Israeli challenge was there.

Tariq Hamdi al-Azmi: [Asks about Sudan.]

Fuller: There is tremendous ignorance about Sudan in the West. The United States, has major problems with Sudan, particularly the cancellation of democracy, the stepped-up civil war in the South and its support of radical movements. People also talk about the Iranian influence. I'm sure there's Iranian representation in Sudan, but I don't think it's significant. I also reject this fear of Iranian influence in Egypt, in Pakistan, and in Algeria. I'm sure that Iran has ties with the Islamist parties, but if Iran disappears tomorrow, it will not change Husni Mubarak's problems one drop.

The perception in Washington is that the Sudanese have welcomed radical movements. Sudan, even before Turabi, has always welcomed virtually any political movement to come in and be represented there. Ben Ali in Tunisia accuses Sudan of giving a passport to Rashid Ghannouchi. You know, this is not important ..., but we hear these arguments and ... Washington is influenced by them. I think it's mainly in ignorance, but, frankly, I don't think the Sudanese regime has been a very satisfactory one either. I think the attempts to apply the Shariah universally in the country ... with a huge Christian minority, is a big mistake.

Bashir Nafi: But Sudan does not do that.

Fuller: But, what has gone on in villages and in the war–Look, it's mixed up with separatism, I know that.

Nafi: The Sudanese experiment, in many respects, is a modern experiment in government, because what has been growing in Sudan is the politics founded on traditional relationships in the country.   ...I totally agree with you. It is not only Zionism, but it is not only economics–what is happening in the Muslim world–it is much deeper than that. [It is a response to imperialism.]

Fuller: My statement simply was that the Western desire to colonize and take over and control these Muslim societies was not motivated by the goal of crushing Islam.   After attempting to take control, they found Islam was a resistant force.

Unidentified Speaker: ... you [in the West] seek to remold the world according to your image.

Fuller: The bottom line in my book about Islam and the West is the conclusion that large powers are uncomfortable when other powers emerge that begin to limit the options of a greater power. And I think you can say this whether it's the United States or Russia, or France vis-à-vis others, or Iran vis-à-vis the smaller powers, or India vis-à-vis smaller powers, or China vis-à-vis smaller powers. But clearly other powers <u>will</u> emerge. There has been a long recognition that single state domination of the world is simply fading. The U.S. simply cannot afford, and will not be able to control the world. We'd like to dictate policy on Iraq, but we have to think about the French and the Russians and the British and the U.N. and everybody else.

The United States also faces a major dilemma of change versus stability. Especially during the Cold War, in the Third World, we saw stability as the number one virtue. Stability was in the interest of the West and instability was in the interest of the Soviet Union. Today, most of the non-Western nations are in desperate need of political, social, and economic reform, and this will take the form of democratization, among other things. Democratization is desirable and it's necessary, yet it's also destabilizing, and this is where Washington gets very nervous.

This process of evolution and reform, by definition, <u>will</u> be destabilizing. When Iraq becomes democratic, and 60% of the country is Shi`ah who have never had much voice in the government, suddenly the Shi`ah become a major power in Iraq–this will have <u>tremendous</u> political, social consequences. So, policy-makers are torn between pushing for change and not wanting the destabilization that will come from change.

Tariq Hamdi Al-Azmi: You didn't comment on Nacmettin Erbakan.

Fuller: I think Erbakan may come to power. I've spent a lot ... [of] time in, and I've written a lot about Turkey. If Erbakan comes to power it will be by elections, and Refah has already, in municipalities and cities, come to power and <u>left</u> power ... so I think that there is a chance the Refah is becoming a normal political party.

Unidentified Questioner: Do you consider that Americans will be friendly towards such a group?

Fuller: No–uncomfortable. They will accept it, but they feel it's unpredictable–untested. People ask me "What will happen in Turkey if Erbakan comes to power? Will Turkey stay in NATO?" I have to say that this is a very big open question. "Will Turkey stay democratic?" I say "probably." "Will Turkey impose the Shariah by force, and then you'll have refugee problems and all sorts of people leaving the country?" I say, "Probably not in that form, no, but there may be some disorders within the state."

Unidentified Questioner: Why <u>probably</u>? You know [Erbakan] from the 70's. You just mentioned that he has come to power and went out of power.... Why is the West not accepting Refah as a party?

Fuller: It will accept Refah. We will be uncomfortable, but we will live with it.

Emad Shahin: The current Islamic movements could be categorized as reform/protest social movements. Sociologists wouold tell you that for a reform movement to remain moderate and not to resort to violence or go underground, it has to function in a democratic environment. This is a prerequisite. Once it faces oppression or suppression, you cannot predict the response of that movement, and I think this is the situation now.

I would also like to comment on the point you mentioned regarding the Islamist movements' lack of programs. I would argue that the Islamists do have programs, but these are not well studied by Western scholars. In fact such programs have been considered by the authorities as evidence for incriminating the Islamist movements under the pretext of planning to replace the current political, social and economic order by an alternative one. Finally, givin the nature of modern politics which now focus on issues and performance more than ideological programs, I believe that the Islamists are more effective on the ground, particularly in providing social services such as medical care, education, social support, and emergency relief assistance to victims of natural disasters such as the earthquakes in Algeria and Egypt.

Fuller: This is one area where I have been impressed by the Islamists—the area of social services. Also, on corruption, because I think at the beginning, anyway, they will be able to do something—although, unfortunately, in Iran now, corruption—this is human—corruption has crept in.

I would simply argue that there is fear of the unknown on the part of the West. And, I'm afraid, the more we move towards democracy in the Middle East, there will be some—I don't want to say "opposition" to it—but nervousness as to what will come out of the woodwork—so to speak—when these things happen. There is a great deal of anger among populations in the Middle East and much of the world for all sorts of reasons—some imaginary, most of them real—and that anger is more likely to be expressed in some ways through democratic governments than through non-democratic governments. There is not a long history of responsible government in the Middle East so far. For example, I think even Hafiz al-Asad would rather have nuclear weapons in the hands of Israel than in the hands of Saddam Hussein. This is not because he loves Israel, of course. It's a question of: "Is this a reliable government?" The more these countries move toward stable and reliable and transparent government, I think the easier the relationship will be, in the end.

Imad-ad-Dean Ahmad: I would like to comment on some points that have come up. The problems that sparked the Enlightenment, the challenge to authority that grew out of the confrontation between modern science and the medieval church are something of which I have also made a particular study. My book *Signs in the Heavens: A Muslim Astronomer's Perspective on Religion and Science* (Beltsville: Writer's Inc. International, 1992) demonstrates how that whole process that lead to Western secularism was a consequence of the crisis that emerged from the medieval West's encounter with Islamic science and theology. The West inherited the techniques that mark modern science from the Muslims, and the Muslims were inspired to them by the Qur'anic commandments to observe God's signs in the heavens and the earth, to think about them, and, above all, to submit only to God's authority. The bottom line answer to your question about where does moral authority lie if all authority may be questioned, is that valid authority is not afraid of being questioned about its credentials. The Qur'an insists that true authority from God cannot conflict with sound reasoning nor with correct observations of "God's signs in the heavens and the earth."

You mentioned the perception Muslims have that the West is engaged not only in economic imperialism, but a cultural imperialism as well. I perceive a presumption in the West that Muslims will always resort to authoritarianism because, given the freedom to choose between Muslim cultural norms and Western ones, Muslims, as individuals, would generally prefer Western culture. Thus, an Islamic state will be forced to coercion to combat it. I would note that the opposite seems to be the case, not only in Muslim countries, but in France where the government has had to ban the headscarf from schools because given a choice, its use was spreading and is seen as a threat to the secularism of French society.

Finally, you express concern about the prospect of nuclear weapons in the hands of Saddam Hussein. I am no defender of Saddam Hussein, but it is a matter of fact that he did not use chemical weapons against the allied forces in the Gulf War. I myself am concerned about any government having nuclear weapons. The historical fact is that there is only one nation on earth that has ever used nuclear weapons against a civilian population and it was not a Muslim country, nor was it Israel; it was the United States of America.

A Diplomatic Perspective
on the Islamic Movement

Robert G. Neumann: I have read with great interest and admiration the analyses of Political Islam which scholars like Dr. John L. Esposito (*Political Islam: The Challenge of Change*, Springfield: United Association for Studies and Research, 1995) have presented within the framework of the United Association for Studies and Research. These studies, while different in emphasis and scope, deserve great credit for inveighing against presentations and policy recommendations which take a monolithic view of "Islamicism" or Radical Islam or whatever expression one might prefer.

I accept, without adding to these scholarly works, that Islamicism is not uniform, not a "world conspiracy" directed by some sort of international, Islamic leadership, not a kind of "Islaminform" or "Islamintern." I further accept that "Islamism" is not a new phenomenon suddenly thrust upon the world. We have seen it develop since the twenties as a debate on how to organize the Ummah, the Islamic World, following disputes over the consequences of the dissolution of the Caliphate.

I also reject the proposition that Islam–or Islamism–now represents a new World Enemy, to take the place of the "Evil Empire" of Communism. Communism, as organized and directed from Moscow, did represent a credible threat. But that is not our subject today. I mention it only to suggest in passing that "evil enemies" like Communism, Nazism, etc., have in fact existed, have constituted a credible threat to our interests, and hence were a legitimate core issue around which the security interests of the United States and its allies were organized.

I also note that among those who would regard "Islam" or "Islamism" as the New Enemy, there are also those who see in such a concept an opportunity to identify our interests in such a way that our principal ally would be Israel. But I must add that this is not a uniform idea in Israel or among Israel's supporters in this country.

In opposing the idea that Islamism, as manifested today, is the New Enemy, however, I cannot accept the connotation the Islamism is necessarily benign.

I must also confess that I find it difficult to handle the idea that only time will tell whether the Islamist call for democracy is only a means toward political participation or simply a means to power. By the time the situation is clear, it is usually too late to do anything about it, and important national interests may have been damaged.

It should further be noted that revolutionary movements, such as political or radical Islam, grow and change as the result of the support and resistance they encounter. Hence American and generally Western diplomacy affect Islamism as Western diplomacy and interests are affected in turn.

It is certainly acceptable for scholars to argue that "only time will tell" how future Islamic regimes will act. But this cannot be the prescription for diplomacy, which must try to devise a policy, a strategy, to shape our action now, when the outcome of the inevitable struggle between moderates (pragmatists) and dogmatists is not decided–if it ever is. These remarks constitute the perimeters of the observations that follow.

A significant part of our diplomacy must also be not only to analyze how our diplomacy might affect the struggle between pragmatists and dogmatists, but also, where possible, to shape our policy in such a way that the pragmatists–if we believe they exist and are sufficiently powerful–may prevail and the dogmatists may not. But one must also realize that the dogmatists are not or do not remain dogmatic on all issues, and the moderates can be quite dogmatic on some issues. Bear further in mind that in an existing Islamic regime, such as Iran, an active power struggle between the two groups goes on and both are affected in their political organization by the way they are viewed.

How this plays out in a country like Iran, where Islamism has been in power for several years and has a track record, is different from Algeria where the Islamists are still fighting for supremacy, using methods which America and the West find difficult to accept. The task of formulating American diplomacy in the face of such differences is further complicated by the rules of the political process in America (and France and other European countries) and also, prominently, by the electoral struggle in America.

In an election year, facing no serious competition for renomination by the Democratic party, President Clinton quite skillfully used the Bosnian crisis to reposition himself as a decisive leader, an impression unsupported by his stewardship after his election. However, the argument occasionally heard both here and in Europe, that the fate of the Bosnian Muslims could enhance Islamic fundamentalism in Europe, has not received much credence in America, not even in pro-Israel circles. Even extreme pro-Israeli circles would find it difficult to make this much of an issue. I mention it at all only because it underlines the need for both Democrats and Republicans to treat this issue with restraint.

Much scholarship has centered on the question of Islam and Islamicists' beliefs. This has been somewhat successful in countering distortion of Islam and Islamic literature. Similar views are found among the present and former officers of the Near East bureau of the State Department and their colleagues in at other agencies and among most members of the staff of the present National Security Council.

But, in following this realistic and prudent course, the American officials and diplomats realize the danger of concentrating too much on "beliefs" where distortions in both pro-Islamic and anti-Islamic interpretations are sometimes produced by dubious scholarship. Studies of the vast literature of Islamic doctrine can lead to highly theoretical debates in a bottomless barrel. It is more practical for our policy makers and diplomats to concentrate on what Islamists do, rather than on what they believe. This is all the more advisable as Islamism deals basically with the questions of Justice, the nature of the moral social order, and perceptions of internal social and economic injustices. In no way would I wish to question the justification of scholarship to examine fundamental Islamic or Islamist beliefs. But as a guide to policy and diplomacy such endeavors are surrounded by pitfalls. What Islamists do is a matter of ascertaining facts; what they believe will be endlessly debated, and language, especially Arabic, is often subject to multiple interpretations which are not static, especially as the failures of the Iranian and Sudanese regimes are beginning to have their effects on the literature.

Nor is it very fruitful, from the standpoint of finding policy guidelines, to argue whether Islam is capable or incapable of accommodating democracy. This is not just a problem for Islam but for all religions since problems of divine and immutable truth cannot easily be subjected to public opinion polls or majority vote. In Islam the question of consensus and its interpretation or evidence are the subject of considerable debate. Nor is this even a purely Islamic question. Was it not relatively recently that Vatican II accepted pluralism–and that, not universally nor unreservedly (Esposito, *op. cit.*, p. 7).

American foreign policy and diplomacy cannot function successfully unless they have popular and Congressional support. That runs up against the fact that some of the methods which Islamicist movements use in their struggle for victory are cruel and arbitrary and cannot be accepted nor condoned by those who formulate American diplomacy. It is true that the Islamic regime in Iran, in power since 1979, has had time to modify some of its doctrines in the light of practicability as the political struggle between moderates and dogmatists continues in its various shadings and as public opinion, our views and those of other groups, are beginning to diminish the rigid demands of orthodoxy. But the evidence of Iranian hands and support in terrorist activities–whatever the definition thereof, cannot be lightly discarded.

Hence the call expressed above, that American and Western policy should rely on what the Islamicists do and not on what they say, does not automatically provide easy answers. And the suggestion that our policy might take too benign an attitude towards pretty grim deeds by Islamists may well carry an excessive price for a government trying to win reelection against considerable odds.

Nor is there much to be gained, in my view, by the argument that the Islamic regime in Iran merely or primarily reacts to the frequently arbitrary action of the Americans (including support for the late Shah and his cruel Savak police). That argument comes under the umbrella of Ambassador Eilts' response to a similar argument—"I understand it, so what?" In any event, it is not a sufficient guide for policy makers. It is merely argumentative.

It is particularly difficult to take a benign view of Algerian excesses by Islamicists, in view of the steady rise of casualties. What makes the Algerian case more difficult for American policy makers is also the fact that the Algerian military government has put itself drastically in the wrong by suppressing a fairly honest election which could almost certainly have brought the FIS (Islamic Salvation Front) to power. Still, a diplomacy of "a plague on both your houses" is a moral cop-out and no guide for the policy of a world power which inevitably has sometimes contradictory interests in all parts of the world. The considerable interest in Algeria of our often ally, France, is a matter of concern for the U.S. government as we need to work with France in other parts of the world, such as Bosnia.

During the Mitterand-Balladur regime in France, American and French policies on Algeria came dangerously close to a collision due to the intransigent policies of French Interior Minister Pasqua who encouraged the extremist "eradicator" wing of the Algerian military regime.

Under President Jacques Chirac and his prime minister, Juppe the French and American positions have become closer. As Foreign Minister in the Mitterand-Balladur government, Jean Juppe, now Prime Minister, opposed Pasqua's extremism. If that trend continues, America, whose interests in Algeria are significant, but clearly not as extensive as France's, might be willing to let France take the leading role in quietly pressuring the military regime to move toward a more conciliatory policy following the achievement of the Rome conference under the auspices of the St. Egidio Circle. (The San Egidio organization of the Catholic church is an organization dedicated to fostering peace and understanding in regional conflicts. It brought to the Rome meeting an unusual gathering of many Algerian opposition parties, including the FIS.) The quite moderate recommendations of the San Egidio Conference were brusquely rejected by the Algerian government but have served to keep alive the idea of compromise which, in different degrees, both the United States and French government support.

What policy we conduct in the Algerian crisis has now become even more important because President Mubarak of Egypt, a very important ally of Washington, has now suddenly embarked on a much more repressive policy against his Islamist opposition including even the relatively moderate and now largely non-violent Muslim Brotherhood.

America is deeply involved with Egypt. Mubarak's sudden turn causes us considerable problems. All American governments, Republican as well as Democratic, have been deeply concerned and determined not to be forced into the appearance of a blanket anti-Islam policy which would greatly hurt our position in the one billion-strong Islamic world. We cannot abandon such strong and faithful friends as Mubarak and Egypt. Without their support, the Palestinian-Israeli and Arab-Israeli peace processes could never have come about. Nor can the Clinton administration place too obvious pressure on Egypt to modify its policies during the election period in America when such pressure could cause trouble electorally and politically, when some important groups could accuse Clinton of being "soft on Islamic radicalism" and "terrorism."

In order to help us put together a viable policy, it is well to suggest here some of the basic principles which might help. Our first priority ought to be a serious reconsideration of our "double containment" policy. Its author, Martin Indyk–then senior National

Security Council aide and now U.S. Ambassador to Israel–argued that both Iran and Iraq were equally determined enemies of the United States and pressure should be put on all our allies to isolate them politically and economically. The aim of that policy was to bring down Saddam Hussein and to force Iran into more acceptable forms of international conduct, especially with regard to its support for terrorist movements all over the world.

This policy, as stated, has a certain rationale but has been sterile and counterproductive primarily because it ignores the considerable differences between the two cases. That Iraq remains a constant threat to Middle Eastern, especially Gulf area, stability need hardly be proven. Despite constant harm to Iraq's own interest, Saddam Hussein has repeatedly tried to provoke Iraq's neighbors. There is little likelihood that Saddam's eventual successor would establish a more acceptable, less oppressive regime. But at least it can be argued that he would be less foolish because Saddam's misjudgments are so obvious to anyone with open eyes. Hence, the personalization of U.S.-Iraq policy is justified. In fact, for the U.S. government there is little alternative as long as Saddam Hussein can maintain his iron grip. Washington admits that the anti-Iraq boycott hurts primarily innocent civilians, but no alternative exists but to make life so intolerable for the Iraqis that internal explosions could eventually overthrow Saddam. That a more contented Iraqi population might be more motivated to rise against Saddam can hardly be seriously maintained. The defection of top-ranking members of Saddam's own family and of the Takriti ruling class also indicates that serious disaffection has now reached the top military strata, whatever other reasons may also exist. Moreover Saddam's occasional attempts to swing the Islamic flag have been unsuccessful in view of the known secular policies of the ruling *Ba`th* party.

The case of Iran is materially different. Its proclaimed "Islamic" character as well as the greater size of its population and resources are not to be taken lightly. After sixteen years in power, it has begun to learn from its mistakes and there exists now a somewhat greater degree of internal debate which has made occasional compromise somewhat easier for the rival "moderate" and "dogmatic" factions, while they remain watchful that such compromises do not excessively strengthen rival accusations of their becoming allies of the "Great Satan."

It is difficult to deny sufficient intelligence information that Iran is involved in supporting and helping to organize terrorist activities in many parts of the world. But it is clear that continued isolation of that country is not going to change its conduct, as no side wants to admit "softness" toward the West. The American government's different policy toward Syria should be noted since Syria has also been accused of supporting terrorist activities.

Neither is continued isolation likely to strengthen the so called "moderates'" who, to the extent that they exist, do not seem politically strong enough to impose their leadership more decisively. Nor do "moderates" and "dogmatists" always moderate or act dogmatically in all matters.

To my knowledge there is no convincing evidence that the Iraq-based "Mujahidin-i Khalq" have sufficient support in Iran to seriously trouble that regime.

All observers agree that there is a deep psychological gap between Iran and America. Even "moderate" Iranians are convinced that America remains an uncompromising adversary and seem unable to understand how deeply the long hostage-taking during the revolution has soured the American attitude, even though a number of former hostages have advocated a more forthcoming American policy. There is not much greater understanding in America for the psychological burden which long American ostracism has created in the Iranians. It will be recalled that then Secretary of State Warren Christopher was the chief American negotiator (as Deputy Secretary in the Carter administration) for the release of the hostages and thus experienced in full measure the humiliation which Khomeini inflicted on America. These personal factors cannot be taken lightly.

This makes rather sterile the long "debate without partner" between America and Iran as to who needs to make a move first. It does not help that the rather smooth and effective handling of claims by the American-Iranian Court in the Hague has not had a visible impact on other American-Iranian disputes.

All this makes for a very difficult situation. While an overthrow of Saddam Hussein makes possible in Iraq the arrival of an at least initially more acceptable regime, no similar situation exists in Iran. The Iranians, having suffered from the cruelties and deprivations of the Iranian Revolution, seem to have no appetite for a second revolution.

A change in American policy can be expected only over considerable time and probably not before the election and while Warren Christopher remains in office.

Still, a beginning could be made by an underclared but perhaps only gradually visible decoupling of the two halves of the "double containment" policy and by a quiet search, mostly through third parties, for items on which a modification of American and Iranian rigidity could be slowly accomplished. One aspect of such a diplomacy is that it remains "deniable" as long as possible. This I maintain, is not deception. Deception is an act designed to deceive. Nobody with any degree of intelligence will be deceived except those who choose to be for political purposes, and they are one of the burdens of diplomats especially during an election period.

Recent trends have gone in the opposite direction, especially the reinforced American boycott of Iran and the prohibition of oil purchases by non-American partners or subsidies of American oil companies (Conoco). This has only created yet another rift between the United States and almost all European governments who have shown no inclination to follow American leadership on this Iran policy, while the same allies have rather quickly accepted American leadership on Bosnia–evidence that leadership in one area cannot easily be transferred to another where policies differ.

A gradual cooling of the anti-Iranian rhetoric of the Clinton administration might be possible, and there is some indication that this has begun. Within the foreign affairs bureaucracy there is considerable support for such a change. But politically even such a minor step is so fraught with risk that even courageous diplomats are unlikely to risk promising careers by sticking out their necks. Even in the Bosnia crisis, where there was considerable dissent in the State Department, the resignation of several career diplomats had no lasting effect. Resignation in protest is not an American tradition. It has a somewhat greater effect in Britain.

An emphasis on Islamist action rather than belief will strengthen American perception of the differences existing and growing among different Islamist attitudes. In this, considerable subtlety is required but is made exceedingly difficult by the American political system in which the Congress constantly competes with the administration for influence, even when both White House and Congress are dominated by the same party. Diplomacy is a subtle game. Politics is not. Quite the contrary, as politics moves in the public arena and fights for power and influence without much regard for the consequences of disclosures and false accusations. Often quite short-range political advantage is sought, and the fight is frequently one for appearance rather than substance. The diplomat who tries to further the long-range interests of the nation faces the constant danger of being publicly accused of being "soft" on this or that evil. Nor can he be sure that his administration will support him even when he carries out the administration policy: when the President wants to beat a hasty retreat, he has no compunction about letting his faithful servant hang out to dry. This situation has been particularly notorious in Middle Eastern affairs where opponents have long been accustomed to tar diplomats as "Arabists" or with other suitable epithets.

Nor can the diplomat count on the support of business which may benefit from a more realistic approach. Business also has to move in the public arena where being labeled in an undesirable form may hurt its economic interests. Since America is the country of lobbies where even the most minor causes have and support noisy interest groups, the courageous diplomat can never lose sight of the danger that he might suddenly find himself alone. That so many American diplomats have shown remarkable courage is a monument to their character, but has rarely made much different on the ground.

Also it is not helpful that Congressmen or Senators may well understand the diplomat's action when talking in private conversation but do not hesitate to denounce him in public. It is a real jungle in which, as in other forms of war, little fairness can be counted upon.

American Middle Eastern diplomacy now has a new problem, or a new version of an old one, as mentioned earlier, with President Mubarak's foray against the Muslim Brotherhood in Egypt. His impatience may be understandable but it complicates American diplomacy. The Arab-Israeli peace process has a high priority for the U.S. government and an increase in "Islamist" influence would disturb that. We are also committed to try to extend democratic tendencies and that is not just a political slogan but is deeply desired by the American public without whose support no government can remain in business. But in Egypt, as in so many other areas of the Middle East, Islamism is a protest against very pervasive social ills. This is an area in which Egyptian government progress has been far from satisfactory, in the face of admittedly mind-boggling problems.

What is the U.S. government supposed to do? President Mubarak's political survival is probably essential to the peace process. But America's influence over Egypt has its limits despite considerable economic aid. There is never enough of the latter and, it is not always used prudently by Egypt. Yet any sizable enlargements are inconceivable in the face of existing budgetary constraints.

Under these circumstances the U.S. government can do little else than attempt to counsel the temperamental Egyptian statesman to calm down, to refrain as far as possible from sudden outbursts such as we have just witnessed. In this, we can and do also work in tandem with those of our European allies who know the region well. But to press Mubarak too far or too openly might undercut his political position as there appears to be no visible alternative to him. This is not a time for some dazzling "breakthrough'" which is simply not available. Politics and diplomacy are the arts of the possible, and plodding forward is far more frequent than breakthrough.

Considering how much is at stake in Egypt, American policy problems toward the other Maghrib countries are somewhat easier. In

Egypt we are the principal players; in the Maghrib we are not, or at least not as much. We would do well to thank our limitations, rather than become excessively ambitious. *"Pas trop de zèle"* is an old diplomatic watchword.

In Algeria the intransigence of the military government, especially the "eradicators," has produced the increasing radicalization of the opposition, especially its Islamist part. Both sides are stuck and stubborn. The cruelties of government suppression have their mirror image in the increasing violence of the Islamists. That the victims of both are largely the civilians fans and the innocents has produced a standoff in which neither side is likely to win, and both sides use terror to make government or political survival impossible. But if neither side succeeds, there is a subtle difference between the government and the militant opposition–and not only in Algeria: the government loses if it does not win; the opposition wins if it does not lose. That favors the opposition, although not decisively.

As in similar situations, more sensible people strain their eyes to seek compromise. The proposals of the above-mentioned San Aegidio Conference in Rome have kept that question open despite the Algerian government's brusque rejection. In such a situation compromise does not mean that government and opposition come closer together, but rather that they split. Those government circles who realize the hopelessness of their situation, and those more moderate circles in the FIS begin to strive toward common ground, both against the background of considerable clash of sudden assassination and destruction. One significant factor is that Algeria's women, not all but a significant number, are strongly resisting Islamist violence frequently directed against them, and that constitutes a considerable weakness in the Islamist position despite their claims to the contrary. As the influence of women grows, that is a factor favoring compromise but only if the long run. This means that a scheme for power-sharing is not exactly around the corner.

America, although a super power elsewhere, does not have the power to affect the outcome significantly, but France does. Its economic support for the government in Algeria is decisive to keep it afloat and France is the principal area for the emigration of Algerian unemployed youth.   That emigration has now been curtailed by France in response to the spread of Algerian Islamic violence to France, but the French government is too experienced and tough regarding North Africa not to use this card with some flexibility. America has little alternative but to encourage French efforts and not develop an entirely independent policy as might have occurred if the Balladur-Pasqua government had prevailed.   To "out-French" the French by a sudden surge of anti-terrorist or anti-Islamist policy, would be sheer madness.

The solution is somewhat different regarding the other Maghrib countries. The Tunisian social and economic structure is sufficiently different from that of Algeria to make it possible for President Ben Ali to prevail in his fairly repressive policy which has, thus far, avoided the degree of violence which has characterized Algeria. It is also a fact that the considerable Tunisian middle class is inclined to support the Ben Ali regime better than is the case in Algeria. There is no special American national interest to interfere with the Ben Ali regime. Our modest economic interests seem to find sufficient commonality with that of France not to opt for change.

Morocco is a different case for a number of reasons. There is a considerable history of good American-Moroccan relations which Morocco's rulers in the past have sometimes called into play to counter excessively colonialist French policies.   Since Morocco acquired full independence in 1956, Washington has consistently held high esteem for King Mohammad V and King Hassan II's flexibility. Both kings had a strong popular support among rural masses, and the present king's policy of constantly increasing and then decreasing the openness of the regime has provided a system which is less brutal than that of Algeria and even that of Tunisia. Even the disaffected political elements have a good idea how far they can go in expressing opposition and are generally content not to rock the boat too violently. This remarkable talent of the king has produced a fragile but not inconsiderable stability. While Hassan II's assertion of being the "commander of the faithful" may not seem terribly convincing to outsiders and even to some Islamist elements in Morocco, it does work in a general way, at least while Hassan remains in good health.

This generally satisfactory although not ideal situation does not call for any American change in policy. America remains welcome in Morocco as a counterweight to excessive French muscle and Morocco would welcome greater American participation, especially in the private sector. But progress has been slow. Morocco's attractiveness is still insufficiently known in America's business world, and America's business representatives find themselves frequently disadvantaged by the personal closeness between French and Moroccan businessmen who have often gone to the same schools.

American government support for Morocco remains relatively steady but is constantly endangered by budgetary restrictions. Such restrictions are not new but are often the result of American inattention since the support for aid to Israel and Egypt remains a priority and cuts have to find their targets among "the rest" of our aid program—for which no bright future can be expected.

This relatively good Moroccan-American relationship could, however, be endangered by excessive American activism in the question of the former Spanish Sahara. Here the determination of King Hassan II not to give way is genuinely popular in Morocco. Moreover, the Sahara region is too poor and underpopulated to produce a viable basis for independence. Hence the realistic choice for the former Spanish Sahara is between Moroccan or Algerian predominance, and the U.S. government has no reason, especially under the present unsettled circumstances in Algeria, to press for change. Also Morocco has changed the situation on the ground by pouring people and resources into the Sahara. The theoretical if not doctrinal American support for "self-determination" has no practical basis, nor does its support by the United Nation's weigh very heavily as the UN's prestige has suffered for other reasons.

King Hassan II is sufficiently realistic to appreciate America's quiet support, and America has no realistic reason to change. There is also no evidence that "Islamism" has any sizable hold on the

Saharans. Support for "self-determination" comes from the Algerian government but is not strident as both it and its Islamist opponents have bigger problems to worry about. As far as American policy is concerned, the old rule of "if it is not broken don't fix it!" is clearly applicable.

In the main, the United States should uphold its principles. By that I do not mean that we should be shrill in pressing for our style of democracy but we should support it when it emerges in natural ways. We are, however, most certainly not true to our ideals if we allow ourselves to slip into an implied position that democracy is alright for us but that Muslims cannot be trusted with it. It is legitimate to raise the question whether they will play by the rules of the game, but that question can equally legitimately be raised with "Christian" Latin American rulers, Israeli right-extremists, or Buddhist generals.

Furthermore, when our interests are involved we may play a very active role in insisting that physical and procedural guarantees exist to ensure that elections are not merely a one time road to power and dictatorship. But if fear leads us into the position that we must prevent Islamists from coming to power by any means, then we are fundamentally perverting our own ideals. The cost of such a policy is too great.

DISCUSSION

Emad Shahin: [One element missing from consideration] in the diplomatic stands or positions of U.S. foreign policy ... is the issue of the people themselves. For example, when you went over a number of countries like Egypt, for example, we see that Mubarak is very important to us for the peace process, or Tunisia, or Morocco with Hassan playing it well, so they're fine; but how about the aspirations of the people? There is a kind of force of change in the Middle East that is really undeniable. You cited the example of "one man, one vote," but the fact of the matter is American foreign policy was forced upon them. Also, there is the issue of Iraq, when you said that measures must be taken against Iraq even though it may have ill effects on the people. Again, the element of the people is missing, because it is at the Iraqi *people's* expense. [Also,] I think Algeria is still important to the French and even to the United States, given the situation in Sudan. There is a very explicit interest for America to step in and try to formulate some kind of foreign aid policy with regards to Algeria towards a democratic policy.

Neumann: I'm arguing for changes, not just for change. How could you start change? One of the very important elements in policy is deniability. If you want to change, the first thing you do is to say you want to change, and then you change. Once a very important leader of one of the countries to which I am giving credit said to me, "Now, when you deny something, it does not mean that you did not do it. It only means that you do not want to take responsibility for it." Now is that lying? Is that deceiving? In my opinion, no. My definition of deception is "an act designed to deceive." But if everybody knows what you are doing, it is not deception. It's flimflam. Therefore, it is in the interest of changing the policy that you deny as long as possible that you are doing it. By the time it comes out and you really have changed it, people are sort of used to it.

Shahin: But the opposite is true, because it can also promote democracy, but you are not supporting democracy. This is exactly my point. You are trying to say, "I'm for democracy, for one man, one vote." But in actuality, you are not, because this is the opposite of denying.

Anwar Haddam: In my small experience in our diplomatic effort for the Islamic movement in Algeria, trying to open channels, as you all know, in the Western world, I find three points which you might ... elaborate upon.

[The term "Islamism"] might, as you said at the beginning, give the impression that there is this Islamic international conspiracy. ...There is no such international conspiracy. This is one of the problems that we face whenever we talk about the Algerian experience. They talk to us about Iran, Sudan, etc. It is very hard to get across the message that ... each and every country [has its own] specific affair, ... [and] specific approach.

The second [point] is about energy sources. This is the main problem in certain foreign policy making decisions in the West. How do we approach the West about the issue of energy resources?

The third [point] is the peace treaty. Especially in the United States, it seems that the peace treaty ... is the cornerstone of foreign [policy]. I'm suggesting that to have lasting peace, you have to have democratically elected political authority in the Middle East. The PLO of the sixties and the seventies is not the same as the PLO of today. We see the direction of Hanan Ashrawi. In my view, the peace treaty did not succeed. All that you have is a new totalitarian regime called the Palestine Authority. That's how the masses look at it. They don't feel that it will be a lasting peace. How would you connect to that?

Neumann: What do we want? I can only speak as an American, and then I will speak as a friend. We hope that some justice comes to the Palestinian people and that the problem of the tension between Israel and the Palestinians will be alleviated. To this extent, and in my long experience with the Palestinian problem, the changes have been fantastic. I remember when I was condemned ... for having written, I don't know how many years ago, that if you want to make peace, you have to talk to the people who carry the guns. Oh! That was terrible. I was accused of being an Arabist. An Arabist, I thought, was a person who studied Arabic. But no, an Arabist is a terrible person.

But now, it's a different situation. Of course we'll talk to the people who carry the guns–at least to some of them. And when you think of the scene on the White House lawn September 1993, that's a mind-boggling change. Now has that brought peace and prosperity to the Palestinian people? No. But there is a great deal of change.... Mr. Arafat is not a great democratic liberator, but what is the choice? You have to talk to the people who are the representatives of those authorizing the fight against Israel. And we've done that. Now I don't know that it has raised democracy in the Middle East. Syria is certainly not a democratic state, but if Syria were a democracy, would it more likely accept the peace? I don't think so. I am very dubious about that, and anyway that is not their choice. They are not in the business of overthrowing governments in the Middle East. There was a time when they tried, but right now that is not a viable policy. But to deal with people who are there is part of our policy.

Now what priorities does the American government have to speed up the process, to redeploy Israeli occupation a little faster, to get some solution above the waters? These are small steps which can make a change. I don't know what else an American government can do. It could put more pressure on Israel. But bear in mind the political situation inside Israel. I don't have to tell you what it is. Today, Mr. Netenyahu has all kinds of foolish things to say.... I don't know what new generation is coming up. What can we do more that prod and push?

I'm very dissatisfied with what I am saying, because I would like to say ... there would be peace, lasting peace. But when in man's history has ever there been lasting peace?

Let me quote something. There was a discussion between two parties and the one said to the other: "You know as well as we do that which is called right and justice can exist only between those equal in power. While the strong do what they can, the weak suffer what they must." Who said that? The Athenians said that to the Malans in a great work during the Peleponesian War written 3500 years ago. I don't say that nothing changes but that nothing changes very fast.

Haddam: What I'm suggesting is that recognizing those who are in power in the Arab world certainly will not help for a peaceful change–which we do certainly aim for, which I am trying to explain. ... [Surely,] change is coming, either peacefully or through revolution. ... Trying to give certain legitimacy to the existing rulers certainly will not help for those who are calling for a peaceful change.

Neumann: I do not see how we can do anything *but* deal with the existing rulers. Maybe we can deal a little less closely. But is there a choice in Egypt? With whom would you deal? Or is America to decide who should rule India, Egypt?

Tariq Hamdi Al-Azami: I would like to make your life easier. I have a rather simple and direct question. Since the goal of this meeting is to clear some of the views that Westerners probably have about Islam or that the Muslims have about the United States or the West in general, you mentioned a very disturbing idea for me. You said it is not what the Islamists believe in, but it's what the Islamists do. I sense in that you are saying that they contradict themselves and they may do things that they don't believe in. So my question is, can't we apply this to the Western powers, particularly the United States, since we are talking about it today? The slogans of U.S. foreign policy, of the democracy and human rights that the United States believes in–do they really apply them? Also, the Islamists would say, it's not what the United States says, but it's what it practices.

Neumann: I have no fault to find with your argument. Do take us by what we do and accuse us if we are not faithful to our ideas. But what I meant is the following. I think the interest of all who are in this room is to help people have a more realistic, balanced idea of what Islam is about and, in that situation, acts undertaken. By now thousands of people are being killed in the most brutal fashions, innocent people, not people who are leaders or officials of the government, but women who are writers in our countries. What strength do you give to the people who say Islam is an evil enemy which has to be fought? And I would ask the Islamists who commit these horrible acts, "Are you really helping your cause?" I understand why people go towards terrorism, why they want to make it impossible for a government to govern. This is true in Algeria; this is true in Egypt. But nowhere does it work unless the government itself becomes weak. It worked in Iran because the Shah suddenly collapsed, was ill, and for many other reasons. But among tough people, it doesn't work. The people in governments go on until the government is just as brutal as the other side.

Think again if it is important to you, if you really want to effect Western opinion not only to come to power, but also to change Western attitudes toward helping out countries that need economic relations and so forth. Are the passions which you arouse, the killing of innocents, justified? And I would like to see a reconsideration of this in those countries among the people who establish strategies for their movements. But by all means take us at our word. You can't say that you are not serving what you claim to serve, democratically. But at least we are not killing people–at least not at the moment. Some of us are accused of that too!

Mazin Muttabaqani: I heard a statement in your lecture about religion–that religion deals with the ultimate truth. I don't know if I heard it correctly, or if something was wrong with my hearing, that Islam does not deal, or religion cannot deal, with ballots and public opinion.... This is a big issue among the secularists that we have in the Muslim world and Westerners who study Islam–that Islam has nothing to do with politics. Read in the Qur'an the number of times the story of Pharaoh appeared or the [government] that the Prophet (peace be upon him) established in Medina, which tells us that Islam can deal with everyday life and every aspect of politics.

Neumann: What I said was not referring particularly to Islam, but to all religions–that when religion becomes a part of the political process, it is difficult, though not impossible, to deal with the aspect of democracy and elections, coming into power, going out of power, because you deal with ultimate truth. After all, the Qur'an was established by the dictation of God. The same is true for Christianity. But, the history of Islam has shown that over time, changes do occur. In the world, over time, governments, kings, presidents, and so forth, have interpreted what ought to be done in different ways, so the original doctrinal concept has been modified. The same is true in Christianity. This is merely, as I said, a problem. It is not insurmountable.

I am very well aware of the Islamic schools that accept interpretation. I don't consider myself a specialist, but I know something about it. I deal with the possibility of differences of opinion and so forth. But it is legitimate to raise the question to a movement that is active politically, but governed by Islam or by Christianity: Will you accept it when you lose your political ability to come to power? Would you be willing to leave power if the machinery of the government that staged the election turns against you? And I don't say that you don't. I reject the idea that Islam is incompatible with democracy, but it has to be faced. And one of the ways to face it is to tell the world how you are proposing to deal with public opinion. I think this is particularly important with the question of religion.

I have heard Islamic arguments that Islamic governance is for the protection of women. And women who have been fighting for generations for greater rights know what to do with the argument that Islamic governance is for their protection. They know what that means. That means to hold you down. And you will not convince them. I have heard a group of African women speaking, and really I was taken aback by the passion with which they rejected the possibility of Islamist government and what it could do to their profession, to their status. Now I don't say they are right. Who am I to make that decision? I say answer them.

It would be very useful to convince the American public that Islam can live with or in democracy. I am sure of it; there is no need to convince me, but even in Europe, people are saying that Islam is a great danger.

Laura Drake: I am intrigued by one thing, and that is the impact of America on Islam. It isn't discussed nearly enough, and it isn't that we're a superpower. I've just attended an event with the American Muslim Council and many of the other groups representing what we might call the number two religion in the United States. They have not got a single Muslim in a professional position on the Hill or in the Department of State. The Pentagon is in a little better position. But I don't know of any Muslim foreign service officers. Well, there may be one, I'll admit. Isn't this a very important factor in our paranoia with regard to Islam?

Neumann: That's an interesting question, but I don't know how to change it. There is of course something now under dispute as to our method of change used in race relations: affirmative action. That is one way. That is the only example that I know where a deliberate government sponsored attempt was made, even by screwing the system a little bit, to give more representation to people who were disadvantaged. It should be a temporary thing. In the long run, a permanent advantage to one race or another is an evil thing. As a step up for a period, it is legitimate and more. And now perhaps people's education has changed. There are a great deal more educated Black people.

Now can that be applied to Muslims? I don't see how. What I would like to see done, but done as quietly as possible, would be to encourage gifted young [orthodox] American Muslims to apply for the foreign service and see what happens. If you feel that they have been discriminated against, then scream. But there would have to be some kind of quiet attempt by your Muslim organizations, such as the American Muslim Council–lots of outreach to American Muslims. Encourage them to try to break into this if they're interested, because they have to be interested. Then they cannot expect only to be used in Muslim areas of the world. You know how the system works. And after 5-10 years, or before that, you take another look and see if anything has changed. If you know that people have been rejected because they are Muslims, and otherwise well-qualified, you have a legal and political case to attest to this.

I don't know how many have tried. For the Blacks, it has been that Blacks have frequently tried to get into positions where they would have an impact on the other Blacks. Foreign affairs was not in that area. But I think the State Department is one of the most open institutions as far as color is concerned. Is there something to be learned from other groups? You know how it was for the Blacks and Republicans, speaking of a Black man as a possible and serious contender for the Presidency. But of course Colin Powell is a very special man in a special situation. People are sick and tired of resisting. People are ready for a change.

Muhammad Al-Asi: I didn't want to bring this up, but now that we have shifted in that direction, I will. I am a second-generation American Muslim, and I was in the American Armed Forces, the Air Force. [My brother and] I applied for a security clearance and were denied that clearance in Lackland Air Force Base back in 1973 without an explanation. Now that was followed a few years later by the same attempt, and [rejection] for the same ambiguous reasons. This happened again even though for the test that we took, a simple Arabic/English translation test, the person who administered the test said that those were [the highest] scores he had ever seen. Still we were turned down. Nothing came of it, and we tried to pursue it within the military.

[In contrast,] a person who came from Romania, ... from behind the iron curtain, and was born in Romania ... applied and he *got* his security clearance. Whenever we bring this issue up, there is total silence. No one would say why, and up until this day, I have my brushes with the FBI. They come over as if to say, "We're interested in not having violence in the United States." Well, I'm interested in not having violence in the United States too. So what is your approach to this?

From one discussion to the next, this issue would come up, and I would say, "Just give me a reason why the United States denied me a security clearance." I still cannot understand until this day why that happened. The person said, "OK, I'll give you an answer in one week." And it's been years and years–not more than a decade–and I haven't gotten any answer for that....

In addition, we have a little simple election that we want to occur at the Islamic Center in Washington DC. Also this issue is sort of off limits. You're not supposed to talk about such issues at a place that is controlled by Saudi Arabia. But on this matter, there is no answer that will come out if you try to pursue it. I've tried it verbally, I've tried it in writing, and it seems like there is a dead end to it and it goes nowhere.

Neumann: I have no doubt about your total truthfulness in this matter. It fits into the picture. We have a history of this in another arena, the history of discrimination against Catholics, and similarly against the Blacks. How have these things gradually broken down? By pushing, by protesting, by going to the public domain, writing articles, or getting someone to interview you or others. The history of how people forced their way into the ruling classes is well known, and I know of no other way. It's not my position to counsel you. You are an American. You know how one gets publicity and recognition, how one embarrasses the ruling people.

Look at tolerance, look at military justice and how they dealt with controversial questions–they said nothing about rules for race or religion. Look at how they dealt with the responsibility of "friendly fire," which shot down the two helicopters in which there were some friends of mine. There is still an iron ring, but we are just seeing how an iron ring is broken. This is something quite different. Five years ago, that wouldn't have happened. It is up to those who feel strongly to battle the case, to talk to columnists, not just on your own, but get people to write, and say, "Look, this is what happened."

Al-Asi: It appears–and I like your approach to the move towards incremental change–that the U.S. government has an attitude of taking the position of the status quo, and hence interacting with the government at the expense of the change that is happening among the people. Now it would behoove American diplomacy in its incremental and pragmatic approach to the issues of the Middle East to begin to unrecognize the governments, diplomatically, incrementally, and pragmatically, and likewise to begin to recognize the Islamic forces that are on the side of history and gaining surely, maybe slowly, the upper hand in this whole Middle East context.

I would like to refer to an incident that you presented, and that is: Abbassi Madani made some statements accommodating democracy, but on the other hand Ali Belhaj made some statements that contradicted the concept of democracy. Why did the American administration pick on what Ali Belhaj said to try to discredit a global popular change in a country like that, and did not pick up on what Abbassi Madani said.

Neumann: I guess I was with you until this last point. On this, I depart. I don't think that much attention was paid to what either said. How many newspapers deal with Algeria very much? The way I addressed the issue is to say that it shows that even among them, there are different views, and, therefore, you cannot expect us to be sure of one way or another.

Regarding the incremental movement of change, could we do that gradually by moving away from supporting governments and towards supporting Islamists? It is not easy to do. How do we deal with that side in the practical world of diplomacy? In dealing with the country, we deal with the government. It is almost impossible to deal on an official basis with a country other than through the government. It was even more difficult in the past, when you were not supposed to have *any* relations other than with the official government.

Actually, there are many ways. When I was ambassador to three countries, I saw to it that somebody had contact with opposition people, but it was not always useful if it had to be myself. In the three countries in which I was ambassador, I had to do it in different ways. I knew in one country that if I was seen with some opposition figures, after a while, the prime minister would call me in and say, "Mr. Ambassador, do you really think this is a good idea? I will tell you anything that you want to know." And I would say, "It is my duty to get the best information that I can. I would be very happy to have more information from you, but in all fairness to my principles and home in Washington, I have to also find some way beyond that." Then we both said our piece and talked about more practical issues.

In some countries, this is very difficult. It becomes particularly difficult when it is government policy not to hear the opposition. That, I think, is generally a bad idea. But during the Shah's regime, that was policy, and largely enforced by Mr. Kissinger. In our embassy in Tehran, during those days when we had one there, there was one very able officer of excellent ability. He had very good contacts in the bazaar among the people who later were part of the creation of the revolution. But his reports were sometimes not allowed to go through, while sometimes they went through only as minority opinion, and sometimes were confined to lower levels. And then there is the bureaucratic problem of careers–that your career may suffer if you do something that the Secretary of State has said that you shouldn't do.

You can fight this, and we have some kind of channels. We ought to find ways to have contacts with everybody, which sometimes has to be done by other agencies, etc. This has to be decided and finely tuned in each place. But to have as strong a relationship with the opposition as you have with the government is not even possible in a democracy. The Ambassador to Germany, for instance, has relations with members of the social democratic opposition, but he cannot see them as much, or as visibly as he sees the chancellor.

There is a difference between the official relationship and the unofficial one, but in a democracy there are ways of dealing with both. I have sometimes had better contacts than the State Department or the CIA with the opposition party or with the people because of particular groups' cultural interests. Sometimes my foreign service colleague would say, "Mr. Ambassador, this group's director has the kind of contacts which I ought to have." And my answer was, "Why don't you? My task is to get the best information I can, and I don't care who gets it, as long as we get it together." I think it has improved. I think we have learned from the Iranian example. I would have to have a number of foreign service colleagues here to tell me whether this is true, though they probably wouldn't tell you because they have careers too.

Anwar Haddam: This is concerning the Algerian woman, the mother, the wife, the daughter, the sister of those who are in concentration camps, of those who are in prison, tortured, among the more than 50,000 who have been killed. These Algerian women are forbidden to even cry for their losses. We should remember that. In a totalitarian regime, we don't have free media.

The second thing concerns the killing of innocent people. I speak on behalf of the Algerians, regarding internal affairs, when I say that the killing of innocent people in Algeria is not the way of approaching the West. Maybe I should thank you for your comment regarding the Rome agreements. As you might know, I was the head of the FIS delegation in the Rome agreements. It was the FIS delegation who assisted in calling for an independent commission to investigate the tactics of what is going on. So the Algerian Islamic movement is against the killing of innocent people. Those who have something to hide in the closet are the ones who are opposing any such independent commission or investigation. Not only do we deny it, but we reject it strongly as it is against our beliefs to attack innocent people.

Finally, concerning democracy and human rights: We as an Islamic movement are not into office yet. The best way to judge us is to see us in office; then we will see. But what I would like to comment on concerns the opposition. First, we have to define what opposition means. I do believe that in a constitutional system, the government and the opposition are part of the constitution. What we have in Algeria, is that the opposition is in power, that is, the opposition to the constitution is in power. The elected representatives are not. We have to maybe review our terminology. I think it is time to discuss seriously in the Islamic movement and in the West also, what the place is of the Muslim world in this so-called New World Order. How do we see international relations? Is it still valid that those who control more than 50% of territory are to be recognized, or should those who are duly elected be recognized? I think it's time to discuss issues of global security, sharing in sources of energy, etc. These need to be discussed clearly.

Neumann: I have tried to improve those type of relations, and there have been some, but the question of why some things worked and some things didn't is a different story on which we might have lunch sometime, and talk about that. Part of the same question is at what level does one relate to people other than the government. After all, an embassy for one government dealing with another government has all kinds of things to deal with, not all of them political, but a great many things such as protection of citizens. In order to deal smoothly with that, you have to deal with the established authorities. That is the priority.

The other question of how to deal with the opposition, about which books and useful articles have been written (and I've written some of them), is a question of how to improve those relations with the idea that you can never have a relation as strong and as official with the opposition as you can have with the government. It's simply not practical. And I'm not talking about Islam or any country. In the sense of American politics, it's perhaps possible with the Irish, and you know why. And even that hasn't worked altogether well.

Ahmed Yousef: How do you see the near future in Iraq?

Neumann: I have a feeling that the end is in sight for Saddam Hussein, and that's really all that we want. I've said that before. The next ruler may be just as devious and murderous as Saddam Hussein, but he could be a little more clever, and that's something. Can you imagine that if we relaxed sanctions, the now better treated Iraqi people would be more inclined to rise up against Saddam Hussein? No. But this is why I made the distinction between Iraq, which is really a personal problem, and Iran, which is not.

Osman Shinaishin: I thank you Mr. Ambassador for the open dialogue and the information you shared with us.

Neumann: I have discussed these issues for years, and this has been a very rational, very subject-conscious audience.

Shinaishin: I believe it was the USIA who invited Mr. Adil Hussein, who is the editor of *al-Sha`b*, the opposition [Egyptian] newspaper, and he is considered an Islamist. It amazed me that the newspapers that are mouthpieces for Mubarak wrote criticizing him for accepting the hospitality of the Americans when he comes to Washington to meet with government officials, when he has always been critical of the West. You can see, [whether he reaches out to the West or not, it seems he] can't win. I do appreciate a great deal that non-Muslim Americans have an open mind and want to listen and really understand, and that may give us an opportunity. The more we work with them, the more we understand each other.

Origins of Political Islamic Movements:
A Western Perspective

Stephen C. Pelletiere: The advice that experts have been giving to policy makers on the rise of political Islamic movements must be seen as suspect. Their theories–almost uniformly–assume knowledge about the movement that is not certain. The phenomenon often called fundamentalism–and I'm aware of the reservations about the use of that term–is terribly complex. My theory is that what is widely perceived as a radical movement actually began as a movement of reform. The rapid dissipation of the reformist current did not occur until the reformers found themselves balked by the regimes that they were trying to influence. Unable to carry their reforms into action by peaceful means, the original leaders withdrew from the movement. Then new elements took over–mainly from among the youth–and initiated what must be viewed today as an area-wide populist revolt.

The movement in Algeria developed in the late 1980's practically out of nowhere. Previously, the avowedly secular government tolerated religion–barely. Though not politically active, a kind of shadow movement of religious influence performed what in the West would be called good works. Very conservative, devout Muslims ministered to congregations of primarily urbanized peasants. A feature of this activity was building so-called "free mosques" in the *baladi* districts of the great urban centers in competition with government-sponsored mosques. The latter were viewed by Algerians as corrupt–mere appendages of the official bureaucracy.

The *shaykh*s who operated the free mosques, however, did not seek to take power from the government. The government left the free mosques alone to provide social services that the government was unable to supply.

After the collapse of world oil prices in the mid-1980's, Algeria suffered an economic downturn which deprived the regime of funds needed to run the country and, in effect, it forced the regime leaders to show their mettle. The past practice of throwing money at problems was now impossible. The people saw that the leaders– notoriously corrupt and inefficient–were not up to coping with the diminished resources, and grew restive. In late 1988, prolonged and violent riots erupted. The blowup seemed spontaneous, although some saw it as a government scheme that backfired. Among Algerians, there is an apparently still current suspicion that the riots were orchestrated by the security forces. Clearly, the government bore much responsibility because the army, in putting down the unrest, is estimated to have killed hundreds of people, fueling a spiraling escalation. Out of the riots, the Islamic Salvation Front (FIS) was born.

The clergy attempted to respond to early government appeals to calm things down. Rallies were held in which the crowds were harangued to leave the streets, or at least to desist from looting. Once the rioting had ceased, certain clerics organized the FIS movement

Initially the FIS formed itself into a political party and competed for seats in the local elections. The ruling party, the National Liberation Front (FLN), seems at this point to have miscalculated the appeal of the fledgling movement, which did surprisingly well in the local elections and thus was encouraged to try for seats in the parliament. The military seized the reins of government, however, and attempted to push through gerrymandering rules that would have favored the FLN in the upcoming elections. The FIS leaders called for a general strike, to protest this action, and the movement leaders were jailed.

Still, the movement might not have turned violent had it not been for the assassination in 1992 of Muhammad Boudiaf. A revered leader of the original 1954 revolt against the French, he had been a member of the High Security Council which took over government after the President of Algeria stepped down in January, 1992. Many in Algeria concluded that his assassination was the work of the security forces. (Western officials I interviewed in Algeria offered this theory.) Deciding that the army could not be trusted, elements of FIS went underground, forming the Army of Islamic Salvation (AIS). This group ultimately split, and an even more radical organization came into being, the Armed Islamic Group (AIG). The movement thus entered into its present violent phase. Commencing in 1993, the FIS began to subside as a significant influence in the country. What followed was tantamount to civil war, which left tens of thousands dead.

Latent hostility against the government for its inept handling of the economy was certainly a factor contributing to the outbreak. The government's housing policy may have been the trigger. Not enough apartments were available in the major cities. Waiting lists were subscribed years in advance, and, to get on a list, one had to have influence. Those who were not so advantaged felt themselves denied, and many of the embittered ones were youths. Without an apartment one cannot marry, have a normal conjugal relationship–in effect, fulfill oneself as a man.

Cultural divisions within the community were another factor contributing to the outbreak. No sooner had the FLN defeated the French, than it proclaimed Algeria to be an Arab country. Nonetheless, the country's leaders succumbed to the allure of French culture. They sent their children to school in France. They vacationed there. They banked there. They favored the French language over Arabic. They even dressed in the French style, and watched French television.

Along with this, the early regime leaders co-opted the bureaucracy that the French had left, filling it with their own people. The bureaucracy became a refuge for elite elements, turning into a *nomenklatura*, as existed in the Soviet Union. The bureaucrats drew apart from the rest of Algerian society, isolating themselves from the general populace, driving an even deeper wedge into the community. Those who were not part of the elite languished, as they had very little hope of bettering their lives.   Most keenly affected were the youth, part of the baby boom that developed after the expulsion of the French and the appearance of the national government. Roula Khalaf, writing in *The Financial Times* ("Algiers Mutiny Heightens West's Dilemma," February 24, 1995) says "nearly 60 percent of the population in Algeria is under 25, and half of them are unemployed."

The period between the early 1960s and 1989 marked the growth in Algeria of a virtual caste system, based primarily on one's position in the *nomenklatura* (and, of course, this included the military). Thus, the country was culturally divided. The masses spoke Arabic and were largely from the countryside, or else had moved to the city at a recent date. These recently urbanized elements had come to Algiers and Oran and Constantine to better themselves. Instead, they were blocked by a Franco-phone elite of civil servants who used their bureaucratic connections to keep them down.

With the fall of oil prices, the government had to trim its welfare system. Many began to face real deprivation and social antagonisms sharpened. Thus, there would appear to have been sufficient grounds for revolt in the underclass. Usually, however, revolutions occur when the middle class becomes disaffected. In Algeria, the middle class certainly was disenchanted with the regime, but it did not abandon it.

Conspiracy theories are an inappropriate line to explain the revolt. The fact that the clergy may have benefited from the revolt cannot be cited as proof that they brought it about. Yet the violence occurred before the clergy became involved. Algeria's unemployed youth were on the rampage before the clergy came forth to calm things down, at behest of the government. Weeks after the rioting had been controlled, the *shaykhs* from the poorer neighborhoods formed the FIS, thus creating what is now the significant movement of opposition in the country.

The original founders of the FIS were peacemakers, seeking to further their aims within the system. Their first action (once they had taken over the movement) was to form a political party, and then compete in local elections. Scoring unexpected gains in this arena, they stepped up their electioneering–all a perfectly good democratic practice. Indeed, one could argue that the FIS lost out because it failed to capitalize on the initial unrest. If the aim of the FIS, from the first, was to seize power by any means, it could have called for an insurrection while the populace was aroused. By participating in the elections, it allowed the FLN to recover, after which the military leaders drove the FIS underground.

The Algerians who created what eventually turned out to be a revolt did not initially intend to do so. They were merely expressing opposition to the regime, raising issues in a democratic manner. The clergy made an issue of the riots and the government's maladroit handling of them to mobilize a protest movement, and they rode that issue to success in the local elections. Further, given the way the elections turned out, it would appear that many in the middle class, if they did not vote for the FIS, at least did not support the FLN. The failure of the FLN to mobilize what should have been its natural constituency was in a large part responsible for the debacle. It seems that both the middle class and lower class elements wanted a change, and–in the early stages of the crisis–that was all they wanted.

Once one adopts the position that revolution was not originally on the agenda, one has no need to discover a conspiracy, or to make much of the Islamicness of the affair. In the Arab world (as in black America, and in Catholic Central and South America), clerical involvement in protest movements is not unusual; religion traditionally has served as a vehicle for such activity. Nor would the participation of the clergy have been a concern to many. It would not have signified a clerical takeover of the government and the institution of an orthodox form of rule (one in which the Sharia was implemented). Algerians likely would have interpreted the clergy's involvement as a sign that discontent was serious, and, had the regime been willing to address the situation, subsequent trouble might have been avoided.

In sum, prior to 1988 and the outbreak of the riots there was no movement in Algeria bent on overthrowing the government. For at least the first few months after the movement had formed no one within it seriously looked to seize power from the nation's rulers, at least not by force.

This begs the original question-where does the unrest, indeed, the terror come from? At some point the FIS became transformed into the AIG, with its attacks on foreigners, blowing up of airlines, and all of its other terrorist acts. Why did this occur; who, or what was behind it?

My answer would be that the Algerian Army initiated the resort to terror by refusing to compromise with, and later by trying to crush, the FIS. Military repression drove the more restless spirits of the FIS to organize the AIS (and subsequently the AIG), and these outfits, operating underground, produced the present bloody confrontation.

In the case of Egypt, an activist religious movement goes back to the 1920s, when Hasan al Banna formed the Society of Muslim Brothers, an organization dedicated to revivifying Islam among the Egyptian masses, and concurrently combating Great Britain's imperial control of the Egyptian state. After the 1952 revolution, the Society ran afoul of the Free Officers, who led the revolution. The deeply conservative Brothers objected to the Officers' drawing close to the Soviet Union. The Officers attacked the Society in 1954 and again in 1965, wounding it grievously. Many Brothers went into exile (quite a few in the Gulf, where some became wealthy), while others went into hiding at home.

In the 1970's, when he sought to move Egypt into the Western camp and to privatize many public sector industries, Anwar Sadat sought to rehabilitate the Brotherhood as a foil against his foes, the Nasserites. (The Brotherhood derives its membership primarily from the private sector-small shopkeepers, teachers, professional workers.) Brothers in exile were called home and offered aid in reestablishing themselves. Those underground in Egypt were urged to come out of hiding. For a time, the conservatives and regime leaders cooperated. Then gradually the relationship frayed, and, ultimately, Sadat launched an attack against elements of the religious community–in particular the Brotherhood–similar to that visited on the Nasserites. At that point Egyptian society polarized.

Sadat was assassinated in 1981, apparently by religious fanatics. The deed has been blamed on the Brotherhood, although, in my view, the evidence does not substantiate this. Still, the religious right clearly was upset over Sadat, and just after he died there was an uprising of sorts in Upper Egypt.

When Mubarak took power, he allowed the Brotherhood to exist, but did not concede to the Brothers on the one issue that really mattered to them–he refused to legitimize the Society as a political party, which would have allowed it to compete in elections. Blocked in this area, the Brotherhood pursued other schemes. For example, it virtually took over several professional societies and labor unions, placing its people in the executive posts. In this way, the movement continued to expand, and thus the tension between it and the government was perpetuated.

Tensions in Egypt took an unusual turn in the late 1980s, with violent outbreaks in Upper Egypt. There were several manifestations of this, including attacks on tourists and intercommunal fighting between Christian Copts and Muslims. As the level of violence rose, the government began to intervene aggressively, until finally the security forces undertook what amounted to another major crackdown. This, however, only succeeded in making matters worse, and then, unexpectedly, there were severe disruptions in the capital. At this point Mubarak announced the discovery of a clandestine fundamentalist network, which he labeled the Islamic Groups, or *Gamaa*.

Following this revelation, fighting between the alleged *Gamaa* and the government intensified. Several assassinations were attempted, in which some high officials were actually killed. A brutal repression launched by the government failed, and, when the violence flared again, Mubarak accused the Brotherhood of being behind the *Gamaa*. Indeed, he claimed that it was the Society's military wing. Today, the Brotherhood, the elusive *Gamaa*, and the security forces are all in an uneasy standoff.

The major mystery is the *Gamaa*. What is it, and what, if any, is its connection to the Brotherhood? The *Gamaa* is, in the author's view, a fiction–or at least it is in the sense that Mubarak construes it. The violence is real–the assassination attempts, the attacks on police, the murders of tourists; all of this is real enough. But, that a single entity is orchestrating these actions, and that this entity is the Brotherhood, using the *Gamaa* as its vehicle, is doubtful.

The violence in Egypt can be broken down into three separate categories. First is the unrest in Upper Egypt, which borders on civil war. Next is the so-called *Gamaa* violence, much of which takes place in Cairo. Finally there are the Brotherhood-regime confrontations, which initially were peaceful, but soon became quite bloody. Mubarak ties all three together, saying that the Brotherhood is masterminding events, with the *Gamaa* cadres functioning as the Society's shock troops. The aim of this combination is to bring down the regime, according to Mubarak.

The problem with Mubarak's proposition is that the most violent activity (that in Upper Egypt) can be explained without recourse to conspiracy theory, as can the so-called *Gamaa* violence, which is connected to the events in Upper Egypt. This leaves the Brotherhood-regime confrontations, which do not appear directly related to either of the other two.

After Sadat's death, the Upper Egypt area experienced a rebellion of sorts–the only real violence in Egypt following the assassination. Mubarak's attempts to forcibly open Upper Egypt to the lucrative tourist industry predictably precipitated clashes between elements of the population and the so-called *khawaja*s (foreigners). Local zealots disliked the way foreign women dressed and what they perceived as the foreigners' impiety. And most of all they did not like the foreigners' attitude towards themselves–being a tribal people, the Upper Egyptians hold themselves in high esteem and do not expect to be patronized.

It is my view that early instances of anti-tourist violence in Upper Egypt were the work of zealots within the community, and that this hostility was not broadly based. At the same time, it seems likely the police overreacted. The provincial administration blanketed the area with police, who made numerous arrests, ultimately setting off an area-wide revolt. Upper Egyptians observe the code of vendetta, whereby physical abuse incurs a debt of honor. The fact that the abuse is inflicted by government officials acting under orders in no way mitigates the offense. Soon, natives were laying siege to the provincial police stations.

Thus it would seem that the crisis was brought on by a combination of events and was not in any way a premeditated affair. The locals did not plot a civil war against the government; the security forces did not mean to incite any such action. Given conditions in the area, the disturbances could hardly have been averted.

The violence in Cairo to relates rural elements who have been immigrating to the capital over the years and settling in the *baladi* quarters there–some downtown within blocks of the great international hotels. Sadat apparently decided to clean up downtown, and so decreed a face lifting for the city center. Under the decree, whole neighborhoods were uprooted, and the citizens relocated. Dissatisfaction among the displaced residents increased when they found themselves relocated into new neighborhoods, in some cases mixing Muslims with Copts. This led to fierce sectarian clashes.

Then, in 1992, a major earthquake wreaked devastation on many poorer quarters of Cairo, and–unfortunately for Mubarak–the bureaucracy did not provide relief quickly enough. The Brotherhood moved in and virtually took over the relief effort. This so angered the President that he ordered private relief workers to be ejected, which touched off major riots. Mubarak then backed down, apologized, and blamed his underlings.

All of the events, reported in the international media, raised speculations that Mubarak was in trouble. Mubarak, however, countered skillfully. On the eve of his visit to the United States in 1993, he charged that his government was under siege by religious fundamentalists. He pointed to events in Algeria where the junta had recently outlawed the FIS, and he claimed that the Algerian fundamentalists and those in Egypt had allied, and that the whole Middle East was coming under assault from the fundamentalists.

Mubarak thus adroitly turned the tables on the media, using the alleged fundamentalist agitation to plead for assistance from the United States. The formula, as Mubarak posed it, was a simple one—support my government, or my regime may succumb, which will not be of benefit to the West.

Though widely credited, Mubarak's version of events does not hold up under close scrutiny. The activity in Upper Egypt, for example, consisted mostly of peasants sniping at tourists from cane brakes, and throwing petrol bombs at police stations. In Cairo, there was plenty of unrest—clashes between Copts and Muslims, and between the locals and the police. All of this certainly was vexing, but it was nothing that Egypt's security forces could not handle. Even the assassinations, which, according to Mubarak, are tied to the *Gamaa*, are suspect. For the most part they involve anti-police actions—most of the figures targeted for execution were high police officials. As the police and natives escalated their feuding, the violence grew more intense; finally, to avenge the debt, the highest police officials were executed. Also, many of the bombs used in the assassination attempts appear to have been homemade. Professionals would be more sophisticated in their methods, and would be likely to have better equipment.

The most telling evidence, however, would appear to be the casualty count. It is estimated that between 1992 and the present, roughly 600 Egyptians have been killed in this struggle. In a country of 60 million, relatively speaking, that is not a lot. The casualty count in Algeria is much higher, as noted above. Annual losses due to crime in a major American city surpass Egypt's toll

In the final analysis, the violence in Egypt seems more a form of anarchy than an organized attempt at revolution. Egypt is going through a period of socio-economic turmoil; the government is having difficulty managing pressures that are accumulating, and is resorting to greater and greater use of force, to which the community is responding with violence.

Egypt has traditionally been governed by autocrats. Sadat ruled that way, as did Nasser. Both were natural successors of Muhammad Ali, the founder of modern Egypt, and, perhaps, the autocrat of all autocrats. Mubarak wanted to institute democracy, as he sensed, correctly, that this was what Egyptians were yearning for. At the same time, however, his instincts were to play the *ra'is* (boss), the style of his predecessors. He made a few pro forma gestures toward democracy but never followed through. Thus, when conditions began to worsen in the country, he found himself alone. The attitude of the Egyptians was, if he (Mubarak) wants to be the *ra'is* (boss), let him work things out. If he cannot do this, the responsibility for failure will be his.

The unrest that developed within the religious establishment at this juncture was ominous for Mubarak. The *shaykh*s exercise great influence over the people–both masses and elite. In this instance, opposition was expressed by massive turnouts for Friday mosque services. At the services certain preachers went so far as to castigate Mubarak's government, stigmatizing it as "godless." This was a serious charge, and one which Mubarak could not let stand. Some of the preachers lost their pulpits, being forcibly ejected by the security forces.

As in Algeria, the mobilization of religious forces evoked a significant popular response, including elements of the middle class. The latter were expressing discontent with the regime, but they were not calling for a revolt. Rather they wanted to move the regime in a new direction, more congenial to their interests. Furthermore, the government seems unable to improve Egypt's dreadful economic state. The country has not produced throughout all of the Arab Socialism years.

Mubarak has appealed for loans from the international financial community. Loans come with strings attached. The International Monetary Fund (IMF) wants Mubarak to impose an austerity program, and, along with that, it has been pressuring him to open Egypt to the global market. This takes us back to the days of

Sadat, being precisely the course of action he tried to pursue, one which ultimately was abandoned due to public hostility.

The President stonewalled the IMF, and to justify his failure to act, raised the specter of a fundamentalist revolt. This has long been a tactic of Third World leaders under pressure from the international lending community. What was disturbing, however, was Mubarak's willingness to involve the Brotherhood. From his standpoint this made sense, enabling him to avoid complying with the IMF-dictates, and, at the same time, to throw up obstacles to the Brotherhood's bid for political legitimacy.

At the same time, however, Mubarak's maneuvers have gained little support at home. If anything, the President's actions have boosted the standing of the Brotherhood, which could develop into a significant anti-regime movement. Mubarak has succeeded in crushing unrest in Cairo, but at a considerable cost. Many Egyptians are disturbed over their loss of civil liberties.

Interestingly, the Brotherhood's strategy in responding to the attacks has been to exercise caution, going out of its way not to provoke retaliation. The Brothers apparently feel that they can stand up to the regime, and that ultimately Mubarak will be forced to back down. This approach may backfire, however–youthful members of the organization are clearly impatient for action, and already significant defections have occurred. It begins to be doubtful whether the leaders can control the rank-and-file.

Turning to Hamas, it is in the vanguard of the anti-Israel fight. Among groups fighting from inside the occupied territories it is without peer. To a large extent, the fundamentalist challenge is taken seriously today because of Hamas. No other resistance organization has caused such concern among Western policy makers. Despite all the attention, however, aspects of Hamas's career are obscure. It can be argued that the Jewish fundamentalist movement–committed to turning Israel into an exclusively Jewish preserve, to encompass so-called *eretz* Israel–turned Hamas into its course of violent activity.

Hamas is an off-spring of the Muslim Brotherhood–whether of the Jordanian or Egyptian branch is disputed. The Jordanian branch of the Brotherhood reckoned itself among King Hussein's staunchest supporters. Thus, when the Brothers went into the territories in the mid-1970's, many assumed that the king was attempting to reassert his claim to the territories by having the Brotherhood become his agent among the Palestinians.

Once inside the territories the Brotherhood created two institutions, an Islamic Center and Islamic University. These became bases from which to proselytize the Palestinian youth, who until then had been only nominally involved in political matters. The Brotherhood's role was a lot like that of Tammany Hall in New York City politics in the late 1800s. It awarded material aid, arbitrated neighborhood disputes, and acted as mediator between the local community and the Israeli authorities. And, in the process of carrying out these functions, the Brotherhood made enemies. Not only PLO supporters but numerous Palestinian leftists opposed the spread of the fundamentalist doctrines.

Two developments, coming in the late 1970s and early 1980s, frightened the native Palestinian community. One was the appearance of a messianic Gush Emunim movement, bent on fulfilling the Biblical prophecies by turning all of *eretz* Israel into a Jewish preserve; the second was the ascension to power of Likud, with its policy of unlimited settlement. Although not formally tied, Likud and the Gush certainly were in sympathy.

Driving the PLO out of Lebanon in 1982 and forcing its retreat to Tunisia, Israel effectively crippled the PLO, creating a leadership vacuum among the Palestinians. Palestinians under the occupation needed someone to look after their interests, someone positioned to be instantly on call for help.

When, in December 1987, the *intifâdah* exploded into a veritable firestorm, the previously docile, noninvolved community of Palestinians was passive no longer. This was the beginning of a great popular revolt, caused in part by confrontations between settlers and natives. Now the need of the Palestinians for a defense force was urgent. The Brotherhood was the logical candidate for this, but it held back. The idea of such a force went against everything that the organization stood for. The Brothers' idea was to proceed slowly, to educate the masses, and then ultimately to take power by peaceful means, but never to succumb to the lure of violence. Now, as the fighting raged, more and more of the younger members of the group began to break away from the parent organization and join the street fighters. Finally, to stanch the defections, the Brotherhood leaders agreed to the formation of Hamas, a completely separate organization. Hamas advertised itself as the Brotherhood's fighting arm.

For a time, the Israeli Defense Force made no move to curb Hamas. Indeed, it seemed actually to encourage its activities. The reason for this was that–even in the early days of the *intifâdah*– Hamas fought the PLO and the "leftists"; it spent as much time fighting them as it did the occupation authorities. At a point, however, Hamas changed, and the IDF moved against it.

The subsequent crackdown of the IDF on Hamas has been quite harsh, to the point that the organization was thrown into disarray and then fractured into numerous quasi-independent gangs. These exist without much organization, and virtually no discipline. How they manage to survive is a great mystery–as quickly as leaders are arrested or killed by the Israelis, new ones rise up to take their place. In this respect, the modus operandi of Hamas is similar to that of the *Gamaa* in Egypt and the Armed Islamic Group in Algeria (about which we will have more to say below).

When, in 1990, the Gush Emunim announced that it would attempt to lay a cornerstone on the Temple Mount–as the Jews refer to the *Haram ash-Sharîf*–mobs of Muslims converged there, to be met with hundreds of Israeli Border Police, who opened fire, killing 21 persons. After that, Hamas announced that it would lead an armed revolt against the occupation, which prompted the Israelis to step up their military presence in the territories. After that *intifâdah* violence became almost uncontrollable.

The Israelis had been pleased to have the religious forces and PLO fighting each other, but there was more to it than that. The territories are a financial drain on the Israelis. When the Brotherhood offered to take over social services there, the Israeli government acquiesced. After all, the Brotherhood was not perceived–at the time– as a disruptive force. Hamas did not exist when the Israelis made their decision. Had the Israelis anticipated the appearance of Hamas, almost certainly they would have acted differently.

Today, in Lebanon, *Hizbullah* is divided between moderate and extremist wings. The moderates have begun to experiment with the electoral process, and recently they elected eight representatives to Lebanon's parliament. The extremists remain determined to crush the Jewish state. The Lebanese Shias' grievance against Israel involves land, which Israel seized from Lebanon along the southern border. This was Shia territory, and the Shia community wants it back. *Hizbullah* is spearheading that fight.

There is only one mystery to consider in regard to *Hizbullah*, and that is why the Lebanese Shias, with relatively little political consciousness, allowed themselves to be turned against the United States. This was an extraordinary step for them to have taken. Heretofore, practically all of the resistance groups had focused on overcoming the Israelis. The Lebanese Shias bypassed that stage to focus on the United States as their principal foe.

The Shias appear to have been influenced by their Iranian patrons. Since the days of Iran's prime minister Mossadeq, when Washington intervened in Tehran's attempt to nationalize British-owned oil fields, a significant portion of Iranians have hated America. They see it as the successor of the British imperialists. In particular, these Iranians harbor a deep resentment for the CIA's 1953 restoration to power of the Shah.

Antipathy for the United States is nothing new in the Middle East. But prior to the coming of Khomeini it was virtually inconceivable that any group–for example, the Iraqi or Syrian Ba'thists–would presume to fight East and West simultaneously. This was what made the Khomeini Revolution so different, that the Khomeinists viewed Washington and Moscow as equally devilish.

When the Iranian Revolutionary Guards arrived in Lebanon, they brought their ideology with them. They indoctrinated the Lebanese Shias to see the world as they saw it, however simplistically. There were the forces of darkness, which included communism and capitalism, and there was Islam. Israel, to the Iranians, was an adjunct entity, subsumed by the greater evil.

This attitude may be gaining authority among the Middle Easterners. Indeed, it has begun to surface among the Brotherhood cadres, who have developed the concept of the "Crusaders." That is, the Brothers look on the growing influence of the United States in the region as a return of the Crusaders, evidence of the fact that the West is trying to destroy the Muslim faith. Whether this is a widely held conviction is debatable; but it is present, and is being voiced with greater and greater frequency.

What is striking about the performance of these religious movements is their ability to attract and to hold popular constituencies. This is most apparent with the Algerian Islamic Salvation Front (FIS). The FIS example is particularly illuminating because it is so clear cut. There was no religious opposition in Algeria prior to the FIS; therefore we must infer that the movement's ability to challenge the regime was built on support picked up after the rioting.

It seems obvious on what this support is based. The clerics speak the language of the masses, particularly the barely literate urbanized peasants. They also have lived among them, whether in the urban ghettoes or in the *baladi* villages. Under such circumstances, trust can be achieved fairly easily.

Moreover, the appeal of the clerics has a material basis. All of the regimes currently beset by the fundamentalists share a common background. They all initially tried to take over the welfare-providing role of the mosques, and failed. When they did so, they turned back to the mosques, and asked them to reassume their charity dispensing activities. The mosques gladly complied, but, then, in the process of doing so, they deliberately set about to undercut the regimes' legitimacy. Thus, there appears to be a correlation between the governments' ability to provide welfare and to maintain community control. Once the regimes stopped looking out for the people's economic well-being, they provided openings for the religious conservatives to expand and take over politically.

We next want to consider the ambivalent behavior of the religious forces. Every one of these movements (with the exception of *Hizbullah*) eschewed violence in the beginning. Instead, the leaders opted to work through the system. And, even when balked by the governments, they still held off. Later, however, the movements became wildly violent; some of them now appear to be absolutely out of control. To get at this requires probing the nature of the clerical establishment under Islam.

The religious leaders traditionally have looked on themselves as intermediaries between the people and the rulers. In time of community tension, they feel it their duty to defuse violence and direct emotion into well-regulated channels where compromises can be made. Given this disposition on the part of the `ulamâ', there would be no incentive for them to instigate a revolt. To do so would be to undercut their position in the society, which they have built up over the course of centuries. What appears to have occurred, however, is that the clerical establishment has undergone change in recent years. Among Muslims today, there still exist traditional clerics, who are conservative and inclined to support the government. Many of these individuals are paid civil servants.

Along with these "establishment clergy," there are increasing numbers of so-called free clerics, individuals who have no government ties, and, in many instances, seem deliberately to avoid establishing such links. These people appear to be caught up in the present violent activities. The author does not know when this phenomenon (of the free clergy) developed, but it is easy to see how it would have come about.

Sunni Islam, unlike Catholicism, does not have a formal religious hierarchy. Any Muslim who has studied at the *madrasa* (religious school), and has received a diploma can set up as a *shaykh*, after which he performs essentially the same role as does a clergyman in Christianity. He must find his own means of support, however, which he does by gathering a congregation. That congregation will, assuming it approves of the *shaykh*, provide for his maintenance.

Those *shaykh*s who decline working for the government, or who may not have had the opportunity, can yet exert influence over the community because they are not perceived as having been bought. Indeed, there may be a relation between speaking out and being taken care of. If a cleric takes stands that are controversial, this may enhance his reputation, which would be of material benefit to him.

To the degree that they are willing to speak out, recalcitrant *shaykh*s perform a service to Muslims at odds with the regime. They can explain to congregants under pressure–those who find themselves slipping into poverty–why this is happening to them. A *shaykh* who blames the woes of the community on the regime probably is telling the congregants what they want to hear.

This would explain the drawing power of small *shaykh*s operating in villages in upper Egypt, but what about the great mosque preachers of Cairo who also speak out against the government? These *shaykh*s, too, are fulfilling a need, for middle class congregations also are upset with the government; they, too, want to be told that the regime in power is derelict.

What is interesting, though, is that the same message is interpreted differently by two different audiences. Poor villagers, told that the regime is corrupt, may take this as a signal to drive the rulers from power. The middle class, on the other hand, may interpret the message as a call for reform.

The point, however, is that the *clerics* are not agitating the *movement*, but are responding to prodding from the people, who are discontented with the regimes in power and want to have their grievances articulated. Why go to clerics for this, when in the West a politician would suffice? First, under Islam, there is no separation of church and state; Muslim clergy have not foresworn politics, as is usually the case with clergy in the West. Additionally, after a half century of misrule under secularist leaders, Muslims may naturally turn toward clerics as more trustworthy.

The secularists had plenty of time to prove themselves during the Cold War years. Not only did they fail, they did so egregiously. The Six Day War, Black September, and the tragedy of Beirut are but a few of the failures of the secularists, leftists and rightists alike. Once the hold of the secularists was loosened–as happened under Sadat–the religious forces reemerged, as if they had never been in eclipse, and they recaptured their hold over the public.

This explains the ability of the Brotherhood to survive after Sadat's and Mubarak's efforts at repression. Similarly, in Algeria, the FLN's belief that religious influence had been done away with proved illusory.

My theory is: what the West regards as a movement of religious fundamentalism is in reality a conservative reaction to over a half century of misrule by secular regimes. This reaction was spearheaded by the clergy, because–given the entrenched nature of the regimes–only the clergy could stand up to them. Even the most obdurately secular ruler would think twice about defying the demands of the clerics for reform. Rather than confront the clerics head on, he would be more likely to try to conciliate them.

When, however, the rulers, in effect, dug in their heels and refused to proceed any further long the path of reform–as in Algeria– moderate clerics who were originally associated with the movement withdrew. Rather than incite the mobs to violence, they simply subsided; to all intents they abandoned the movement. Mubarak, and the Algerian junta, both maintain that this pullout was a sham, that the conservatives are still involved; they are orchestrating the activities of the radicals from behind the scenes, they say.   I doubt this explanation. It seems more likely that the conservatives were not interested in, and indeed had cause to fear, a mass uprising, since this would strike at their interests.

At the same time, however, the elders' unwillingness to confront authority changed the tone of the movement. Rebellious youths took this on themselves. They kept up the agitation, and, in the process of doing so, won support of elements of the clergy who were themselves radical. In this way the movement preserved its religious cast. In fact, however, it is not, as it exists today, primarily a religious movement anymore; it has taken the form of a populist revolt, which has broken out in at least two important Middle Eastern states.

The question now becomes where is all this heading? Is this movement going to spread? And, if so, which states are next in line to be assaulted? This would appear to depend on the regimes in power. To the extent that they are willing to open up to the people, they can probably avoid confrontation. But, as the examples of Egypt and Algeria have shown, the rulers are not disposed to be so yielding. In the case of Algeria, the army seems to feel that it must repress the popular forces at all costs. Mubarak has been somewhat more compromising, but even he of late has shown himself to be obdurate. As for the Palestinians and the *Hizbullah*is, the outcome depends on the peace process.

Unaccommodated by this explanation is the matter of violence against individuals who constitute no threat to the movement. The stabbing of Naguib Mahfuz is a good example of this. Such actions apparently are crimes, egregious acts of violence, which serve no useful purpose. Indeed, Mahfuz would appear to be the last person one would want to attack. By winning the Nobel Prize he brought honor and glory to his country.

The key is to understand what happens when a regime is stigmatized as "godless." In fact, it is stripped of its legitimacy, which means that Muslims need no longer obey such a government. The injunction may be construed as binding, that is as an obligation not to obey.

At the same time it appears that, under the Qur'an, there are any one of a number of permissible responses. One can simply withhold cooperation, while on the surface appearing to obey— observing the forms of submission while hardening one's heart against the regime. Or one can speak out against it. In the most extreme case, one can take it on oneself to correct the un-Islamic condition that obtains. This last scenario would appear to be what is going on with much of the *Gamaa*-type violence in Egypt. Individual Muslims, acting on their own initiative, pass judgment on perceived offenders, and then execute the judgments.

One could argue that this does not, or should not apply to Mahfuz, since he is not part of the repressive government apparatus. True, but he does represent something noxious in the minds of a particular class of Muslims. He is seen as someone who has sold himself to the enemies of the faith by writing blasphemous articles and books about it. Thus, his presence within the community was perceived as an abomination, which must be expunged. No one has taken a contract out against him. Nonetheless he has become a target for any Muslim who has the opportunity to strike him down.

If this interpretation is correct, it reveals something about what is going on, not only in Egypt but throughout the entire Arab world. Mubarak, Rabin, and the leaders of the military junta in Algeria, have all claimed that the fundamentalists are highly organized and obedient to central authority. This does not appear to be the case. The character of the violence belies this–it is much too random and spontaneous. Much of it appears to be committed on impulse, and indeed this may be precisely what is happening. Once the *shaykh* has pronounced against the regime, it is up to individual Muslims to decide how they will respond. The *shaykh* does not tell them how to act; nor does he help in carrying out the action. This is solely up to the individual. It is really not much different than workers performing acts of sabotage. In fact, this would appear to be a good description of what is occurring–a form of sabotage.

Individuals in Muslim society who are only marginally effective are acting out their frustration and rage by attacking the system whenever the opportunity to do so presents itself, or when their rage becomes insupportable. Such activity may seem quixotic; it may ultimately be doomed. The authorities certainly are going to fight back, and they have the will and organization to do so effectively. Still, the attacks are taking place.

One of the criticisms leveled at the fundamentalists is that the leadership seems incapable of generating effective tactics. It has been claimed that, were there effective leaders within the movement, the regimes under assault long ago would have been swept from power. This theory overlooks the extraordinary resources on which the regimes have to draw. The Israeli presence in the territories is overwhelming; Mubarak has legions of security forces; the Algerian army is equipped with the most up-to-date equipment. Given this massive security presence, the tactics the militants have devised are fairly shrewd. Stabbings, suicide bombings-these are the sorts of actions that security forces cannot easily deflect.

These actions are in the tradition of anarchist violence that flourished in Europe in the last century, specifically in the Mediterranean countries of Italy and Spain. If this is a rebirth of that type of anarchism, then it is more serious than has been recognized, and it certainly is something that should concern U.S. policy makers.

U.S. policy makers need to rethink their attitudes toward the fundamentalist movement. Unless Egypt is. to explode with unresolved class tensions, there must be some move toward democracy. A system in which the Brotherhood was enfranchised would offer an outlet for some of the pressures. Nor does it seem there would be much to fear from such a move. The Brotherhood is the party of conservatism, and thus it does not seek radical solutions to Egypt's ills. Egypt's political system, with the Brotherhood included, would certainly change, but as long as the radicals were kept in check, this would not be so dire.

Algeria is more problematical because the destruction there is so far advanced. Many members of the middle class appear to have already fled the country.

As for Israel, there has to be a compromise struck here as well. For awhile it seemed that this was a possibility. The Declaration of Principles seemed to signal a new beginning of the peace process. It appeared for a time that this was a true breakthrough, and that the parties on both sides–the PLO and Rabin government–would compromise to move the process along. At present, however, chances for peace appear to have dimmed considerably.

The Palestinians insist on some form of statehood and they want East Jerusalem put under Palestinian control. Israel remains adamantly opposed to either of these demands. Given the mood of the Palestinian people, it is hard to envision a solution that does not compromise on one, or both of these issues.

Finally, there is *Hizbullah*, which the author views as a *sui generis* case. Created by Tehran, this organization has consistently deferred to the Iranians. It is therefore, to a large degree, lacking independence. Nonetheless, a careful study of the career of *Hizbullah*, and in particular of its behavior lately, indicates that it, too, is seeking to become autonomous. Indeed, were the Shias to get their land back, it is likely that *Hizbullah* would go out of the guerrilla business.

The United States must not become implicated in the machinations of regimes under assault by the fundamentalists. If the Islamic resurgence is a system-wide social upheaval affecting the entire Middle East, it is only a matter of time until areas that have escaped will be caught up. The United States must not be overwhelmed by this phenomenon, and that is a matter of positioning. When the wave breaks, as seems to be inevitable, we must be able to maneuver ourselves to safety. Policy makers should ascertain how the United States can facilitate change, without undercutting U.S. interests, which in this part of the world are vital.

To a degree, the United States is on trial. Up until now the anger of area natives has been directed at unresponsive governments, but these groups could just as easily turn against Washington. We must keep in mind the example of Iran, and the conviction of the hard liners there that America is the number one enemy. U.S. policy makers should do everything possible to resist the appearance of a Sunni variant of the Iranian revolution.

DISCUSSION

Imad-ad-Dean Ahmad: While Iranians may have exploited Lebanese Shi`a's hostility towards the United States, I think it is more accurate to say that the hostility was inflamed not by Iranian influence so much as 16-inch shells hurled by the U.S.S. New Jersey at Shi`a villages in the mountains over Beirut. As Gen. Colin Powell so astutely observed in *My American Journey* (New York: Random House, 1995): "What we tend lo overlook in such situations is that other people will react much as we would. When the shells started falling on the Shiites, they assumed the American 'referee' had taken sides against them. And since they could not reach the battleship, they found a more vulnerable target, the exposed Marines at the airport." We know from Powell's book that the President made this decision at Bud McFarlane's urging over Casper Weinberger's objections.

Dr. Pelletiere wishes it to be clear that his responses to the following questions are his own opinions and not those of the United States Army or of the U.S. Government.

Muhammad Mosleh: Do you conclude that the dynamics of radicalization originate outside the Islamist movement and that the original reformist motivation of all Islamic movements can gain ascendancy if the policies of the United States and the European countries would aim to remove these external radicalizing causes?

Stephen Pelletiere: Yes and no. My focus was on those regimes in the Middle East that actively sought to ally with the West, and what happened to them, and to the societies they ruled, at the end of the Cold War. My finding was that a lot of the pro-Western governments (Mubarak's in Egypt is an outstanding example) found themselves without a role once the Soviet Union collapsed. At the same time, elements of their societies, which had countenanced the regimes' continuance in power (largely, it appears, because they opposed Communism), now saw them as corrupt and wanted them removed. It was the clash between the secular rulers, who had to justify their rule, and the people, who wanted reform, which led to the eruption of discontent, i.e., what we in the West have characterized as Islamic Fundamentalist agitation. I don't see how specific interventionist moves by the United States can turn this situation around. Perhaps if the United States were not to prop up these regimes that are coming under attack, that would help. I guess to that extent I agree with you.

Mosleh: Would it be a more productive methodological approach if we first study the forces that drive Islamic activism before we study the internal dynamics of the Islamic movements. Should we not reverse our definition of cause and effect by developing a conceptual framework or ... theoretical paradigm to study and analyze the dynamics of the history, current developments, and probable future of the Muslim movements around the world?

Pelletiere: You have to try to understand why I chose to proceed as I did. I saw Islamic Fundamentalism as a unique phenomenon, and thus as something worth studying. But, it is my belief you cannot understand a thing unless you know where it comes from. I saw a number of scholars (and a lot of journalists) speculating about Islamic Fundamentalism on the basis of, as I construed it, no real facts. As a consequence, what they were claiming was nonsense. I decided to go back to the origins of the various groups in order to fill what I perceived to be gaping holes in our knowledge about them. What I found was extraordinary, or at least I think it is. It's hard, once you know how these groups came to be, to go along with the widely held view that they constitute a great threat to the security of the United States. They are not targeting the United States, as far as I was able to learn; and certainly they are not being directed by a controlling authority (such as Iran, for example). You can go ahead and attack the problem from another angle–construct a different theory from mine; you can concentrate on the dynamics, if you wish. But still you might want to try to incorporate my findings in any investigations of your own.

Anissa Abdulfattah: My gut feeling is that much of what is mentioned here is true and should not be news to American policymakers, who are intelligent enough to understand the pitfalls of "unconditional" support for regimes that stand in contrast to popular opposition movements, or even resistance. My question is why does the United States not use its economic leverage to encourage democratization in the Middle East and North Africa? And why does the media, both domestic and international, not do more to clarify the interests of the various players in the democratization movements in these countries, since the media has been supportive of democracy, at least in principle?

Pelletiere: I don't think the media in the West is going to act as you propose. The media's function is to entertain, and its role is to make money. Expecting the media to take the lead in educating public opinion about what's going on in the Middle East and North Africa, is delusory. As for the United States using its economic leverage, I think to a degree it has done that. For a while, the Labor government in Israel–under Rabin–seemed willing to trade a meaningful peace with the Arabs for tangible economic rewards. I think the United States supported, and to a degree leveraged, that determination. Of course, once Netanyahu came to power, any movement in that direction died. Whether the United States has the will to pressure Netanyahu, remains to be seen.

Abdulfattah: [I suspect that analyses of] the religious thrust behind the evolving movements [evince] an attempt to neutralize any fear that it is really "religion" coming to power over secular ideologies. Can you examine this fear of the religious politics of Muslims? ... There appears to be little fear of religious politics in Israel. Are they equally feared? Why or why not?

Pelletiere: I think most of the sensation over Muslim politics, has been generated by the media. The Islamic Fundamentalism craze, if I can call it that, was a media event. As a former journalist I know how easy it is to manufacture these campaigns. All you need is a few techniques, which are fairly simple to learn and easy to replicate. Also the fact that media control in the United States is in the hands of a relatively small group of people makes it that much easier to do. Why doesn't the media mount a similar campaign inquiring about religious politics in Israel? Because the people who run the media aren't interested in going into that.

Robert Crane: You have emphasized that the Brotherhood movements, the Ikhwan, originated as non-violent efforts at reform within the existing system of governance. Yet today many of even their moderate leaders speak of change from the top-down. They call for systemic change without any well-thought-out or actionable agenda or program for what changes they would introduce, and have no strategy for working within an alliance of like-minded but not overtly Islamic groups. They would seem to be supporting the utopian view that if only they had power all problems would disappear. This suggests a mentality which is not reformist but revolutionary. You say that the Brotherhood leaders are basically conservative and that their reformist movement has been challenged by younger radicals. What difference would it make for American interests if the Brotherhood would ascend to power in various countries rather than the radicals?

Pelletiere: I think it would make a lot of difference. If my conclusions are correct, the difference between the Brotherhood and the radicals is, to a large degree, generational. The Brotherhood leadership tends to be older, more established, and less anxious to risk substantial holdings built up over the course of years in a potentially ruinous confrontation with the authorities. The radicals, being younger and less well established, have less to lose, in a material sense. I think if the latter come to power, change would be more far reaching, and could not be effected without considerable violence. Since America supports the status quo, our interest would be adversely affected, if the radicals took over.

Crane: Is there any evidence that Islamist leaders are learning from their failures and that the radicals have alienated much of their support by their violent excesses?

Pelletiere: I think it's too early to say. The initial clash between the religious forces and the secular leadership took place, by my reckoning, just about five years ago. The secular forces were able to suppress the religious groups (this was particularly true in Egypt), but not utterly destroy them. Now we see the conflict building up again—in the Occupied Territories and Algeria, most notably. We will have to see how the second round plays out.

Crane: How can the U.S. government and the private sector, perhaps through two-track diplomacy, encourage any moves toward pragmatic moderation by both the Islamists and the secular governments in ways that would promote political stability and economic prosperity? Can this be done simultaneously with continued U.S. support of existing regimes?

Pelletiere: I think the only thing the United States need do in the Middle East is to get the Arabs and Israelis to agree to a meaningful peace, and to lift the embargo on Iraq. After that, I think the less we get involved in the politics of the region the better.

The Intersection
of Islamic Resurgence
and Democracy

Charles Butterworth: As a student of political philosophy, I want to focus on the significance of political Islam. By way of introduction, I would pose the following kind of question: Why is there so much emphasis in the West on liberty, and so much criticism on Islam for not being liberal? Does that mean not being "secular"–why does that happen?

The second question is, "How can we present an accurate picture of what's going on in the Arab and Islamic world?" I realize that to say "Arab world" does not do justice to all of Islam, but that happens to be the part of the Islamic world that I'm most familiar with.

I'll try to get at what's going on behind the scenes or at a deeper level by focusing my remarks on three separate topics. First of all, what I'd call "Republicanism" and "Islamism", secondly, "religion" and "liberty", and then thirdly, on the way we can come together.

Where do Islam and Democracy meet? I've been thinking a great deal about the model of the French Republic, "Liberty, Equality, Fraternity," and it seems to me that it would be interesting to take that model or those groups of words and ask ourselves what an Islamic Republic would look like in light of those three categories. With respect to liberty–there would be liberty from poverty, even liberty from penury as well as liberty from the oppression of the passions.

Second, there would be equality before God, but an equality of human beings before God without destroying a traditional set of hierarchies—hierarchies that are based on natural phenomena such as sex, age, and intelligence. And, if you wish, I can come back and explain why I think that <u>would not</u> go away, and why there is a good reason for it not going away. Thirdly, fraternity—now, for somebody like myself there is one problem about that fraternity, because I see it as primarily a fraternity among co-religionists, and so that excludes me.

Without getting too bogged down in contemporary events, I'd like to talk about an article published recently in *The Wall Street Journal.* It deserves mention because *The Wall Street Journal* so often does such a bad job of reporting on Islam and the Middle East. So when they do a good job, they should be commended. And then I'd like to talk about an essay that Amos Elon wrote in the *New York Review of Books.* And finally, I would like to share with you a few impressions from a trip I made recently to Tunisia.

Peter Waldman, whom I do not otherwise know, wrote an article called "Leap of Faith" that was published in the *Wall Street Journal* on March 15, 1995. He tried to make three points that I thought were very interesting. One—to see what's going on in the Arab-Islamic world today as being primarily a movement that has an emphasis on human rights and on democracy. And somebody led him to think about the verse in the Qur'an—2:256—*lâ ikrâha fi dîn,* "There is no compulsion in religion." He tried to show how that guided some of the movements that are going on. What Waldman walked away from after all of his interviews and what he presented the readers of *The Wall Street Journal* with was the notion that the major desire now is a desire for modernizing society and the institutions of society, without losing Islamic identity. The final thing, in keeping with that notion of modernizing, the emphasis, is on renewal rather than on reform.

If you think back to what was going on thirty years ago, even twenty-five years ago, even, perhaps, until the death of Fazlur Rahman, the notion now, as then is *tajdîd,* renewal. Amos Elon, an Israeli now living in New York, who strikes me as an interesting observer of things that are going on in the Arab world, and who writes very frequently in liberal journals about these things, drew an interesting picture. It was primarily a picture based on his recent trip to Cairo. He entitled his essay, "One Foot on the Moon." Thinking of what happened when he went to interview some of the journalists in the *al-Ahram* offices–looking not only at the opulence of the building, but thinking about how he had been forced to go through metal detectors as he came into the building and searched or frisked by security guards, how he saw security guards before all of the eleva-tors–he then contrasted that with what he saw outside the windows and especially outside on the street when he left. Any of you who have been down in that district of Cairo know that you go from opulence to utter heart-wrenching misery. The *al-Ahram* offices are in one of the poorest areas of urban Cairo. Then Alon went on to draw the fascinating contrast between luxury cars one sees–as you remember there was a time when everybody used to speak not of Mercedes-Benzes but of "Misra-cedes"–and the wretched streets. The other thing that is so shocking when you look at what's going on in Egypt–the extravagant weddings in five-star hotels and the poor hanging on, looking for a few pieces of money or some kind of food or something that the wealthy attendees at the wedding are going to give in a moment of joy.

Second, Elon pointed at the incompetence of President Hosni Mubarak today, and how awareness of this is now very widespread among almost all Egyptian intellectuals. The economy is stagnant–the economy has been stagnant for years, but it's still stagnant. Mubarak has not changed anything. What is worse is that, more pointed than ever before, the affluence of government officials continues apace even though the economy remains stagnant. So, why is there Islamist sentiment? Because of utter frustration. There seems to be some willingness on the part of the government to let this go, that is, to let the Islamist sentiment be expressed–to let it continue. And the reason for this–despite the harsh crackdowns in upper Egypt–is because of the government's fear of what Israel will ultimately do economically: the whole fear of Israel's ability and certainly, desire, to usurp the whole area economically, to usurp the old Egyptian role that has been so very important.

Now, one thing that I think, Elon was trying to put his finger on is something that impressed me mightily when I was last in Egypt, namely, what is happening among people like Mustafa Mahmoud with his mosque and the centers that he's formed both within the mosque and outside the mosque. Let me share with you what I learned from Mustafa Mahmoud himself once when I had the privilege of spending an evening in conversation about his precise goals and his hopes for the future. Mahmoud would like to see an Islamic regime, but not today. And he does not know when one will be feasible. Before it comes about, he realizes that the well-being of people has to be provided for, that he has first to get to the material conditions of the people, eventually get to their moral conditions and then, at that time, he can begin to think about some political solutions. One of the best contemporary Islamist works I have read is his autobiography, *My Voyage, From Doubt to Faith* (*Rihlati min ash-Shakk ila'l-Iman*).

My third illustration: In March of this year, I was at a conference in Tunisia put on by the Tunisian Society of Philosophy. It was very impressive because, to the best of my knowledge, all the costs connected with the conference were paid for by the Society itself without state funding. (If there were funds that came in, they were very modest; for example, Tunis Air may have helped with a couple of air tickets.) It was very much a "grass roots" kind of thing. The theme of the conference was *Ibn Rushd al-Yawm, Averroes Today*. It was not very clear what the organizers meant by that title, but I do not for a moment think that they espoused the goals of Murad Wahbah when he organized a conference on Ibn Rushd in Cairo just a few months earlier (December, 1994), namely, to promote the notion that there was an enlightenment movement in the Twelfth Century or earlier on in Islamic culture and thus to encourage people to think about, even to emulate, this.

But the president of the session at which I gave my paper–a woman professor who specializes in Spinoza–was noticeably disappointed by my presentation. So as to entice, but also so as not to reveal too much, I had to entitle my paper: "Averroes: Precursor of Enlightenment?" When the program was published, the title was transformed to "Averroes and Enlightenment," either due to wishful thinking or human error, who knows. I was scheduled to speak on the last day of the conference, and as people chatted with me, I realized they were expecting me to say: Well, he was the voice of rationalism in the Arab world and all we have to do is follow his guide. I did not say that, for I do not think that is accurate.

What I tried to show, as a matter of fact, is that Averroes does not represent enlightenment–at least not Enlightenment as it is understood with respect to 18th Century France and also Germany. That kind of enlightenment considers religion nothing but a tool for the people; it is a kind of a "sop" you have to use to bring the people along and lead them where you want to go–you, i.e., the ruling elite. I do not for a moment think that this is what Averroes is about. I tried to show that he is a man well aware of the importance of religion, that he deemed it very, very important to keep people's faith in religion strong because it was so important for their moral well-being. The president of the session expressed her disappointment at my having failed to see how close to Spinoza Averreos really was. Well, in the discussion period we tried to dispel that misunderstanding.

In addition, there are three impressions I took away from this voyage. The first is how well education was working. There was among the professors–but, more importantly, among high school teachers and people who simply were interested in philosophy because they had studied it in high school or in university and continued to be interested in it–a kind of desire, which we seldom see elsewhere, to learn more. The first speaker–who happens to be a very well known figure in the world of letters, and quite well known to Muslims, Professor Muhsin Mahdi from Harvard University–and I talked about this, and we were simply astonished. Not only is this unusual for the Arab world, it is unusual for the West. There was a cohesiveness among the people at the conference–among university professors with one another, among university professors and high school teachers, among them and the people not involved professionally at all in the pursuit of philosophy–a willingness to talk that is, sadly, all too rare. This was an interesting kind of "side effect" that shows part of what is going on in Tunisian society.

Second, Tunisia is poor. There are problems, but there is a better sense of economic well-being there than I have seen elsewhere in the Arab world. And I thought I noticed an attempt on the part of people to keep that going.

And, finally, what impressed me was the openness to the West expressed by the people I dealt with. (Now to be sure, I was only there as a visitor, and later as a tourist; so I am speaking of my relations with merchants, with people in hotels, but also with my professional colleagues, that is, the university professors and high school teachers at the conference.) This was an openness they clearly desired, but one they considered to threaten in no way their Arab or their Islamic identity. The Islamic identity was not worn openly; it was not expressed as openly as I noticed it, for example, in Egypt–but it was there–and, after a little bit of discussion, one found that they all desired to preserve this Arab-Muslim identity. There was one exception–a man a few years older than I am who openly longed for the old days of French colonialism–which just shows that there has to be a reactionary in every crowd.

Now the final point I want to make regards a book written by Olivier Roy that has recently been translated from the French, *The Failure of Political Islam*. I think it is important to think about Roy's argument and also about the reply Graham Fuller made to the effect that Roy is wrong in what he takes to be the precise failure. Roy's problem is in claiming "well, there's nothing new," when that is not really the issue. What we must do in order to determine what political Islam is doing and to judge it correctly is to look more deeply than Roy has done.

In this vein, let me talk for a moment about religion and liberty. In the book William Zartman and I put together, *Political Islam*, I tried to express concern about why we in the West think liberty is so important and want to judge all other political phenomena in terms of liberty. I criticized both Leonard Binder and his new book on development and Frances Fukuyama and his book on the end of history. It seems to me that if you look carefully at what is going on in politics, liberty is not the goal we should focus our sights on. The real goal is virtue–what we are trying to do is to guide a nation. We want to shape our citizens' goodness or moral virtue. Let me try to persuade you of this argument by turning to more authoritative thinkers.

The first authority I would bring forth is Jean-Jacques Rousseau. Now I know that Rousseau raises hackles on all sides, but if you can remember for a moment how carefully he tried to think through the problem of human dependence upon government and to see how human beings might achieve liberty without losing self-governance and without losing religion, then you will see why I call upon him. In *The Social Contract*, Book One, Chapter Eight, entitled "On the Civil State," he says: "the impulsion of appetite alone is slavery. Obedience to the law that one has given oneself is liberty." Well, if you happen to be a follower of a law that has been given you, you make that law your own by the understanding you gain of it–and so that is the way that applies, I think, in this context.

Further on in *The Social Contract*, in a note to Chapter Two of Book Four, a chapter entitled "On Suffrage" or "On Voting," Rousseau says:

> In Genoa, one sees in front of prisons and on the chains of galley-slaves, the word 'libertas' [freedom, in Latin]. This application of the motto is fine and just–in effect, it is only the wrongdoers of all states who prevent the citizen from being free. In a country where all those folks would be galley-slaves, one would enjoy the most perfect liberty.

And, if you think about it, when we establish and then apply penal codes, we do so in order to safeguard our own liberty or freedom.

Another way of thinking about this and trying to draw on this other Western tradition that I am more familiar with is to reflect upon Plato and his famous dialogue called *The Laws*. What is set forth in that dialogue is the notion that virtue is "the unending courageous fight against evil." Now the greatest virtue that the main spokesperson in the dialogue, the Athenian Stranger, tries to bring forth is something called "perfect justice." He defines perfect justice as "trustworthiness in the face of evils." It is when he talks about trustworthiness in the face of evils that he introduces the concept of liberty or freedom for the first time. In other words, virtue–that is, excellence or, for our purposes, moral goodness–is the manly struggle to be free. Allied with your fellow citizens, you struggle against foreign oppression. Allied with some citizens against others, you struggle to repulse the oppression those other citizens would like to place upon you. And, within yourself, you struggle against the passions that would allow you to be easily enslaved by other human beings.

Now, if you think about this, the word I am using as "struggle" is very readily translated into Arabic as *jihâd*. My point is that this last struggle–the struggle within oneself to prevent oppression by, or enslavement to, the passions–is really central to religious struggle. And, of course, there is also a need to struggle against the oppression others might wish to force upon us.

Consider for a moment now our status as human beings in history: the love we have for liberty is really fairly recent. As you think back through time–I will dwell here on Western figures, but you can also locate many of these ideas among thinkers within the Arab-Islamic tradition–Plato and Aristotle did not prize political liberty that much. They prized the liberty or freedom I have just spoken about, but not political liberty. Nor did St. Augustine. And even Marsilius of Padua tried to break the hold the church had over political things, he did not think it should be broken in order to have individual political liberty. I think the first time liberty or freedom becomes an issue is with Machiavelli and with the people who follow Machiavelli. What Machiavelli, Hobbes, Spinoza, Locke, and so on mean by this is that we then stop asking ourselves how we can live well within a political regime and insist upon living freely. The danger that we have now come to is the danger that is represented by Nietzsche and then by the person who has made Nietzsche most prominent, Martin Heidegger. This danger is the inability to see clearly or the inability to determine whether there is anything to see at all. That danger comes from Nietzsche's supposed insight into the historicity of all human thought.

A similar line of reasoning is to be found when we look carefully at the philosophers within the Arab-Islamic tradition. I constantly look back to Alfarabi and to Ibn Rushd for guidance in these matters and am amazed to see what little importance they attached to liberty or freedom as the goal of political life. Now, the problem is the following: if you had to choose how you want to live, you would always want to be in a situation where a wise person or a wise group of people provided for you–assuming they were willing to use their wisdom for our sake. It is only because we have come to doubt either that there can be wise people, or that they will have our best interests at heart, that we claim we want to rule. If you look back over the whole struggle between the people and the few in the history of mankind that doubt has been at the core of the argument against rule by an enlightened few or–the other way around–at the core of the argument for rule by the majority. Either bitter experience has shown us that the wise–that is, those who claim to be wise–really are not so or, wise or not, that they are more interested in their own advancement than in ours.

But once again, I call upon Rousseau to shed some light on this. And I refer again to *The Social Contract*. In Book Two, Chapter Seven, entitled "On the Law-giver," Rousseau speaks of this extraordinary individual and says:

> To discover the best rules of society which suit nations, one would need a superior intelligence who sees all the passions of human beings without experiencing any of them; who had no connection with our nature and yet knew it fundamentally; whose happiness was independent of ours and who, nonetheless, wanted to busy himself with ours; and, finally, who, preparing for himself a distant glory in the passing of time, could work in one century and

revel in another. Gods would be necessary to give laws to human beings.

This is what Rousseau has to say about the law-giver or legislator. Then in a footnote to this passage, he adds: "a people does not become famous until its legislation begins to decline. We do not know for how many centuries the institutions of Lycurgus made the Spartans happy before anybody heard of them in the rest of Greece."

I will cite one last passage, if you permit. In Chapter Eleven of Book Two, "On the Diverse Systems of Legislation," Rousseau says:

> If we were to look into what precisely the greatest good of all consists in, which ought to be at the base of every system of legislation, we will find that it is reduced to these two principle objects–liberty and equality.   Liberty,   because   every   particular dependence is so much strength taken away from the body of the state. Equality, because liberty cannot subsist without it.

So this is how Rousseau thinks his way through to preserving, to arguing for and preserving, liberty or freedom and equality.

Now it seems to me that the problem we have all inherited, the problem common to us all as we sit here today, is how we can preserve liberty and equality along with dignity.   I take that combination to capture what we normally mean by moral virtue: being sufficiently free and equal to act without impulsion or impediment and conducting ourselves in an upright, dignified manner. And as somebody concerned with what is going on in this country, in the United States of America, I look at what we have tried to achieve more or less intelligently, for the last two hundred years. Remember, the best education is called liberal education or education in the liberal arts. We send our young people to the university so that they can be taught to use liberty or freedom wisely–that is the point of liberal education.

Differently stated, and resorting to a somewhat far-fetched image, in a certain respect, we long for a vision of the Roman citizen–this firm, proud, strong individual who stands for duty and for what is right. We long for the image of that kind of person and juxtapose it to the petty, narrow-minded bourgeois who is only interested in making money, to the democrat who is only interested in what the mob will say, and, above all–and this is the gravest problem today–to the relativist, the person who says "well, it's all equal, I can't make any decision."

So, I come now to the last point: where do Islam and democracy meet? Taking a line from Charles Péguy–a fascinating Christian socialist from the beginning of this century–I would say "the revolution is moral, or it is not a revolution." If we are to meet, it must be on that ground. We, here, and people everywhere who are interested in making Islam political have to reflect upon the virtue proper to self-government. What is the virtue we need to govern ourselves? I will quickly make two suggestions, then draw on something we thought we learned from the founders of this nation. Reflection is needed, and we have to go back and think about not only how we got here, but what is best about our getting here–what makes sense about it. And secondly, what seems to be missing so much today is that we have to think about what informs choice. Now, the mark of the democrat, the mark of the free human being is free choice or the freedom to choose. But free choice without deliberation is senseless, and so what really marks choice is this ability to have intelligent awareness of all of the alternatives.

In one respect, we lowered the standards amazingly when we founded this nation, or those who founded the nation lowered the standards amazingly–and they came across a very interesting solution. I am thinking of the solution that is put forth in *The Federalist Papers*, No. 51. It provides a very interesting insight into the human dilemma, into the problem of politics, but it has also now come back to haunt us:

> Ambition must be made to counteract ambition. The
> interest of the man must be connected with the

constitutional rights of the place. It may be a reflection of human nature that such devices should be necessary to control the government. But what is government itself, but the greatest of all reflections on human nature? If men were angels, no government would be necessary. If angels were to govern men, neither external nor internal controls of government would be necessary. In framing a government that is to be administered by men over men, the great difficulty lies in this: you must first enable the government to control the governed; and in the next place, oblige it to control itself. A dependence on the people is, no doubt, the primary control on the government; but experience has taught mankind the necessity of auxiliary precautions.

This policy of supplying, by opposite and rival interests, the defect of better motives, might be traced through the whole system of human affairs, private as well as public. We see it particularly displayed in all the subordinate distributions of power where the constant aim is to divide and arrange the several offices in such a manner as that each may be a check on the other—that the private interest of every individual may be a sentinel over the public rights. These inventions of prudence cannot be less requisite in the distribution of the supreme powers of the State.

Now, there is a great deal of very good common sense there and, and as a way of trying to figure out how you are going to form a constitution it is very, very sound. There is a problem, however, and this is one I think we are living with today: the problem is that in espousing that doctrine, the standards have been lowered too much. And I think it is now time to think about raising them again.

DISCUSSION

Imad-ad-Dean Ahmad: As is fitting for a philosopher and someone with classical training–Professor Butterworth has gone straight for the fundamentals and left the details for later discussion.

Ahmed Yousef: What you had said is really interesting, but still, the question is still there: Is political Islam a militant movement or a grassroots renaissance?

Butterworth: The problem with the question, of course, is that there are as many responses to it as there are political Islamic movements. I think we'd have to decide what we're really looking at when we talk about this. In the volume that I've mentioned that Zartman and I edited, a number of authors addressed different kinds of movements that are coming up as militant because of the context, but at same time trying to draw on the people, trying to get support from the people. The impression I have is that, really, I don't think there is any such thing as grassroots, if by grassroots, you mean all of a sudden people organize themselves and move. There's always somebody who sees first, and I'll take one example just to show you what I'm thinking of– Hassan al-Banna. He clearly saw that something was wrong with the world in which he lived. He wasn't the only one who saw that–before him, Muhammad Iqbal had seen it. Before them, Jamal ad-din al-Afghani had seen it. But that idea of a great past which had somehow been trampled upon–frustration at that and a question of "What have we lost? How can we regain our former grandeur?" then gets different kinds of answers.

I do not think that there is such a thing as spontaneous movement, but I think that what you are really trying to ask about by your question is militant, as opposed to peaceful, political Islam. And there, as nearly as I can see–but I really have to defer to those who have studied this much more closely–the movement is militant only when necessary; militant in response to others.

A few of you were present at a discussion we had at the University of Maryland with the Ambassador of Tunisia some time ago. He fielded a question from a Palestinian Christian who asked: "I

have read a little bit of Rashid Ghannouchi, and I do not see him to be
so terrible. Why did he suffer the fate that he suffered at the hands of
Tunisian authorities?" The question was never answered. Yes, what
is going on in southern Egypt is militant; it is something I would
criticize. But some of the things that preceded it, if people had not
been killed, I mean, this was a "Keystone Cops" kind of business—
where a bunch of police go into a mosque and spray people with
machine guns, and then find out they are in the wrong mosque. This
is ludicrous!

Imad-ad-Dean Ahmad: Obviously you're correct—militant can be
grassroots and grassroots can sometimes be militant—and I think you
identified the role of circumstance quite correctly. But on the other
hand, I see the question as aiming at two particular sub-cases:
grassroots in the sense that even though one particular person or some
small group of people may conceive of the idea, they find a
responsive chord in the masses, and therefore, it spreads in a
grassroots manner—it becomes easy to organize; militant—meaning not
so much, necessarily, militants against the established powers, but
that a militant methodology is necessary just to organize the
movement. I will use concrete examples in Afghanistan where we
can take Hekmatyar on one side and the Talaban on the other. Here
we have someone who is trying to use force in order to impose his
vision on the society, and another group which, while not averse to
force—they're engaged in armed struggle—has had an easier course
because they have received popular support. Perhaps you could
answer in that context, if you have an additional comment.

Butterworth: I would like, somehow, to bring it into a focus of
asking what's going on in places like the United States. If by
militancy all you mean is seeking to stir people up to get them to
shake off their diffidence, clearly that's there. That's what a preacher
is all about. I think I would continue to say that I don't see action
without a cause. It seems to me that with grassroots, you have to keep
asking yourself, well, who put the seed in?

Ali Ramadan Abuza`kuk: I have to really bring to the discussion a
few accepted definitions or precepts or conceptions I have difficulty

in dealing with. The first one is when we say political Islam. As a Muslim, I have never felt comfortable with this, that there is something in the jungles called political Islam. Is there something behind it? The second thing is that I have some difficulties in grasping the concepts of renewal and reform. I consider the word "reform" as *islâhi* and a renewal as *tajdîdi*–they are really two sides of the same movement.

Butterworth: Zartman and I had the title "Political Islam" imposed on us. Try to think back twenty-five years back to 1970. People didn't talk about political Islam in the 1970s. This is something that has come about recently. We tried to show what the vocabulary imposed on us by others meant. We were so dissatisfied with that paradigm that we took the chance to do a conference, and then from the conference, after getting the papers revised, a book will be forthcoming. We called it *Between the State and Islam*. When you think about the Middle East, North Africa, you see state apparatus– very heavy-handed rulers,–or you see a call for Islam being taken more seriously, becoming powerful in the lives of the people. And yet, all sorts of other things go on in people's lives. And we wanted to get people to talk about that and to show that there was a lot more going on between these two great monoliths.

I think you're right, you can push the renewal/reform and find that they overlap. There's a common core, but then, as you draw them out you see where reform does not mean necessarily renewal, and vice versa. That's all I meant. I think that what's going on in this article that Waldman wrote is "Oh, if we present this movement as renewal, it's less frightening than reform." This is "take advantage of what language allows you to do, so that you can communicate what you want."

Ali Ramadan Abuza`kuk: Do I understand from the usage of the two concepts–reform and renewal–that when we speak of renewal we speak of the realm of ideas and when we speak of reform, we speak of the society?

Butterworth: Yes. That's very good. And not only the realm of ideas, but also some kind of personal commitment–putting faith to work. That goes back to your question about "political Islam." I don't know, to say it in Arabic just sounds so strange–.

Abuza`kuk: But, is it because of the secular paradigm? I mean, it is the secular paradigm imposing itself?

Laura Drake: They have to distinguish Islamism from praying and ritual and belief in God.

Saleh Saleh: Are Arabs playing with the language trying to bring these terms into the discussion?

Charles Butterworth: That's a good point. And, remember that the whole coining of this term "Islamism" or "Islamist" was an attempt on the part of people like myself to get away from the "Fundamentalists."

Muhammad Alami: I think this has to do with Western-world thinking–the separation of church and state, and we don't have such a thing in Islam. Probably that's the source of this problem in names. You mentioned seventies–that's a very good date–because in the [late]-seventies was Iran's Khomeini, a new Islam for the West, not the Islam of Saudi Arabia, that's militant anti-Western, anti-Washington, anti-Moscow....

I think Algeria poses an extremely elegant example of this militancy, political Islam, and the West. There was *coup d'etat* in Haiti–one of the poorest nations on Earth, with two million people or three–... and the White House was obsessed with this issue for months and months. But when the only free election was held in the history of Nigeria, and the military stepped in, nobody cried; the United Nations passed no resolutions. Actually, some Western capitals were backing the military government. So, even grassroots movements become militant because of what you see as the hypocrisy of the West. Why is Aristide worth bringing back, but our embassy is not worth fighting for? I asked this question to an ex-official of the State Department and he could not give me an answer. Why is the Algerian democracy not worth even mentioning? Clinton, over the last three weeks, received three heads of state: Hassan, Hussein, and Hosni [general laughter]. But he never mentioned political freedom; he never mentioned human rights; he never mentioned anything because the fear of the alternative–who's going to replace this guy?

Butterworth: I wish I knew more about what was going on in Algeria. I was a student in France when the Algerian war against the French for independence was at its hottest. I have always had great admiration for the backbone of these fighters, these people who stood up to that wretched French colonialism. I just do not understand what is going on now, and of course the Algerians whom I see here are Algerians who are disgusted with the FIS. No spokesmen for the FIS can come to the United States to talk about these things.

I do know that there are many analysts in the West who condemned the military coup–they were not listened to. I am in an awkward position, because I cannot say very many nice things about Clinton and his foreign policy. What bothers me about Clinton is the people who are advising him on the Middle East, people who–without beating an old dead horse–all have one particular, very narrow, conception of the Middle East. It seems to be power and power politics.

Ten days ago, I was in Paris and gave a lecture before a group of conservative French, who wanted to hear something about what Islam is all about and how it stands in relation to freedom and things like this. Well, they wanted to hear it, but they wanted to hear it on their terms, not on my terms. It became very clear to me that the market was the only thing that counted in their eyes. Every other time I have had any dealing with the French with respect to Algeria, this fear of what is going to happen, of Algerians and Tunisians coming down on them, on their southern shore predominates. You hear, you read in the paper about the debate over whether young girls can wear the *hijâb* in class. The argument is "no." The claim is that it would be terrible, it would be against French laicization of the school. But it is quite all right to wear an open sport-shirt with a cross sticking out of it. And, I found out, much to my surprise, that it is quite all right for Jewish students to wear the kippah or yarmulke. This last visit, I began to question this discrepancy. And people replied: "Oh, well, you know, those things don't matter; they aren't as 'closing off' as a hijab is." You know, that really is hypocrisy–it is either sheer ignorance, brutal ignorance, or it is hypocrisy.

What I think is the most important thing about freedom is that it is a condition–we cannot live as human beings without freedom. But that does not mean that it should be the end. That is where I take my guidance in this philosophical quest: freedom is a condition permitting us to do something else. We cannot really do the good if we are not free. But just to be free–and that is where we are today, that is the problem in the United States today. Free? For what? For freedom! In the sense: Don't tell me what to do.

The other thing I just cannot help but mention–when you say, "Yeah, the seventies was a very good time because of Khomeini, etc." There is another figure who somehow passed out of the picture, whom I was always very taken by–Ali Shariati. And, he got a little bit of coverage here, because of Hamid Algar, his translator, at Berkeley. But I hear that he was very, very important among the youth; now, since I don't follow Iran that much, I don't know what happened.

Tariq Hamdi Al-Azami: There is a school now, [headed by] Abdolkarim Soroush. He is a physicist who's also [following] the same footsteps in Iran now.

Butterworth: And he's accepted?

Al-Azami: He is–it's a trend now.

Jafar Shaikh Idries: I think it is important for the Islamists to discuss the relationship between Islam and democracy and what the Islamic position is regarding freedom, but I don't think that that is the problem. The problem is that there are people in the Arab world who are supported by the West who think that there can be no modernization, their country cannot be developed, their country cannot live a modern life without secularism. So, the problem, in fact, is secularism. And no one here in the West asks whether secularism is a grassroots movement, because the question is very easy. I mean, it can be easy to answer–it has no roots at all. Secularism was something that was imposed on the Arab and Muslim world by the

West.... And it lived for some time. There was secular democracy in Egypt, in Syria, in my country, Sudan, and so on. And, because at that time all the political parties were secular, there could be democracy. When the Islamic movement came, the secularists supported by the West started to feel that secularism is in danger, and so I think the West preferred despotism, secular despotism or whatever you would call it, to Islam. And now I think it is impossible, it is impossible in the Muslim world for any Arab country to be both secular and democratic.

Butterworth: Why is that? Why do you think that is?

Shaikh: Because, if it is democratic, then this means that it would allow political parties—they would be Islamic political parties, and some of these parties might win the elections, as they did in Algeria. So they have to decide—would they just sit back and see the Islamists come win the elections? For many people, I think, in the Arab world and in the West—they prefer secularism. If it is democratic, well and good. If it is not, then secularism should be preferred to Islam. I think that is the problem.

Now, I come to the concept of freedom. I've thought about this for a long time, because for us it is not only just an intellectual problem—it is something that we live. I think that there is a concept of freedom in Islam, and it is more positive than the concept of freedom in the West. I learned a long time ago, I think from Solzhenitsen, ... that the problem was democracy. Now, in the West, he said that democracy was good when people were religious, because democracy only gives you the freedom to say and do what you want, what you choose. Religion told you to do the good thing. Now, if there is no religion, democracy becomes the freedom to do evil. Now, in Islam, of course, the most fundamental, the most important thing in Islam is that you worship God, you worship Allah. And you are called the "Abdullah." The emphasis is here, but there is something which many people forget—that Islam says, by being "Abdullah," you liberate yourself from the passions that you were talking about; you liberate yourself from being a slave of other human beings; and so on.... Islam has a political aspect. I often say that, in Islam, dictatorship is *shirk*, because a dictator who imposes his will on the people and who becomes a lawgiver puts himself in place of Allah.

Muhammad al-Asi: The real freedom is the total submission to God. You said following a system that is imposed on you is slavery, but being obedient to a system you believe in is liberty or freedom, right? That is exactly the Islamic concept–because a person, when he submits his will to God then he becomes free. Why? Because he is submitting his will to nobody else–only God. And God is not a human being. ... If you submit to anything lower than that, you are becoming a slave, but when you submit to God you are a free person.

Imad-ad-Dean Ahmad: In Islam you don't become a slave of human beings, because no human being–no matter how good he is–can benefit you, even if he has the best intentions. He doesn't know everything about you, and so the laws which he, or they, meant for you will not be to your interest–real interest–whether spiritual or material.

Islamic Movements at the End
of the Twentieth Century: Where Now?

Michael Collins Dunn: The topic which I have been asked to address is a broad one: "Islamic Movements at the End of the Twentieth Century: Where now?" A comprehensive response would require a book or perhaps several as well as an ability to foretell the future, which I do not claim. I believe, however, that it is possible to discern certain trends and characteristics in the evolution of Islamic movements from which we can extrapolate a few inferences about future developments.

First, some definitions are in order. I have taken "Islamic movements" here to mean those with a political agenda, those movements sometimes called "Islamist" or "political Islam" and, by their enemies, "fundamentalist." There are, of course, other elements of the Islamic revival which are not political in their goals: some Sufi movements are also experiencing revival and growing membership, but while they are in a sense "Islamic movements" and part of the Islamic revival, they do not generally except in Africa and the Caucasus involve themselves in political matters. As a matter of convenient shorthand, I will be referring to those Islamic movements with a political agenda as "Islamist". This is not a particularly satisfactory term, but it is far better than "fundamentalist," a word borrowed from Christian vocabulary, and I believe it is a bit more precise than simply saying "Islamic," for while these movements are certainly Islamic in their orientation, so are many other movements and ideas which do not seek social and political change.

I should also note that as a non-Muslim observer of these movements, and as a Westerner though one trained in Islamic history and culture, my views will probably not please some adherents of modern Islamic movements or, on the other hand, their opponents in secular regimes. I am offering my own analysis, which does not accord precisely with that of either side in the growing polarization between secularist and Islamist.

There is an irony in attempting to discuss the future of Islamist movements. I, and many other observers of these movements, have tried for years to convince policymakers and the media in the West that we must not stereotype these movements, by seeing them as a unified global movement or monolithic structure. Just as the countries in which they have emerged are quite different from each other, and the societies differ profoundly at times, so too these movements differ from one another in precise goals, in tactics, and in their own view of their role in the existing system. The responses of the existing regimes also differ enormously, from accommodation to outright hostility. To ignore these distinctions is to encourage the Western tendency to see "Islamic fundamentalism" as a monolithic, united phenomenon which is often perceived as a threat to the West. Each of these movements is different, and its prospects for success differ according to the nature of the state and society in which it exists. Its goals and its implications for the West may differ enormously from another such movement in a very different society.

Having said and written many times that we must not characterize these movements as a monolithic phenomenon, I am now asked to venture into discussing the future of Islamist movements as a whole. Therein lies the irony, for a short presentation such as this one leaves little time for the distinctions required by the diversity of these movements.

I should also mention that my own experience is limited. I know very little about Islamic movements in Sub-Saharan Africa and Southeast Asia, including Malaysia and Indonesia. I know a bit more about South Asia and Central Asia. But I am primarily a specialist on the Middle East, and so most of the examples I draw upon in my analysis will be Middle Eastern, either the Arab world or Iran and Turkey, though occasionally citing an example elsewhere. This by no means implies that Islamist movements in other regions are unimportant, merely that they are outside my direct experience.

To set the stage for our look ahead, a few words are in order about the evolution of Islamist movements to date. It is important to recognize that throughout Islamic history there have been frequent movements to reform, renew, and purify both religious practice and society, including the political sphere. Sometimes these movements have been primarily reformist, sometimes more messianic, in the sense that they have believed that they represent the beginning of the last days. These historical movements have sometimes had enormous political consequences: the *muwâhhidûn* or Almohads of North Africa and Spain were such a movement, as was the original Wahhabi movement. These historical movements to reform or renew the Islamic world were not, of course, identical to the movements with which we are familiar today, but they shared many things in common: a sense that the existing political regimes lacked Islamic legitimacy, that Islam itself had become stale and weak through inadequate observance or outright apostasy, and a desire to revitalize the faith and society along with it.

Twentieth century Islamist movements draw from these same feelings and also from some changed circumstances. Initially, modern Islamist movements, particularly the two pioneers, the Muslim Brotherhood in Egypt and the *Jâma`at-i Islami* in India/Pakistan, also grew up in response to the presence of European colonialism. With the end of the colonial era, they have continued to seek to offer alternatives to the pervasive social mores of the West. That need not always mean that they are opposed to the West politically or economically, though it sometimes does. (Westerners who denounce Islamic revival as "medievalist" often are puzzled by the importance of modern technology in the spreading of its ideas: from audio cassettes in the Iranian revolution to computer diskettes today. To most Islamists, however, it is not the West's technology that is deplorable, only its social mores.)

Although the Brotherhood and the Jama 'at grew up in the 1930s and 1940s, they had to compete with other ideologies, particularly the new nationalisms, in their countries of origin. While Islamist groups and political parties have been in existence for decades, it is only since the 1970s or so that they have begun to display their strength, as other ideologies–socialism, various types of nationalism including "Arab nationalism"–have faded or failed.

For Westerners, and particularly Americans, political Islam did not really demand a place in their consciousness until the Iranian Revolution of 1979. Though Ruhollah Khomeini's ideological and religious beliefs had much in common with other Islamist movements, and the social and economic mainsprings of Iran's revolution also have echoes elsewhere, the distinctively Shi`ite elements of Khomeini's thought mean that the Iranian experience will never translate precisely in a Sunni context. Despite a Western tendency to see every Islamist movement as seeking to create "another Iran," the Iranian model will not be precisely repeatable. In the Sunni world, Mawdudi and Hasan al-Banna and Sayyid Qutb have far more influence than Khomeini.

I believe that there is also a clear distinction to be made between those Islamist groups which seek to engage and reform the secular state and those which consider the secular state unredeemable. This is sometimes linked with the doctrine, attributed usually to Sayyid Qutb's later years, of seeing the secular state as jâhili and thus non-Muslim and the proper target for *jihâd*. Those movements which embrace this idea of the secular state as deserving destruction and secularists as not really fellow Muslims tend to be much more violent and unwilling to compromise than those which seek to transform society and the state through playing a role in the existing political structure.

As Islamist movements have evolved, we have seen a number of transformations in their goals, their tactics, and their roles. The role of underground organization and of the use of violence is one area where varied approaches have evolved in response to events. Sometimes, when efforts to work within the system are thwarted by the regime, more radical responses result. The apparent shift of influence from Algeria's Islamic Salvation Front (FIS) to the more radical and extreme Islamic Armed Group (GIA) is a case in point.

There is also a diversity of leadership in Islamist movements, ranging from traditional *'ulamâ'*, through educated persons with religious training but without traditional credentials as religious scholars (Hasan al-Banna was a schoolteacher), to young revolutionaries with little formal religious training. This too makes a difference in the tactics applied and the willingness, or lack thereof, to work within the system. The nature of the supporters also matters. In Egypt, for example, the Muslim Brotherhood still draws much support from the professional classes, educated middle-class people, and has much influence in the doctors', lawyers', engineers', and journalists' syndicates, though that is being eroded by government action. On the other hand, the radical, violent *al-Gama'a al-Islamiyya* and *Jihâd* groups draw their support from more socially dispossessed groups.

Differing responses by existing regimes have created very different approaches on the part of the movements. In addition to certain countries where Islamist movements are in control of the government—Iran, Sudan, and (arguably) Afghanistan—there are other countries where they participate along with secular parties. The role of the Yemeni Reform Rally in the Yemeni government is an example here, and that party is itself an alliance between traditional tribal groupings and urban Islamists. The role of the Islamic Action Front in Jordan is another case in point: in the past it has held cabinet posts, though today it leads the opposition.

Islamists make up one of the major blocs in Kuwait's parliament. Even in Egypt, where the state is engaged in open war with radical Islamists and is increasingly pressuring the Muslim Brotherhood, the Brotherhood still has its role in civil society: in the newspaper *ash-Sha'ab*, its alliance with the Labor Party, and in most of the professional syndicates. Until it boycotted the last elections, it was the largest opposition force in Parliament.

Then there are a number of countries where the major Islamist groups have always been illegal or, as in the case of Tunisia, have been made so in response to challenges to the state. The Tunisian case is particularly interesting. The Nahda Party did participate (though not as a Party) in elections in 1989 and outpolled all the secular opposition parties. But Shaikh Rashid Ghannouchi left the country soon after and in the months that followed an-Nahda and the government became more and more polarized. The government accused an-Nahda of maintaining a parallel secret organization (like that of the original Egyptian Muslim Brotherhood's *al-jihâz as-sirri*) and crushed its internal leadership. Some violent incidents did occur and one of an-Nahda's leaders, Abdelfattah Mourou, quit the party. The government cracked down hard, and today, though an-Nahda is visible and vocal abroad, it has been suppressed rather effectively inside Tunisia. We seem to have here a case of a movement which, though it did better in the elections than other opposition groups, decided that it would seek to use other tactics and moved prematurely.

There are a number of other examples of the varying relations between Islamist groups and the state. Of course in many cases, such as Saudi Arabia, it is difficult to judge the influence of such groups as there is no political process as such and thus no way to test the strength which they often claim in press releases.

Of course the model of a democratization process which failed is Algeria. The Algerian tragedy is still unfolding, but with tens of thousands dead already, and the country in a virtual civil war. Had the elections not been voided, there is no doubt that FIS would have controlled the new government. Unlike other countries where Islamist groups have not had a chance to prove their strength, in Algeria the strength was demonstrated at the polls. When Chadli Benjedid was forced to resign and a new military-backed government cancelled the elections, it did so when Islamists had already shown how influential they were. It was an invitation to disaster, and disaster ensued. Even today efforts continue to find a formula for restoring some kind of democratic structure, including FIS, but hard-line resistance within the government (and radical resistance on the part of GIA to any FIS deals with the secularists) have frustrated any breakthroughs. There are many different ways in which states can deal with Islamist groups, but one thing is unarguable: the Algerian approach was a disastrous failure. Some secularists argue that the mistake lay in allowing FIS to run candidates in the first place, while Islamists obviously argue that the mistake was voiding the election.

Having briefly looked at some of the models which exist of relations between Islamist groups and the state, we can move to the original subject of this presentation: where do we go from here? Obviously the future of Islamist groups will differ enormously according to the individual case, and is not going to evolve in the same way in Yemen or Jordan, where these groups work within the existing system, as in Egypt or Tunisia, where they are excluded, or in the large number of states where there is no open political system to participate in. A few comments are, however, in order. Let me offer them in terms of the existing relationship between the Islamist groups and the state.

Revolutions do not end when the palace falls, but often revolutionaries are not certain what to do once they achieve power. Running a state paying payrolls, picking up the trash, making the trains run on time requires a different set of talents from organizing an underground movement. Islamist groups which have succeeded in taking control of a state apparatus have, I would say, at best a mixed performance so far. On the other hand, at least in the Middle East, no Islamist group has taken over full control of a state through an electoral process. The Iranian regime was the result of a revolution, the Sudanese was produced by a military coup against an elected regime. In both cases there have been clearly visible divisions within the leadership over how to proceed. In Afghanistan, though the various factions have proclaimed an Islamic state, the state itself has essentially come apart.

Many Islamist groups working against secularist regimes have used the old Muslim Brotherhood slogan *Islam al-Hal*, "Islam is the Solution." It is a powerful and, to the believer, true maxim, but it is not in itself a blueprint for running a state apparatus. The Islamic experience is too varied, and the original Muslim *ummah* too remote in time, to provide obvious answers to running a modern nation-state. This is not to say that there cannot be a genuinely Islamic state today, merely that even the most sincere Islamists may differ about how to bring it about. Qur'an and Sunna may contain all the answers, but it will take wise men to find out how to extrapolate and apply them.

In the Algerian case, it is worth remembering that FIS had controlled almost all of the municipalities for about a year before the cancellation of the parliamentary elections. During that time, the results appear to have been mixed. In some municipalities FIS was able to rally broad popular support, even bringing people into the streets to help collect garbage, while in others local councils spent more time putting up slogans and taking down symbols of the FLN than they did running the town. This sort of mixed result is natural, and perhaps better than the old regime could have accomplished, but it is a reminder that once in power, the challenges are different.

And here we come to a crucial question, one which secularists invariably raise against the idea of an Islamist party in power. If an Islamist party comes to power through democratic elections, as FIS very nearly did, will it in turn yield power if it does not deliver what the people expect and they vote it out of office? Since, in the Middle East, Islamist parties have not taken control of any central government through elections, there is insufficient evidence. (Examples such as Malaysian state governments are too far afield culturally and in other ways to depend upon.) Western democracies have long relied on the old axiom *vox populi, vox Dei*–the voice of the people is the voice of God. But some Islamists have openly said that Western democracy is not Islamic, and that while the Islamic concept of shura guarantees the people a voice in affairs, ultimately they cannot overrule the laws of God. Does this mean that an Islamist government, once in power, would refuse to accept a vote to oust it? No, it does not, and certainly many Islamist leaders are sincere when they say they will play by the rules of democracy. But the uncertainties are sufficient that many secularists believe that for many Islamists the slogan is "one man, one vote, one time" and that the Islamist party would never yield power, on the grounds that it is implementing God's law.

This issue will confront any Islamist party that does come to power democratically in the future. No answers can be derived from the Iranian or Sudanese examples, since they have both, in effect, abolished opposition parties. This is true in effect, though not in law, in Iran, and true in law in Sudan.

For those Islamist parties which are already working within existing systems, the issue just raised is an important one: they must convince their secularist partners that they will play by the rules if they win power, and yield it up if they lose the next elections. In Jordan, the Islamic Action Front has moved fairly smoothly from being a member of the government in 1991 to being the leading opposition bloc. Its opposition to the peace treaty with Israel has created new frictions with the King, but so far it seems to still be playing a functional role within the system. The role of the Yemeni Reform Grouping in Yemen has been enhanced by the victory of the ruling coalition against the southern secessionists last year, a civil war in which the Yemen Socialist Party (the southerners) tried to brand the northern government as "Islamic fundamentalists" in order to win Western support, without success. In Egypt, the Muslim Brotherhood's role as the main opposition grouping is being rapidly chipped away by government arrests of Brotherhood leaders and pressure on Brotherhood organs of opinion. In Kuwait, the Islamists play a prominent though not dominant role in the Parliament.

For all of these groups, the challenge for the future will be to maintain their position and, if possible, enhance it. Any attempt to consolidate power without going through proper electoral channels would alienate the secularists and, possibly, lead to a Tunisian-style decision to stop tolerating Islamist participation. On the other hand, so long as these groups can continue to function within existing systems, and demonstrate that Islamist parties can be part of a democratization process (as in Yemen and Jordan—the Egyptian and Kuwaiti models are at best pseudo-democratic), they may provide a model for persuading other regimes to tolerate a growing role for Islamist participation in the system.

It is actually harder for an outsider to judge the future of Islamist groups that are excluded from, and working against, the existing regimes. The committed and convinced will, of course, believe that their victory is inevitable. But, in fact, few things are inevitable. I might add that another group which tends to see the march of Islamist politics as inexorable are those who strongly oppose political Islam. Israel and some of its friends, and the allies of some secular regimes, are the mostly likely to subscribe to a sort of "domino" theory of Islamism: A success in one country will lead to the "fall" of others.

On the other hand, the basic elements that have led to the rise of Islamist movements in the first place are not about to go away. While improved economic conditions may strengthen the existing regimes, as the Tunisian economic boom has helped reinforce the success of the government's crackdown on an-Nahda, generally speaking economic problems fuel social discontent. The broader demographic problems, including rapid population increases in Egypt, Iran, and North Africa, add to social dislocation and discontent with existing regimes. These elements will not go away in the new century: they are likely to get worse. An Islamic state may not in fact bring genuine social justice, but to many of those deprived of power and uprooted from the familiar past, Islam's traditional emphasis on justice offers a promise of hope.

Democratization has made some inroads in the Middle East, though less so than in other parts of the world. If democratization moves apace in other countries of the region, the role of Islamist parties will be increasingly debated. Where fairly genuine democratic experiments have been tried, as in Jordan and Yemen, they have given influence to Islamist blocs but not control. The one case where an Islamist party was poised to win outright control, Algeria, led of course to a military move to abort not only the elections but the entire democratic process. Any assessment of the future of those movements which have been excluded by the state therefore must begin with Algeria.

Personally, I believe it is clear that there will be no peace in Algeria without an Islamist participation in government.   But the situation has grown so bad that a generalized collapse of civil society and a fragmentation of the country could occur as easily as an Islamist success.   Signs of struggle between FIS and GIA are not good news, for they add to the danger that instead of a victory by either the Islamists or the military, the result could be an Afghan situation, with local areas controlled by their own warlords.   The polarization in Algeria today between the secularists and the Islamists is probably greater than in any other country, and whatever happens in Algeria will be used by secularists, Islamists, and others elsewhere as an object lesson for why one should, or should not, pursue particular policies.

The Egyptian situation is more complex.   The present government is seen as corrupt and unpopular, but so have been most Egyptian governments. Secularist Egyptian society has a breadth and depth which differs from the Algerian case both in its strength and in its Egyptianness: the Algerian elite model themselves on France, while Egypt's secularists are clearly Egyptian.   The security services have effectively ended serious Islamist attacks in Cairo and most of the Delta, while the ongoing violence in Upper Egypt appears to have turned into a regionally-limited exchange of vendettas.   Despite the claims of some Islamists and the impression sometimes given by press reports, the Egyptian regime seems secure for now, though the lack of a successor to Mubarak could be an Achilles heel.

Tunisia does not now have any visible internal Islamist resistance to the state and is enjoying one of the highest economic growth rates in the Arab world.   It appears to have succeeded, by its crackdown in 1990-1991, in eliminating an-Nahda as a serious challenge for now.   There are certainly plenty of Islamists in the country, but they are not an organized threat.   An economic downturn or other significant change could, of course, revive the Islamist appeal.

The Gulf states are harder to judge because of the lack of political representation or an open press, with the limited exception of

Kuwait, where Islamists work within the system and do not generally constitute a major threat to the present social structure. The recent troubles in Bahrain have a sectarian element that makes them a poor model for comparison. There is certainly a growing Islamist critique of the state in Saudi Arabia, but it is hard to be sure that its echoes in the country are as loud is its noisemaking abroad. Islamist movements in Syria and Libya, long suppressed by the regimes, are hard to detect or describe. In Morocco, both the Islamists and other potential opposition groups appear to be biding their time, emphasizing social and labor issues rather than political ones, recognizing that change is unlikely while King Hasan reigns, but may be inevitable after him.

For Islamist groups challenging these regimes from which they have been excluded, there are many tactical issues to be addressed. Do they seek allies from secular or other groups that are similarly excluded from power? After all, the Iranian revolution succeeded because the Shah managed to alienate a broad range of critics, from the left to the right, from the clergy to the Communists, and including the Bazaar. Or do Islamist groups seek to maintain their doctrinal purity by refusing to compromise in order to forge alliances against existing regimes? Do they demand the right to participate in the political system, or do they seek to overthrow and dismantle the political system in order to establish one they consider more Islamic?

As with every other issue we have raised here, some movements will answer one way, some another, and some, being umbrella movements representing varied ideas, will answer in more than one way. Each movement must debate these questions, and the ones already mentioned, of how one will actually govern once an "Islamic state" is achieved, and whether, if power is achieved through elections, power will also be surrendered if elections go against the Islamist party.

I have not addressed the question of how these movements relate to the West in any detail, because it is only rarely a major issue with them, something the West often ignores. While opposing

Western sexual and other moral lassitude, they are only occasionally extremely hostile to the West politically, and then when the West is perceived as being hostile to Islam or to their own movement. When movements achieve power, however, they must make choices about their international relationships.

I do not believe that political Islam is either monolithic in organization or of one mind about what it seeks to achieve. Perhaps all believe *Islam al-Hal*, but how Islam brings the solution about is seen differently from case to case. As these movements differ from each other, and the regimes they challenge also differ one from the other, so the future will see both success and failure for various movements. Islamists may take over here and there by revolutionary effort (Algeria seems the likeliest candidate) or by negotiation (again, possibly in Algeria) or through elections. Some movements will fail because they do not provide the answers sought by their own specific society, or because they have chosen to employ a radical rhetoric or tactics (or violence) which alienates many who might otherwise support them.

It has sometimes been said that if the Islamic revival could produce a single charismatic leader, with both the religious reputation and the public *persona* to lead–a sort of Lenin of the Islamic Revolution–then it might become a genuine international movement. But no such figure has emerged. Khomeini was too Shi`ite, and too Iranian. Hasan at-Turabi is clearly a brilliant man and someone who can eloquently state his case in English and French as well as in good classical Arabic. But Sudan is on the periphery of the Middle East, and while he has influence elsewhere he has not been able to forge a genuine international following. One can not predict the emergence of charismatic leadership, but experience so far suggests that no such leader is likely to emerge, except perhaps in local areas.

Islamist politics–or political Islam–will be a major feature in the Islamic world for years to come, and it will continue to help force the debate about democratization, legitimacy of existing regimes, and the future of Islamic societies. That debate will proceed whether individual movements succeed, fail, or forge alliances with secular groups to win power. Future patterns are likely to parallel the past in one sense: the results will be as varied as the nations and societies involved, and as different as the Islamist groups themselves.

DISCUSSION

Imad-ad-Dean Ahmad: In what violent acts did an-Nahda engage to justify, in the eyes of the Tunisian government, forcing them underground, or the punitive actions that were taken against them?

Dunn: It was essentially one action, an attack on a ruling party's headquarters there. That led to one death and one person crippled, which is actually fairly violent by Tunisian standards. The people who did it were accused of being with an-Nahda. Ghanouchi left the country right after the 1989 elections, and though he kept indicating he might come back, he spent most of his time traveling around the Arab world or in London, and didn't come back. There are several different ways of interpreting what happened. There's a question as to whether the government completely made up all the evidence in the case against an-Nahda (I don't think so), or whether there was a more radical wing of an-Nahda which began operating underground–particularly after Ghannouchi was out of the country, or, as the government would put it, whether the whole thing was a plot to begin with. I don't accept the government's case. I don't completely accept all of an-Nahda's denials either. I've done some work on the subject and I think there certainly were some radical elements within an-Nahda who were organizing within the army, within the national guard, and with other elements. The government cracked down *very* harshly when they got wind of it. That's what I was referring to. I don't have all of the specific details in my head.

Ahmad: Do you know what was the nature of an-Nahda's denials? Were they claiming it didn't happen, that it wasn't them, or did they denounce it? Did they say that this is not the kind of activity that we engage in?

Dunn: This is where we begin to have a split. This is where Fatah Muro–much more of a traditional `alim by training than Ghannouchi–

split over the issue of violence and suspended his membership in an-Nahda. Ghannouchi always insisted, as I understand it, that an-Nahda's leadership never authorized violence, in his break, Muro seemed to be saying that there was something to this in that he was denouncing violence. The an-Nahda leadership, as far as I know, while they said they did not authorize it, did not specifically denounce it either in the way that Muro did.

Tariq Hamdi Al-Azami: You already mentioned Turkey as part of your interests, but you did not mention it in detail, so I want to say a few things about Turkey. 1) You said that Sufism in general is not politically inclined. But Sufism can be a political force. [There is] a discussion ... in Turkey [about] forming a political party. Although some of them support Refah Party, they have the feeling that they may form their own political party. 2) On the question of what to do with trains and trash: ... the Refah party, now ruling many parts of Turkey–Istanbul, Ankara, etc.–are dealing with these daily issues: the price of bread, how to deal with rent, and all of these things. Many Turks support them. Islamists have six radio stations in Istanbul and two main TV stations, so they are reaching the people, and that is all that Islamists want in the Muslim world. The Prophet (peace be upon him) said: Let me talk to my people; give me room to talk to my people. In Turkey they have this. So if they came to power, they wouldn't have the problem of what to do next because they are very practical with the daily things of life.

The other issue I would like to address is based on what ... you said would make Islamist groups anti-Western.

Dunn: I said that in the Iranian case, there was clearly a historical reason for the anti-Western sentiment. I think Islamist groups tend, not necessarily in every case, but tend to oppose certain Western morès and so forth–sexual lassitude, etc. If the West assumes, though, that this means in every single case that an Islamist party is going to be politically anti-Western, the West helps create a self-fulfilling prophecy.... By excluding them and working against them and supporting the people who are working against them, [the West] is going to make the Islamist movement naturally anti-Western. I think that the West needs to recognize that in many cases these movements do not have a particular approach one way or the other.

I don't know Turkey very well, but obviously Turkey is a very special case. The most secularized–or at least attempted to be– the most secularized Islamic country in the world. Ataturk's efforts went to what most Westerners I think would consider absurd extremes–moving the day of rest from Friday to Sunday, and so forth. This was just excessive Europeanization. And of course he banned the Sufi orders. Probably the surest way to make Sufi orders political, is to ban them. This is true of almost anything. If you ban the Boy Scouts, or the Elks Lodge, we would probably turn them into an underground organization. The secularization of Ataturk went so far in one direction that you naturally have a response in the other. Again, I think Turkey is a special case and I didn't get into it for lack of time.

I need to say that particularly in the first few years after the collapse of the Soviet Union, there was a real wave of fear that Central Asia would be subject to Iranian influence and a real wave of fear rising that the natural counterpart to that is secular Turkey. Why would Central Asia be particularly subjective to Iranian influence? There are very few Shiites in Central Asia–there are some but very few. Tajikistan, it's true, speaks Persian, or a dialect of it, but they're not Shiites for the most part, and those that are Shiites are mostly Ismailis. Why would Iran have any greater influence in Central Asia than elsewhere? Most of these people have been under official atheism for 75 years anyway and the strongest organizing elements in Central Asia were always the Sufi orders. So why would Iran have such great strength there?

I don't think anyone ever really explained why and I don't think that the Islamist movements that have emerged in Central Asia have a particular Iranian coloration to them, but more likely a Sufi coloration. Now, it has been in the interests of the pro-Communist leaders in Uzbekistan, Turkmenistan, and the Russian government as well, to try to portray the opposition in Central Asia as Iranian-style Islamic fundamentalists. The one place where I know anything about them–the Islamic Renaissance Party in Tajikistan–did not show much sign of that at all. They tended to be a coalition of various political groups who happened to have an Islamist identity. That included a lot of Sufi orders and so on. I don't really think there was much to this nightmare of an Iranian threat. Just as the Iranian threat in Central Asia proved to be somewhat of a phantom, I think the Turkish savior proved to be something of a phantom as well.

What does Turkey have in common with Central Asia? Language. Now, the languages are not real close–Turkish is written in a Roman alphabet; the languages of Central Asia were written in the Arabic alphabet until about 1920, and then in Cyrillic. Ironically, originally, Stalin was going to put them into Roman, but then when Ataturk went to the Roman alphabet, he realized then they would be able to read modern Turkish, so they switched to the Cyrillic alphabet so they couldn't read anything. Language and culture are about all that Turkey had in common with Central Asia. One thousand years ago, you had some great common ancestors, but today, language and culture are primarily what they have in common. And Turkey has been helpful in providing television programs and some other things and in trying to help people learn modern Turkish in these Turkish-speaking countries. But essentially, it's not as if they spoke, wrote, and read the same language exactly or that they had been part of the same nation-state only 75 years ago.

I think a lot of the sense in this country among analysts who thought Turkey would be the great counterpoise to Iran and Central Asia came from people who talked to the Turks. Turkish nationalists have long tended to identify with that Central Asian cradle of Turkish civilization. But just because romantic Turkish nationalists identify closely with Central Asia doesn't mean Central Asians identify with romantic Turkish nationalists. If anything, the existing regimes in Central Asia are run by the old Communist nomenclatures anyway. So I think this is one of the fundamental errors a lot of Westerners made, and, without knowing specific cases, I think that one reason was because they talked to Turkish leaders who were very enthusiastic: "Yes. We have the secular model and the Turkish language. That's exactly what they need. We will be the great counter poise."

Well the problem is that Turkey has neither the extra funds nor the time on its hands to be the great cultural savior of Central Asia. Turkey's got enough trouble controlling its own Southeastern provinces where it's got a major Kurdish revolt going on, and invading neighboring countries as well. Turkey is not in a position to become the great cultural center of Central Asia. The one country in the former Soviet Union where Turkey can, and I think may very well, end up having an enormous influence is Azerbaijan. But there the reasons are contiguity, fairly recent historical links in being part of the Ottoman Empire at various times–although Azerbaijan was shifting back and forth between Iran and the Ottomans at times–and the almost identical language in that except for the alphabet the language is virtually the same.

Al-Azami: I was watching a Refah member talking in parliament, and he said that the Turkish government opened one secular school and an Islamic group opened twelve schools. The one opened by the Turkish government was closed after a few months because people didn't like it.

About the TV station that was, and still is to a certain extent, for the Turkish secular regime, there were a lot of complaints by many Central Asian Turks who said that it was too Western for them, that they were more conservative than that. They lived 60 years under Communist rule, but the Communists didn't do what was then being done. So they complained, and now you see that the women are dressed more modestly. So this shows how Central Asia looked at Turkey and will really in the future get more influence there.

Dunn: But again, do you see much Iranian influence? No. It's not there either. There is an Islamist influence there but it's coming from the traditional sources of Islamic identity there. Azerbaijan again, is caught between Turkey, Iran, and Russia.

Osman Shinaishin: The question of Turkey should really be looked at in isolation from the rest of the Islamic world. One thing that I think is very significant is that the problem that the Islamic movement sees in Turkey is the same problem that is emerging in many of the other Muslim countries. Unfortunately it is not a problem created by the government, but is created by Islamic movements themselves with the help of the government. Some might not agree with me on this, but it seems to be the case. ... The problem is the extremism in the projection of Islam. And that is even creeping up in the United States itself.

The question of what these movements mean by Islam is extremely important. I hope we can reach some closure on it because it has some very significant points that we should stick by and others that we should not stick by. Among the things that we should stick by are the fundamentals of Islam–not in the way of "fundamentalism," but the fundamentals of the religion–namely, allegiance to one power, namely the Creator. And from there, you give tremendous freedom to act within that framework. Having said that about Turkey, I repeat that the problem also exists in other countries. I am currently very disturbed with the trend of many of the Islamic movements in the Muslim world. They are very different from what Islam truly is and what has brought success.

Dunn: I don't really have a comment on that because, obviously, I make a lot of distinctions among the different kinds of Islamist movements. Obviously too, sometimes Islamist politics is used basically as a socially reactionary vehicle.

Clearly, it scares the heck out of a lot of women, particularly women in prominent professional positions. This doesn't mean that every Islamist is aiming at reducing the role of women. Women have a fairly important role in Iranian society today and in Sudan. But at the same time, if you listen to the advocates of Islamist politics in some countries we are talking about, it sounds almost as if their first priority is to get women out of the workplace and out of sight. This is, I think, not helping their cause, certainly among women. Modesty is one thing and invisibility quite another, especially in countries where women have struggled for a great many years to try to achieve social, political, or professional presence. Turkey is certainly a case in which women are quite prominent in many areas. Obviously, I doubt that they are going to be very enthusiastic about some political Islamists. Now not all Islamists are reactionaries on the role of

women, but some are. I think also we have seen some things that
upset women and a lot of other people in Egypt recently. Although
he's not really an Islamist, but more of a government clerk, the
Shaikh of Al-Azhar's comments on female circumcision a few weeks
ago certainly fueled the argument of the secularists that the Islamic
society these people are trying to create is a reactionary one that will
put women back into the Dark Ages. And they are in that sense
helping to fuel or helping to support their own opponents because
they are sounding like precisely the kind of medieval reactionaries
that they are accused of being.

Ahmed Yousef: What about modern Saudi Arabia?

Dunn: Modern Saudi Arabia is unfortunately what a lot of secularists
in the rest of the Arab world think the Islamists want to create.
Modern Saudi Arabia, after all, has its own pretensions to being an
Islamic society, however little we may give credence to that. This is
why it is important that when you say Islam is the solution, [you
should say] what do you mean by Islam? I know what Islam is in
general, but when it comes down to specific requirements, specific
answers to specific questions, specific issues of social or political
importance, I don't know what Islam is. The Saudis say Islam says
women can't drive cars. The Iranians say they're an Islamic state, and
women can drive cars. I don't know anywhere in the Qur'an or
Sunnah where it is clear … one way or the other, that … has anything
to do with it. What I'm trying to say is that there are extremists or
people who have their own particular social issues.

Nihad Awad: You said that one of the challenges for Islamist
movements and even for the governments is to answer the question of
[what the future of] the country will be. The Islamic movements I
think will focus principally on social and political reform and will not
talk about what car they will prefer to drive or if they have Islamic
machines to replace the Western machines, because technology is universal. My question is: What do you think defines the relationship
between the Islamic movement and the West, concluding that there is
a cultural and religious gap or prejudice.

You also talked about Palestine as a political point of vision, but I don't think it's only that–not just because of Palestine. You also have to look at Bosnia and I see who represents the enemy there. The Bosnian Muslims have proven themselves as mostly cultural, often very moderate, even to their Jewish and Christian neighbors. Yet the West has been ignoring them. I'm really confused, so what are your thoughts?

Dunn: The Islamic revival has political implications and sometimes it does not. This revival is not created by economics or social requirements or anything else. It is, I think, built into the general tendency toward spiritual revival in a lot of cultures today as the failure of imported colonial era ideology has become more obvious and old nationalisms have failed and people are going back to that which is richest in their own spiritual tradition. And that's happening in a lot of areas, not just in the Islamic world. The Islamic revival is one thing and it is not particularly fueled by economics or other issues. I think that the strength of Islamic groups with political agendas does draw some, but by no means all, of its support from those who want to change the social or economic situation in their own countries. Now that doesn't mean that only the poor are supporting these movements. Clearly the Muslim Brotherhood for example draws support from all kinds of professionals–doctors, lawyers, etc. I'm not saying it's a direct relationship.

On the other hand, genuine political revolutions generally don't take places where everyone is economically secure and socially happy. If we're talking about Islamic movements driving political change, that is going to have it's greatest success in an area where there is a general social and economic problem. I come back to Tunisia. I'm not saying they've solved the problem forever, but I think the economic boom in the last few years has undercut not those who genuinely believe in an-Nahda's message completely, but a lot of those who would have supported them in order to bring about change, had things not gotten better economically.

Obviously there is a hard core of committed Islamists in an-Nahda or in any other group whose primary concern is not economic.

They really believe they need to change society in this way. But a lot of the people who are going to support them may do so for economic reasons. There's a famous quotation about the early Islamic conquests: "We did not come for Qur'an and Sunnah; we came for bread and dates." A lot of people do things for the wrong reasons. A lot of people support Islamist movements for their own security and their own survival. And as I said, revolutions don't take place in countries where everyone's comfortable.

So on the one hand, I'm not trying to suggest that poverty and economic troubles are the only reason for Islamic political movements. And they're certainly not the main reason for Islamic revival generally, but they do have something to do with the success or the growth of these political movements when they are in opposition to the existing government I think.

On the question of the West and Islam, I don't think there are any two cultures in the world that have so interacted with each other over so long a time as Western culture and Islamic culture, usually interacting in negative ways. It amazes me that the stereotypes that Westerners have about the Muslim world are absolutely contradictory. "They are dangerous warlike fanatics and they are untrustworthy, lazy, and unwilling to work." Well, wait a minute, those two don't go together at all. But why do we have these stereotypes? Because we have got fourteen centuries of being neighbors and rivals. Because, for the first few centuries, Islam was such a far superior civilization to that of Western Europe, Western Europe always kind of looked up at it with the envy that anyone has of the richer, fancier, smarter neighbor. And then, as Islam went into decline and Western Europe went into expansion, Western Europe moved out as a colonial power and began to see the Islamic world as subservient, to be dominated, to be exploited. This is a gross over-simplification of history, but here we have both elements. First, you say Islam is a stronger rival, and then you see Islam as a subsidiary culture that works for you. Now we're trying to deal with the Islamic world in a post-colonial environment and the West still has a lot of old stereotypes. And those who want to do so know how to play on those stereotypes.

The two countries that I tend to think of in this area are Israel, which is obvious, but in the last two or three years, less obviously, Russia. When Russians try to defend what they are trying to do in Tajikistan or in Chechnya, they always start turning to: "Do you want a bunch of mullahs like in Iran? Do you want an Iranian-style fundamentalism?" Russia is almost becoming another Israel in its attempt to see the devil in Islamist movements everywhere, the same Russia which for years tried to show itself as a friend and a protector of the Islamic world. But what we're seeing here is that I think we're still playing with old stereotypes. So are Muslims, and so are many Islamists when they look at the West. I'm not suggesting that the educated folks in this crowd are, that anybody here is, but a lot of Muslims in the street are still thinking in terms of old stereotypes.

There are some parallels between Israel and the crusader states, but there are some big differences too. I think the Western response in Bosnia is a lot more complicated than some Muslims appreciate. They appreciate quite well what's happening on the ground in Bosnia. But the reasons that the West is so ineffective right now are not just because the Bosnians are Muslim. That may be a part of it, subconsciously somewhere, but it's also because the West does not have any idea how to use its power right now. The United States wants to do things, the British and the French say no. But this is in Europe and the United States has difficulties doing it without British and French support. Besides, there's no political support in this country for military action, and so on.

Imad-ad-Dean Ahmad: Don't do anything, just lift the embargo.

Dunn: On that, I'm with you 100%. I've been saying that for a very long time.

Ahmad: But I think the point is that given that's all that's being asked of the United States, why is it so hard for the United States to do that?

Dunn: You have to ask somebody who's against it. I'm for it.

Saleh Saleh: I think the West generally has decided to make Islamist movements anti-Western–particularly with the issue of Palestine.

They have been supporting the Israeli occupation and the Israeli atrocities since 1948.

Dunn: I think that certainly this is a very useful element for Islamist groups to use against the West. At the same time, I think that realistically the West is not going to back off from supporting a peace process, particularly one that creates some kind of a Palestinian authority, even if its an inadequate one. I don't expect a Palestinian to applaud where things are right now. But I think the United States is trying more than it has in past years to create some kind of Palestinian legitimacy that could evolve into a Palestinian state. It's highly unlikely that the United States or anyone else is going to be able to undermine the existence of Israel even if they wanted to. Israel is a nuclear power, a major military power. I'm not going to argue the peace process here because that's a whole different issue that we could get into for hours and hours. It is clearly a divisive issue and an area in which the West and the Islamist groups are not likely to agree any time soon. I recognize that. I'm not suggesting that they will never agree on anything, but I am suggesting that you don't necessarily have to see the West as the main enemy or the primary enemy of Islamist groups. An Islamist group in Algeria may have very strong feelings about Palestine, but in fact, the reason people are out on the streets usually has much more to do with their own economic and social problems and their own search for political expression.

Ahmad: I disagree with the notion that the United States couldn't undermine the existence of Israel even if it wanted to. The role that American aid plays to Israel is indispensable, and I think most, if not all Israelis, see it that way. The fact that Israel is a nuclear power has nothing to do with it, because what good will a nuclear weapon do them unless they want to use it to blackmail the United States to continue giving that aid? If Israel feels that Hamas is a problem, they're not going to nuke the Gaza Strip. The winds blow to the East, and the radiation would carry over to them.

Dunn: Gaza is not going to bring down the state of Israel. The only way that Israel would disappear is if Arab states make war on it.

Ahmad: When Israel is not supported by the US, it could fall in a number of different ways, not least among them is economic collapse because of the inherent instability of its socialist system.

Dunn: There are a lot of Israelis who recognize that U.S. aid is not open-ended forever, that the mood in the United States is not for taxpayer money to continue to go to any foreign country for very long. There are certain Israelis who are recognizing that they are going to have to learn to structure their economy to try to live with less, if not without, U.S. aid over time. It would be disastrous for Israel if U.S. aid were cut off tomorrow, but it's not going to be cut off tomorrow. We're living in a real world; we're not speaking in a theoretical world where the United States suddenly decides that Israel is going to disappear. The U.S. political process is not that; that's not the will of the U.S. electorate. It's not going to happen. It's not even the will of most Arab regimes frankly and it's not going to happen.

Ahmad: I was only addressing your point that the United States couldn't do anything if it wanted to. If it wanted to, it could do something.

Dunn: It couldn't want to.

Bashir Nafi: I'd like to hear where you stand on the relationship between the Palestinian Islamists and the terrorists.

My comment is about democracy and the democratic process in the Muslim world, basically in the Middle East. I think there are three major reasons why democracy is not going to work in terms of Islamists vis-à-vis the establishment:

1) Among the ruling establishments in the Muslim World there is the perception that an Islamic government entails a fundamental shift in the world-view and in society. *Why* is not important, but it is a fact now everywhere.

2) There isn't a consensus. There is no unified view or opinion that if the Islamists won the elections this year and lose it four years later that they will give up power.

3) Among the Atlantic powers, namely Britain, France, and the USA, unfortunately, the [negative] perception of Islam is deepening. Whether we like it or not, that's what's happening now. The test for whether democracy is going to work or not is going to rest on this point. I cannot really see that if the Islamists win the election, they will be given the chance to run the country. I remember in 1981, the minute the army realized that the old Refah party was gaining popularity, they took over power with the agreement of the major democratic forces in Turkey.

Dunn: A few months ago, I was on a panel at the Middle East Policy Council with John Esposito and Daniel Pipes, taking the obvious opposite sides. I think I was supposed to be a commentator somewhere in the middle there. One of my comments, though, was that I was astonished to find that I had lived long enough to hear Daniel Pipes urging negotiation with the PLO. The reason of course was to keep Hamas out. Suddenly Arafat looks very good to Dan Pipes.

I think the Palestinian issue continues to be and will continue to be, unless some kind of solution is found, a divisive issue even with the PLO-Israeli agreement. Whether the creation of an actual functioning Palestinian entity in most of the West Bank could lead to evolution into something else is something we can only hope for. Clearly, you cannot simply deny the role of Islamists, particularly in Gaza but throughout Palestinian territories. They're there; they're a major force. The Israelis do seem to feel that, just as they tried for years to deny that the Palestinians existed altogether, they can deny the that Palestinian Islamists exist and deal only with the secularists and the PLO. I think the PLO is smarter than that, but at the same time, they're caught between two fires. They either give up the process altogether and get nothing, or they keep trying to negotiate with the Israelis and get a bit. But as they do so, they're caught in this quandary that they're under enormous Israeli pressure to crack down on Hamas and Islamic Jihad. It is a very delicate and difficult situation and it could blow up at any moment.

Saleh Saleh: On the question of the programs [Islamists] present to specify what they are planning to do: I think in 1989, the days in which Jordan had no party system in the election, the Islamic movement was the major force in that election. They had their own programs and they had printed their own understanding of what it meant for them and for the citizens of Jordan for Islam. I myself looked at that program that they presented. I find that it is close to the kind of modern understanding of what's going on these days. The Islamists in Jordan won three major cities out of six city elections in which had participated. They won about 25 seats out of the around 70 people that they presented to be elected. They won about 35% of their participation. So it's not as big a loss for them as has been said. Why is it that always, when Islamists come closer to the Western understanding, the Western standards of life, the Western standards of women, or the Western standards of human rights, when Islamists are progressive, are open-minded, when essentially there is a far smaller distance between Islamists and the West, then they are [portrayed] as a reactionary force and they are not welcome.

Dunn: You're speaking of how the media portrayed this–that they lost a few seats and the media is portraying it as a serious setback?

In my own newsletter, I didn't even report on the municipality elections. I thought that it was the sort of thing you would expect as new municipality elections are held and so forth. It's an evolutionary thing and it's going to go different ways. People look to try to see more than is there. I may have used the term reactionary talking in terms of some attitudes towards women and so forth, but ultimately, Islamists groups do not have to convince me or the West or the media. They have to convince whoever it is that has to be convinced to gain power in their own country, whether it's an electorate in a vote, or an established authority, or enough of the population to rise up against the established authority. Essentially Islamists have to convince, if not the secular elites, then the broad mass of people who are neither Islamic activists nor establishment, but just the ordinary man in the street. When the establishment goes so far as to alienate the man in the street–and It's happened clearly in Iran, and I think it's happened in Algeria–then obviously something happens, something snaps, something changes. Ultimately Islamists don't have to convince Bernard Lewis or Daniel Pipes or even their friends in the West. They have to convince their own people in some way. In a genuine democracy–there aren't a lot of those–they have to convince the voters. In any other society, they have to convince enough people to bring about change either peaceably or otherwise. Yes, the Western press doesn't know much about this area, or didn't before 1979; after Iran, they started trying to educate themselves. They naturally deal in stereotypes. It's almost impossible not to when you're going to write six paragraphs on something today and then write about some totally different part of the world next month.

Saleh: My second question is on the crack down on democracy now in Egypt against the Brotherhood. Today they have arrested 200 Muslim brothers; the other day they arrested about 20 leaders of the Brotherhood. This crackdown frustrates the Ikhwan and the Islamists in general, and I think the governments, by doing this, are fueling the violent groups. In trying to push the moderate Islamists, those who understand that there can be a kind of coexistence with the government, to the corner leads them to being more violent and more extremist.

Dunn: I don't think the Egyptian government is in any danger of falling, but that does not mean that I approve of some of what they have been doing. I think one of the more intelligent things Mubarak did when he came to power was to open up to the moderate Islamists, as a way of excluding the more radicals who are trying to bring down the government and shot Sadat. Sadat, after all, in his last months had been arresting everybody. He not only arrested Asaadi and the Brotherhood, he arrested the Coptic Pope. He was cracking down on everybody, and Mubarak's first instinct seemed to be right: "Yes, find a place for moderate Islamists. Those who are trying to break society apart, we can't really deal with. Find a place for those who want to work within the system." And for a long time, it seemed to be working. But the fight with the radicals and the violence used by the radicals seems to have led to the government's decision of cracking down across the board. It decided to push Islamists out of the professional syndicates.

Now, I think far more serious implications than arresting twenty here or two hundred there has been the government take-over of the syndicates. And they had some fights on their hands with the engineers and so on. But this is pushing Islamists out of an area where they did have some real influence in civil society. Now I think that's a mistake, because I think in the long run, it pushes moderate Islamists into the radical camp. Yes, practically, I think the way in which Western media portrays it is a mistake. All I can say is that I'm only responsible for one element of the Western media, which is my own newsletter, and I try to be fair and balanced.

Mehmood Kazmi: My question is in regard to "pan-Islamism." You discussed Islamic movements within different nation-states, but what have you seen in your research in terms of the relations among these movements? Do they bring up the issue of pan-Islamism or do they try to put it on a back burner, not selling it to their people right now? Maybe it's not a very popular issue. Where does it fall in their priorities? Or is it in any movement's agenda?

Dr. Dunn: I can't speak for movements. The first question is, what do we mean by "Pan-Islam?" Do you mean the notion that some had classically of trying to create one big super Islamic state? I think, given the fact that even efforts at Arab unity don't work, the notion of a genuine Islamic nation state is not likely to come about. ... It would be *very* hard to achieve. Do you mean there is only one *ummah*? I don't think any Muslim is going to deny that, and not just Islamists. Yes, there is one community of Muslims. Obviously, there is coordination among Islamist Muslim groups. There is a lot of sympathy. There have been some efforts by Iran, by Sudan, and so forth, to support movements elsewhere. Not usually to the extent that some regimes claim, but there have been some elements of support flowing back and forth. But I don't think there is a coordinated international Islamic movement in the sense that there was with Communism. I think most of these movements would in theory support, of course, all Muslims living in one just Islamic society, and that probably means one political entity. But how do you do that? Do you restore the Caliphate? If so, how? And whom do you choose? Some of these movements do debate these things, but I think most of them would say that the first issue has to be establishing an Islamic society in our existing nation-state, and that farther down the line, you can worry about a broader pan-Islamic unit of some sort. But it's not something that's going to happen overnight given the fact that even regional units haven't held together very well in many parts of the Muslim world. It's a long way down the line, and I don't know of any major groups with a lot of influence who spend much time worrying about this. I'm not saying there aren't some small groups somewhere that are trying to proclaim someone Caliph, but they're marginal and peripheral, and not part of the main stream of Islamist thought.

Muhammad al-Asi: When mentioning Iran you said its Shiite peculiarity makes it stand apart. Could you explain a little more what you meant...?

Dunn: In Khomeini's system, as elaborated by Khomeini and as institutionalized in the Iranian constitution, there was the principal of *Waliyat al-Faqih*, of government by *faqih* (the Islamic decision maker/jurist/judge or however you want to translate it).   This [conception] grows out of not just the Shiite but specifically the Iranian Shiite clerical system as it has evolved over the last 400-500 years with the whole structure of ayatollahs ... and so forth. The `ulamâ' in a Sunni country do not have the same type of hierarchical structure.

Sunnis also do not have, although many Islamist groups would give it to them, the use of *ijtihâd.* I think essentially, the fact that a Shiite religious scholar is a *mujtahid* and that 3 of the 4 legal schools of Sunni Islam have insisted that *ijtihâd* is closed, makes a major difference. I'm not going to say that it makes the only difference or an absolutely decisive one, but it's an important difference because it gives a certain religious authority to the individual as opposed to the consensus of the `ulamâ' generally. It is an authority to the individual that Sunni Islam usually does not concede.

Now it is true that a lot of Islamists want to open *ijtihâd*. It's also true that the Hanbalis, especially our Saudi friends, have never insisted that *ijtihâd* is closed, but the notion that the *mujtahid* is speaking for the hidden Imam gives a more direct authority, a more direct "pipeline to God" to some extent than exists with the Sunni *`ulamâ'*.

Finally, as Khomeini forged his system in which the *faqih*, who is sort of the chief *mujtahid* of all, has the ability to override all other elements of state, including parliament, means that the political system as created by Khomeini (which may not really be the political system as it functions today in Iran, but is in theory) has theoretical elements in it that just don't exist in Sunni Islam because they come directly out of the Shiite tradition. This is because they come directly out of a doctrine of a hidden imam, and they come to some extent out of a very different attitude towards *ijtihâd* than exists in Sunnism.

Al-Asi: [Regarding] the generalization "Islam is the solution...." How do you characterize generally–because you spoke specifically about the Arab Islamic countries–the development of political thought of these Islamic movements? How much have they developed their political thought that is needed for their response–whether it's an electoral response, an area response, etc.? Where would you place them on a scale of one to ten?

Dunn: I won't claim to have read everything written by every Islamist movement. I haven't and I wouldn't try. I do feel that many of these movements still have some way to go in articulating their own systems. A lot of what has been done in the last ten years seems to reiterate and reflect what was done in the previous forty or so. A lot of people are still going back to Mawdudi and Hassan al-Banna and so on. I think that there has been a lot of creative work done, and that there is a lot of thinking going on. But I think a lot of these groups have a long way to go. Consider democratization, something that I didn't address. For reasons totally unconnected with this, when you look back at the development of the British parliament, we do obviously see a lot of parallels. We do see groups attempting to keep other groups out or to allow other groups a certain amount of say; we see the system breaking down periodically; we see the English civil wars and the Glorious Revolution of 1688. And as you go back, obviously democracy in Western Europe and the United States–the

U.S. system is essentially an outgrowth of Western European systems–took a long time to form. France took several revolutions. England took one civil war and a *whole* lot of change so that parliament has grown bit by bit and really wasn't a genuinely democratically elected body until the present century.

When you look at that, you see that democracy in the West is something that grew slowly. This doesn't mean that it's going to have to take one thousand years for it to grow in the Middle East. But I don't think that the Jordanian and Yemeni cases are examples of genuine equal sharing of democracy. Yes, they're there in part to show either that this really is a fair system or for the government to show: "We recognize that Islamists make up a significant part of the population and they're too big for United States to ignore."

If I have a conclusion, it's that this debate is going to go on. As we look into the new century, we're going to see the Islamist vs. secularist debate going on with all of the questions this raises about the legitimacy of existing governments, what democratization ought to be, how it works, what it means. There isn't going to be a sudden transformation across the board one way or the other. Islamist politics isn't going to disappear and it's not going to be universally triumphant. On the other hand, we are seeing the evolution and the Islamist agenda is a very important part of the debate. We're watching a historical evolution. We're not going to know what Islamic society will look like one hundred years from now in our lifetimes. But, whatever it looks like one hundred years from now will depend on what the answers are to some of the questions that we talked about here tonight. History has a way of answering questions that you can't always predict beforehand. You can't always be sure how these groups are going to evolve, how Islamist thought is going to evolve as it does have to sometimes....

I think now is a very important time in Islamic history. I think we're seeing that a lot of countries which had downplayed the Islamic elements in their tradition are having to rethink it, even to the point, of course, that secular leaders are frequently adopting external, superficial Islamic props to try to claim some Islamic identity of their own. We saw Saddat do it for example. This is not surprising either. They are recognizing that, once again, Islam has become an extremely important element of their respective societies and that for many people it has become a factor that helps to determine their political position.

Imad-ad-Dean Ahmad: Certainly, the fact that people in the Muslim countries and in the West don't know what an Islamic state is going to look like is a problem, an impediment. On the other hand, to ask them to outline it in advance is also unreasonable. When the United States formed a constitution, it was the first time in history that a man-made constitution was going to be invented. Before that all constitutions evolved or were divinely revealed. The idea of a man-made constitution was totally new. And yet, no one said: "Well now before you can do this, you have to tell us what are you going to walk out of that hotel room with." It would have been a stupid question. We don't know what we're going to walk out with until we go into that room and we argue *because* we know we disagree. Certainly, it is clear that Muslims do disagree. You're absolutely correct in making that observation and you can find almost any kind of view you want somewhere owned by some kind of Muslim. Therefore, we don't know what they're going to come up with. But we can ask some questions, one of which, I think, is: If we look at what the different groups are saying, how do you rank what the different groups say? If you can get an overview, then you get sort of a general picture. Similarly, you could look at the delegates who went into the Constitutional Convention in Philadelphia, and while you don't know what the Constitution is going to look like, you have an idea of the range of views that are going in, and you have a rough idea of what's going to come out.

Dunn: I think the range of views is enormous. I think it ranges from people who are virtual socialists to people who are capitalist at its most extreme. I think that from that point of view, the agendas vary enormously from country to country and it usually has a lot to do with the nature of the regime they are opposing. I think too that you are absolutely right: I don't have a right to ask Islamist groups to answer any questions in the first place. I don't live in their countries. I have a right to ask them only when they start running an Islamist party in the United States and ask me to vote for it. Then I have a right to ask some questions. I don't expect anybody really to say exactly what they're going to do. I do however think that neither the ruling secular elites nor Islamist political groups as presently organized represent the majority of everyday ordinary people in most Muslim countries. And I think that those everyday ordinary people in most Muslim countries are not saying that they want to know everything the Islamist groups are going to do or everything that's ever going to happen. I think they do want to know a little bit more of what those groups are going to do before they do away with the present system.

When those people sat down in Philadelphia to write the constitution, they had already thrown out the king. "We have already thrown away the British. Now we need to think of something new." O.K., you couldn't answer everything about the future, but you had already made one big decision. Now, a lot of people in many Muslim countries are not willing to say "Let's rule out the present established elite. As corrupt as they may be, as unrepresentative as they may be, as illegitimate as they may be, let's throw them out, tear it down, and let this guy over here take over because he says, 'Islam is the solution.'" Well, I think the man in the street, before he's ready to say that, wants to know a little more. "What exactly are we going to be throwing out the present system for, to replace it for what?" This is the question that I'm asking, not can you tell me everything that will ever be done?–unless the present system is so bad that you have to get rid of it and we'll try anything. But if you're not yet convinced that the present system is *so* bad, I think you have a right to know what it is the Islamists are offering in place of what's there now.

Ahmad: You can see that in the case of Algeria, the public did feel the system was that bad.

Dunn: Of course–FIS won the election.

Ahmad: In British history there was a great convergence of ideas on concepts of society or government that people were coming together either peacefully or, in certain cases, by violence. The crux of the debate and the conflict in the Middle East is basically the lack of consensus.

Dunn: Maybe France is a better parallel.

Emad Shahin: Still in France, people who are fundamentally opposed to the political system there are marginalized. In the Muslim World, generally they are gratified. Exactly as you said, none of the groups really holds the majority–not the Islamists, not the ruling elite–whether secular or not.

Dunn: I opened this can of worms by bringing up British issue. But I can also say that we can get into this deep political sociology that could go on for hours about the Middle East. This is a wonderful intellectual discussion, but I know we have to cut it short. In fairness, I raised the issue and I should carry it through, but because of time, we should cut it short.

Muhammad al-Asi: All the Islamic political consciousness that has been fermenting for the past couple of decades or so has one thing in common that [Islamists] absolutely agree on without any questions, and that is the eradication of Zionism as a political expression in Palestine.... This so-called Middle East process that we are witnessing right now is actually bringing Israel to another war front with the Islamic movements. The Islamic movements may have had a political or a religious argument against Zionism previously, but now added to that, they will have a social and an economic argument simply because there is an infusion of Israel[i power] into the Arab government[al] system throughout the area. What troubles my thinking is that you made the comment that the United States is not going to release or let go of this peace process, which I interpreted, as I guess most Muslims would..., as the automatic type of support that the U.S. government always is willing to [lend] to the Israeli or Zionist side of this whole problem. Could it be that the United States, with all the analysts and decision makers and experts in the field, cannot see that not only are they not helping ... [to solve] the problem by reducing its religious and political dimensions, but they are exacerbating it by adding to it the economic and social dimensions which are built into this so-called peace process?

Dunn: Without getting into the peace process, I do not by any means support everything the United States has done in its support for Israel, and I've been a strong critic of U.S. policy towards Israel for a long time. But, at the same time, the only way you will convince most Islamist movements that the United States is doing the right thing would be to support the destruction of Israel, which is not going to happen, given the fact that Israel is a nuclear power. The one thing we can hope to do is to persuade Israel to make some accommodation with Palestinian nationalism, and that's what's going on in the peace process. It may not be a completely just accommodation–complete justice is often hard to achieve in this world. I don't see though what the alternative is. Is it to bring about hard core Israeli expulsion of Arabs on the ground? I mean, Israel is a nuclear power with formidable military force. It's not a country that's going to disappear, unless it does so from within, and that's not going to happen so long as it has an external enemy to rally against. It seems to me that while you're quite right–there is no Islamist movement that I know of which is not resolutely opposed to the existence of the state of Israel–some of these Islamist movements farther afield simply don't have to spend a lot of time worrying about it, because there's nothing they can do about it. In point of fact, there's not much anyone can do about it. The best that you really can do about it realistically is to try to find some kind of outlet for Palestinian nationalism that can, over time, grow into something greater. That's one reason I do support the peace process. You are accomplishing something that is too little, that is not enough for genuine justice, but it is what you can realistically accomplish, given the situation on the ground now, and hope that over time, Israel changes, or that the situation on the ground changes so that more can be done.

Imad-ad-Dean Ahmad: The final point I wanted to make is regarding the claim that democracy cannot overrule the will of God. I think that interpreting this statement to mean that a democratically elected Islamist government would not give up power if it lost the next election is going too far. That's not what the phrase probably means. I guess it depends upon to whom you are speaking, but I think it's only a minority of Muslims who would mean the phrase that way.

For the majority of Muslims, they are merely making a comment that is identical to the comment made in the West by the proponents of natural law–that there are some things which the majority cannot be allowed to do and that you have to draw the line somewhere. There are many examples of this in U.S. history. I'm particularly fond of the Supreme Court upholding the views of the jurors who refused to convict people who had clearly violated the fugitive slave law. They were clearly guilty, but the jurors acquitted them on the grounds that the jurors felt that the fugitive slave law itself violated God's law and they were not going to convict anyone. The Court conceded that it does have the authority to overrule the jury, even though they have violated the democratically made laws of the state.

Dunn: I think basically you are right here. And I think in my paper, which I did not read all of, I did make the point that one of the problems is that we have no experience to draw from. The only existing governments that are theoretically Islamist have been established either through revolution or military coup. We have no Islamist government in power through election in a position to give up power. We've had Islamist parties in coalitions as in Jordan which have then left that coalition and then functioned as opposition, but we do not have any experience. And this is one of the many tragedies of Algeria. We had an elected Islamist government. In theory, the army could have perhaps sat back, and then if the government a few years later refused to yield if they lost the election, then maybe the army should have moved. But since we never had that experience, then for the army to say they would not have given up power is to assume something that we have no evidence for. We have no evidence that they would not give up power; we have no evidence that they would give up power. We simply have no evidence, and that's the tragedy, because it makes it impossible to draw conclusions elsewhere. I think it is a much better approach to trust that they will until they don't, than to assume that they won't and bar them from power for that reason. But this is a question that is regularly raised by their secularist opponents.

Ahmad: There is no evidence, because their secularist opponents keep destroying the evidence.

Dunn: I said that. I agree.

Ahmad: I'm not just talking about Algeria, but there's Bosnia. Even though the Bosnians are notoriously secular, Izetbegovic himself would consider himself a kind of Islamist.

Dunn: I could name the head of another Muslim state that considers himself a kind of Islamist, but that doesn't make him one.

Ahmed Yousef: I have seen a dissertation suggesting an approach to dealing with the democratic dilemma in the Middle East and in the Muslim World and with religious radicalism. If we have to have democracy for everybody and we have to accept the rules of democracy, then the Islamists will come and take power. And then, if they fail after 4 years, who is going to guarantee that the Islamists will surrender or let others take over? In the dissertation, it is suggested that we guarantee that the military will be like a third party which will not indulge in politics, but just keep watching and guarantee that when the term ends, the party will leave even if it changes its mind.

Dunn: What happens when the military decides that since it is the arbitrator in these things, it can do whatever it wants? This is a problem.

Yousef: The people will decide.

Dunn: Hopefully that's the answer. They say that "the voice of the people is the voice of God."

Islamist and Secular Regimes:
Is Violence Inevitable?

Joyce Davis: First, I'd like to thank you, *shukran jazîlan*, for inviting me to speak. I'm not really accustomed to such an esteemed audience, people who clearly know what I am about to talk about. I'm used to dealing really with Americans, both policymakers and just average Americans, who as we all know have a very distorted image in many cases of Muslims and of the Islamic world. And that's something actually that I am trying to address in the work that I am doing this year and with the United States Institute of Peace and in the work that I'm doing at National Public Radio. It isn't easy, because as you know, when people get stereotypes in their minds about anything, be it Islam, be it African Americans, be it people in India, or wherever, it's hard to get those ideas out of their minds and so it is a constant and continuing process.

The book that I'm working on is entitled, *Profiles in Islam*. The project focus, the focus for which I was invited to the Institute of Peace, was finding common ground with Islam. I proposed to go around to as many countries as I can to talk to leaders of Islamic movements to find out what their perceptions are of the West, to get them to answer questions about how they feel. Instead of our always telling the Islamic world what you can do for better relationships with the West, I'd like to go to the people who are shaping these movements and ask them what the West should be doing to improve the relationship with Muslims.

I came up with this idea in stepping into the issue of women in the Muslim world. We've seen all the stories about Muslim women. I stepped in frankly about three and a half years ago with that idea of doing another story on "oh how horrible it is for poor Muslim women." I sat down and began some interviews and I said, "Wait a minute, I'm not getting the same story." I was clearly getting something different. I have to credit Sharifa Al-Khateeb who is with the North American Council for Muslim Women, for her patience. One Sunday she brought me into her home in Great Falls and she had women who were in this area but from many different countries–from Turkey, from Saudi Arabia, from wherever she could find them–sit down and listen to me ask the stupidist questions imaginable. They showed me things to read in the Qur'an–gave me sets of sermons basically–and it was just really enlightening. From that, I decided why do the same old, same old story? I can also go to Mexico or any other places where there are Christian women living in difficult situations and talk about what's wrong. Let's talk about what's right. Let's take a look at what really are the teachings. That's how I got involved in this issue in the first place.

A great chasm that exists between Muslims and the West. There's really a great prejudice many Americans have toward Islam. I realized, frankly, that I am partially responsible for that prejudice. I, being a journalist in this country share the guilt, because we are helping to continue to propagate the erroneous stereotypes about Muslims. So my project is really two-faceted. One facet is trying to get a message out to average Americans. I believe reaching average Americans is important because in a democracy they do help shape foreign policy and the policy toward the Islamic world. I do this by a series of seminars, by articles that I am writing, by talks, that kind of thing, and the other aspect which is also as important, is to talk to policymakers. I have also, of course, participated in seminars sponsored by the Institute. I was recently invited to the Pentagon to talk with Naval officers who are about to be stationed in various parts of Islamic world, and also to World Affairs Councils and the Council Of Foreign Relations. Basically what I'm doing is bringing them a message. That message, first of all, is that there are one billion people around the world who call themselves Muslims. That this is not something that is going to go away. If there is fear of Islam, we have to deal with it, take a look at it and see if it's based on any rational logic at all, and also try to figure out how we can better the relationships.

There is growing hostility between the Muslim world and the West. I say that based on my interviews with Islamists in many parts of the world and also based on interviews and talks with Americans here. I will point out to you a poll, that I was, I believe, commissioned by the American Muslim Council, in which they asked Americans what they feel about Islam as a religion. Apparently, the responses were that it was the least favorite of all religions, which is rather shocking considering from the study that I had that there are so many similarities between Christianity and Judaism. Why is there this prejudice against it? One interesting aspect of that poll is that about 41% of the people questioned said they couldn't answer because they knew so little about the religion that they couldn't even offer an intelligent answer. Now this is cause for optimism in any case because perhaps if you reach these people with some truths about Islam, if you help educate them, you will see the tide of public opinion change.

And I think also there's hostility in the foreign policy community in many regards. Frankly, I don't think it's the majority of the people any longer. I think that many Americans, including people in the policy arena, are seeking more information. They are searching for some way that they can at least begin real dialogue.

My focus with the policymakers is to help them answer some questions. The primary one that I addressed is, "Is violence inevitable between Islamists and secular regimes?" Also, "Should the United States and the West fear all Islamic movements? Are all Islamic movements violent?" Based on my interviews with a wide cross-section of Islamists, as well as their secular opponents, I've come up with some tentative conclusions. First, that U.S. interest would be best served by promoting democracy, and that there appears to be fewer incidents of religiously inspired violence in countries where Islamic parties are allowed some degree of political participation. For comparison, I offer you Pakistan and Jordan, where Islamic parties are allowed to compete. And then there is Algeria and Egypt, where they are not. Those are two clear cases. In Pakistan, Islamists are into social work but they're not really one of the major parties. But then you turn to Jordan, and the Ikhwan there is clearly a major political party in that country. So, you still have two cases where their political participation has minimized the level of violent reaction to government. And at least the examples of Pakistan and Jordan show the Islamic parties can be responsible and stabilizing influences in government and in society. In these two countries, Pakistan and Jordan, Islamic parties and candidates stand for election, and most importantly, accept defeat. This is a theme that comes round and round again when you talk with policymakers and they say yes, but what about this idea of, "one vote–one time?" Clearly, this is not the case where the Islamic parties have been allowed to participate in politics. Islamists are committed in many cases, from what I can see, to active participation in government to change, by evolution, within a system, as long as that system is really a fair system representative of the people.

My second and rather controversial recommendation, one that raises eyebrows when I talk outside of Islamic circles, is that the United States should try to begin to understand the causes and reasons for violence from Islamic groups. In many cases, Islamic organizations are fighting corrupt regimes that refuse to allow plurality and democracy. There definitely are cliques that jealously cling to power and wealth, while their people suffer. As I see it, if Islamists are a threat, their major threat in the Muslim world is really not through violence but through the ballot box.

My message to American policymakers is that they should be aware that there is great sympathy in many parts of the world for Islamists. Why? They are some of the smartest, most charismatic, most dedicated people in the Muslim world–people with a platform of opening and cleaning government, and of caring for the poor. In many of these countries, this is a very powerful message as you very well know, but it is one that I do not think is fully understood in this part of the world. To sit down and talk with a man like Rashid Ghannouchi and to come here and to talk to people who never met him and who have barely read any of his writings, and to see him portrayed as someone who's advocating violence, or assassination of people, it's just ludicrous. Yet you have people who are spreading that kind of message about a person like Ghannouchi, who clearly wants to see the Tunisian government overthrown, but is not necessarily calling for people to take to the streets to kill people to do it. In fact, he has called for moderation, for not using violence. My book contains a chapter on him, and it is really quite revealing about his platform and about how he would promote change.

There are other things that some of our policymakers should know. Islamists are now involved in intense debates about issues ranging from the rights of women to relations with the Western world. Believe it or not, some of the most passionate voices for women's rights are coming from people, both men and women, who are members of Islamic parties. All those people we would call fundamentalists. I advocate abolishing that term and not using it. People continue to use it anyway, even though they don't know what it means. Every time we use the term fundamentalist, we basically are using it as a synonym for terrorists or a synonym for a radical, when it doesn't give us a full flavor of all of the various types of people who are involved in Islamic movements and their various philosophies. I have come to realize that there is a wide spectrum of people involved in Islamic movements. There are some who are quite violent and who are ready to use violence to overthrow regimes to promote their cause, and there are some who are the opposite and quite peaceful, and then there is a whole range of people in between. This is the primary message that I try to get across.

It should also be noted that the people shaping the debate are not all in the Middle East. Many Islamic scholars and most Muslims are in other parts of the world, with the most concentrated in Southeast Asia. Throughout the Muslim world, there is also great sympathy for those who advocate shaping government and society around Islam's religious principles. That does not mean that every Muslim—certainly not everyone that I interviewed—wants to live in an

Islamic state. But it is undeniable that many do, and many more want religious voices to be heard in their government. This sympathy is often profoundly felt in countries where democracy and plurality has been stifled, where opposition parties are suffocated, and where government corruption is rampant. This sympathy does not necessarily translate into support for attacks on innocent people, such as what's happening in Egypt and especially in Algeria, but it can and does translate into support for attacks against the government–against governments that are staying in power by force and subterfuge. Elizabeth Meyer put it well in her book, *Islam and Human Rights*. She said in Algeria, Tunisia, and Libya, and in Muslim countries generally, Islam has become the primary and most potent language of political protest against oppressive dictatorships and military regimes. In many countries, especially in the Middle East, it is the only way to register protest against unpopular governments. In my interview with Dr. Turabi, it was quite interesting that he sounded a note similar to this. He said, "If you look at the thinkers and all of the various movements out there, there's nothing that compares with in dynamism and potential for galvanizing people." There just isn't.

I was asked by some Christian organizations (and I am a Christian), "What is it that's attracting people to Islam, and why aren't people coming to Christianity?" I simply had to say that I come from a long line of Baptist ministers. My father was a Baptist minister, both my grandfathers were Baptist ministers, my uncle is a Baptist minister. Yet, I clearly see the attraction of Islam for a thinking person and the dynamism that now exists amongst committed Muslims. It seems as if in the United States and in the Christian world people have gotten lazy. Their religion is no longer really a vital part of their lives. I went to a dinner party not long ago, and we sat down to eat and we just began eating without a thank you God, or anything, which happens a lot. But, afterwards when the lady who was there realized that I wouldn't have been offended by saying grace, she pulled me aside and said, "You know we usually do say grace. We usually do thank God for the meal but we don't do it with other people because we are embarrassed about it." Now this is a religious person who at least has some private devotion to God or religion, but in public, religion has become an embarrassment. I don't see it that way among people who would call themselves committed Muslims. They would not be embarrassed about Islam. They would be promoting their religious faith. So there's the dynamism, there is something that I think that Christianity now in the West certainly is lacking.

My finding is that it is inevitable that governments that seek to smother Islamists, and that do not allow strong opposition parties, will face continued turmoil and unrest. This is a point that I need to make as strongly as possible: this phenomenon is not going away. The opposition will indeed come from Islamic radicals who believe they must fight corruption, and they will be backed by the support of people from all strata of society. American policymakers unfortunately will be forced to decide whether to uphold the principles of democracy, or cave in to their fear of Islam as a political force. Time after time, Islamists told me that Islam and the United States needn't be foes, that they wished for better relations with the West and with the United States, but they believe U.S. foreign policy was erratic and often widely different from the values we espouse as a democratic country. This leaves us with the question: "How should U.S. foreign policy deal with and respond to Islamic influence in politics?" From my interviews and research, I'm offering some recommendations. Our policy should be benevolent toward Islam, a religion that shares many of the briefs and values of Christianity, and Judaism. Our policy should support plurality and democracy but it should be willing to expand its definition of democracy. It should have confidence in the Muslim people to develop a system of government that is their unique political expression, even if the structure of the government is based on religious principles. Our policy should distinguish between Muslims and militants and we should not use these words as synonyms. Our policy should take into account the reasons for militancy. In Algeria, for example, the Islamic Action Front took up arms after democratic elections were voided by those who sought to maintain power. Of course, Algeria has now degenerated into a chaos that is far from Islam's teachings. And hiuman rights monitors say it's impossible to tell who's killing whom, whether its government agents or Islamic extremists. But it really cannot be argued that Algeria was saved for democracy by considering the catastrophe that has ensued from queshing the elections. Still, U.S. policy should stand firm against any groups (even governments) that promote despotism, be it secular or religious despotism. This would include Islamists. I believe that the government and Americans should reinforce their ties with moderates. We should make every effort to reinforce cordial relations with moderate Islamists and with those who may be engaged in a legitimate struggle to free their people from corrupt regimes.

Finally, the message that I'm really profoundly giving, is that we should encourage Americans, especially those responsible for our foreign policy, to learn more about Islamic movements because it is undeniable that their influence is growing in the world, both abroad and here at home. That's the general basis of my work and my book. There are some special reports here and I'm giving you a list of some of the people that I've interviewed. I'm ready to take questions, as tough as they may be.

DISCUSSION

Ahmad AbulJobain: I would like to know how much access you get to editorial pages in major newspapers: *The New York Times, The Washington Post*? I frequently see anti-Islamic articles and never have seen anything pro-Islamic. I saw in *The Herald Tribune* a very silly opinion piece on Islam. It was not something that you thought an educated person would write. As far as policymakers are concerned, I share that feeling that they have this hostility and I'm even skeptical of to what extent they really are open-minded [about] what Islamists have to say. Having said that, I [sometimes] address people within the State Department, in the Foreign Service Institute, [and there seems] to be a willingness, but you don't feel comfortable. You're not sure if people are being nice because they don't want to put you in an awkward position while you are there. When we talk about the idealism of democracy, the United States should promote democracy. Do they really think that? In the U.S. Peace Institute they have the book, *Morality of Foreign Policy*, and George Kennan's views are still very much prevalent. On the question of Jordan and Pakistan, secularists claim that they might not be violent, but when they do come to power, they start implementing Draconian laws, they start implementing the segregation of men and women; they start doing all these terrible things that are backwards. How do you respond to them when they say things like that?

Davis: Well that's three tough questions. On access to editorial pages, I don't know about *The New York Times*, but I've written articles for the *Post*. I've had some actually published, for example, in the *Times Picayune* in New Orleans. But no, it is very difficult and there does seem to be a block. Even worse, the kind of story that I write about Muslim women is not what they expected. This happened with me with a recent article I turned in to *Mademoiselle* and unfortunately, I had to say that, you know, there are clearly examples of attacks on women who are covered. Americans don't understand the reasons. The covering is not saying that I am submissive and stupid, or anything like that, but to the contrary, These are the kind of issues that I am trying to bring out but there is not a ready audience for them yet.

I would kindly chastise you for in any way giving up. The one thing that is clear to me about people who are committed to Islam is that it is not easy to get the truth across to anyone, and that there is a commitment that you must have to do this. There clearly are people to whom there is nothing that you could say that would make a difference, for whatever reason. You can come up with a million reasons why they don't want to have any faith in any religion, let alone, Islam. But, I would really tell you that there is really a large group of people, inside the policy community, first of all, who don't have anything against Islam, they really just don't know anything about it. Their first concern is, my interest. Let's face it, we're living in the West, the first concern is American interest. So, one of the things that I point out to them, I say look, I have people saying here, that if you deal with us fairly, we'll deal with you fairly. Clearly there are some ways that Islamists and the West are not going to get along, but you can agree to disagree, as long as people remain civil–as long as there is tolerance on both sides. Tolerance is the key. But I will tell you that, now is the time not to give up, but to really continue. Why? You have people like Prince Charles, did you see the article? When I saw that, I said, "This is a beacon of sunshine into this whole issue." Now is the time to pursue. But you have to pursue on many fronts. You have to pursue maintaining ties with congressman and the people and the lower level people, but also with the media. There needs to be lots of work done with the media, and I would even encourage you all to have sessions where you have education about Islam sessions for the media. And you can do it once a month, you can do it once every six months, or whatever, where it's clear you are inviting people to come and this is for journalists. Be ready to deal with any questions the journalist may have in a patient and caring way. I think that alone will do more good than almost anything else you can do.

I don't think that most people hate Islam. Sometimes I go and I speak to people who are really conservative. These people are the most warm. Take, for example, the little retort I had with Dr. Turabi over alcohol. I said, "You would be beaten just for drinking?" I said, "That seems a little draconian to me." He said, "Listen, when we look at your society and we see all the damage that has been done, curbing it in this fashion is the least we can do to avoid all these other problems of fathers who are alcoholics, of mothers who are not taking care of their children, of drunken drivers." How can I argue against that? I can't sit and say, "Well I should be able to have a glass of wine so that all of this can happen." When you tell that to con-servative Americans they say, "Well right on for him." Even the punishment that I still have a problem with, the punishment that Islam in many cases does allow you to chop off hands, well, I get a little squeamish. Dr. Turabi would say, "This is not done at just the drop of a hat. You don't do it because a child steals a loaf of bread, you do it for heinous crimes. Something where someone has risked the life of someone else."

When the full picture of Islam is presented, along with its tolerant aspects, the kindness is there. This is one of the messages too. I went to Howard University to talk, because there's very much interest in Islam, as you can imagine, at Howard. The message I give them is about how Islam is revealing itself to me as far different from what is revealing itself to Farrakhan. The beauty of Islam for African Americans, frankly, is that it is an equalizer. For a people who are accustomed to being oppressed, you have a religion here that says everybody is equal. You get on your knees and you bend and you pray with someone who has blonde hair and blue eyes and someone who may be from the blackest group in Africa.

You have to have faith in the democratic process. I don't think there is any way around it. Yes, when people come to power, they do things that they believe is fair, that is right in keeping with their principles. When Reagan came to power, I didn't like it. He did a lot of things that I believe really hurt Affirmative Action and African Americans in this country, but it's a democracy and I have to tolerate this until I have a chance to change it. If Islamists come to power and they are elected, people clearly will vote for them realizing some things will change. You must have faith in the people, as long as it's an open process that people can have an effect on their government. They will make it clear if they like this and if they don't like it. And, frankly, if the Middle Eastern people or a people in any country, in Jordan or wherever, vote for an Islamic party and that Islamic party then begins to have segregation of sects or whatever, and the people like that, so be it. We're dealing with countries where Muslims are the majority, where, if there is a democratic society, they can shape their own societies. And, if it is not exactly the society that I would shape, I'm not living there. You have to let people decide. Frankly, I think Islam has a chance to teach us some very valuable lessons about the role that religion and morality has to play in shaping society, because we've gone, I think, a little too far in this country on the other side of the coin.

Ahmed Yousef: Americans raise the slogan "democracy and human rights." I think the Islamists accept that challenge, and they would like to accept the democracy and the human rights. But this could take a few years. They can be patient for five years, ten years, to see exactly what is going to happen. If they accept democracy and human rights and the oppression is still there, and they see the American government support those regimes who still abuse the people's political rights, then maybe they will change their minds about democracy and human rights. If democracy and human rights will serve the interest of the established government, the American government will support this slogan. Then if it doesn't work this way, as in Algeria, the American government or the Western governments do not support that slogan, then there might be violence and a terrorist response to what they see in the political arena.

Davis: That's a very good question. It would depend on the relationship that the new governments, Islamic governments, would have with the West. I think that we are witnessing evolution if not revolution. There must be changes. You cannot go on and have these kinds of elite cliques when you have young men and women educated who can't find work. My concern for the United States is: What does it mean when we see Algeria go Islamic and we haven't helped? In fact, we hurt. We're creating all these little enemies all over the world and we don't have to.

Abdurrahman Alamoudi: I have [several] questions. I'll just lay them out. What are we as American Muslims or Muslims in general doing wrong? There has to be something that we are doing wrong, and I'd like your input there. Number two. I think we should look into forming coalitions. How can we work with the people [with whom] we think we can communicate easily? That's the African American community in general, and in particular, the activists. Third is the politicians. If we invite Rashid Ghannouchi, do you think the Institute of Peace would like to entertain him for a session or two or more? Would you help us get that invitation? Why is it in South Africa, Mandela and the ANC can come to power without people knowing what they will do? But when it comes to Algeria, people would like them to say that they will outline [their program in detail]–and all of that. And, I'm interested to know from you what we as institutions or American Muslims can do–and hopefully I think you are ready to go and open some African American doors for us. The African American community is very skeptical about Islam in Africa, just because of what they hear from policymakers and others.

And finally, the issue of Israel and Islam. Where is the Institute of Peace? I thought the way you are talking about Islam, the sincerity you have, the Institute would not tolerate you.

Davis: Let's take the easiest of the questions, the coalitions. I think you are absolutely right. African Americans in this country are probably the most open that you'll find of all Americans who don't already know something about Islam. Why do I say that? Well for one, the whole question, for example, of violence, is one that you will find less off-putting in some cases for oppressed people. Anyone who has suffered any form of oppression, I think, grapples with the issue of how to throw off the oppressor. So that in this country, African Americans, including people that come from strong religious backgrounds such as mine, say, "Well, was Dr. Martin Luther King right or were the other people right?" And, did the other people's existence, the Malcolm X's or the Black Panthers, actually make it possible for a Dr. Martin Luther King to have some influence? So, when I approach the issue of the *Gamaa* for example, and Jihad, and all of those groups, I look at it: No I don't condone this, and no I don't think it's right, but on the other hand, do people have a right to use whatever means that they can to help their suffering people?

The thing that I fear is: which African Americans are you now attracting to Islam? You won't attract everybody. Islam is a religion that's for everybody, but, I wonder, if now you're attracting people who are coming on a superficial basis without the real understanding of the doctrine and teachings of the religion without the study that's necessary. Before you can convert to anything–certainly something as serious as religion–you should delve deep to find out what you're getting into. Many of us are born into religion. You all were privileged to be born Muslims. I wasn't. Before you take any step like that, you have to just really research the religion in order to do it. I don't think that's happening. So I think you find African Americans who are coming in on a superficial level and being led by people like Farakhan. What you want to attract are the solid people who are really going to become a vital part of your community and I'm wondering if you're really getting the message out to those people?

Are Muslims doing something wrong? I don't know that you are. I think that you're beginning to do more things right, now. At one time nobody saw you. There was a recent conference last year that I thought was profound. It really helped me and I saw lots of people there who needed to be there. So those kinds of things, I think, should happen and they should happen far more often. And, I think you should do the small briefing things. Hold press conferences and you invite people. And, begin identifying people who are either dealing with the subject of Islam or with whom you believe there may be an opening.

I didn't quite understand the question on Israel and Islam, but I will say this. So far, at the Institute, I have not had any attempts at all to stifle me or to repress. In fact, they came to me and asked me to help come up with a special report that they issued. The Institute now is under a new president: Dr. Richard Solomon, who was former Ambassador to the Philippines and under Secretary of State for East Asian Affairs. He so far seems to be very open, very encouraging. I had the briefing I spoke about when I came back, he attended that and was really involved in the questions, with some concern. I mean, he again is coming from a position of: but can we trust them?

You're right in South Africa a regime has come to power and clearly there was some concern about Communist leanings, but we are more willing to take a chance on that than we are on Islamists in Algeria. I think also you need to cultivate more of an image. As one person expressed to me: Boy! You're going to interview people that, you know, Americans generally don't care about—this whole realm of moderates here that don't make news headlines. I think that you need to push people like that more to the front and, frankly, you need to use your women. I mean the Muslim women should be there because one of the biggest criticisms of Islam in this country is that women have no place—which is the farthest from the truth from what we can see. So get the women out there and get them known to other women, including the feminists to say: If you're looking for some protection, if you're looking for rights, you shouldn't necessarily discount Islam.

Ahmad AbulJobain: I think you should expound on Islam and Israel. A lot of ... Muslims believe that as long as Israel is there ... [the foreign policy makers are] just not going to accept Islamists, because of ... [America's] very close relationship with Israel.

Davis: There is a close relationship between the United States and Israel. I think that's undeniable. I don't necessarily think that will alone encourage the hostility with the Islamic world. Why? If the peace process is able to achieve some semblance of prosperity for its people, if it's able to work in some fashion, and if it is pushed even further so that more territory is given, you may begin to see a normalization in some regards in relations between Israel and the Palestinian people. I think that's a distinct possibility. As that happens, I think you may be able to see even more productive contacts between Islamic groups and Israel. I think though that Israel may always be a sore point with Islamists. But, also, practically speaking, I think many of the Islamists that I spoke to in Islamic groups are pragmatists. Yes, there was a grave injustice done. Am I going to let it be a festering sore? Am I just going to be consumed with anger for here and eternity? I can, but it means that I get nowhere. It means, you know, that my children still suffer, and at some point you have to say, "We're going on with our lives, we're going to do the best from here."

Jafer Shaib: Back again to the question of the American national interest and how that conflicts with the emergence of Islamic movements in the world. Is that a problem only of the American mentality in thinking about the short term of their national interest? Or should Islamic movements show more willingness to provide guarantees to show the Americans that they will protect interests: security or economic guarantees? I've been trying to bring up the issue of democracy and human rights in the Gulf Region every time the Congress and State Department raise this issue of national interest. Also, you mentioned a new definition of democracy or expanding the definition of democracy. When it comes to a situation like, for example, Saudi Arabia, what they say is that we don't interfere there, because that's the way the people like to be, and rule with this type of government or this type of Shura, that tribal way.

So, we can't enforce our Western model and democracy in that region. At the same time, in Algeria or some other places, when it comes to a democratic election, they interfere there.

Davis: If I say we're concerned or worried about Muslims, well, we have very good relations right now with Saudi Arabia. What it finally boils down to is who needs whom the most. If an Islamic group comes to power in Saudi Arabia and the United States still needs that oil, it's going to try to find a way to improve the situation. Now the question is: How do you encourage the West to perhaps support people who would like to come to power? The only thing to do is to show, here are our leaders, they're moderate, pragmatic people who can deal with you. Show them the people, show them. Often they say, "But we don't know what the Islamists want." Well here is what they want–it's written down here. It's clearly in the constitution of their Brotherhood. You look at Hamas: It's there; it's no secret; it's no mystery. Show them how you can have better relations. I think that's really important. Clearly, we should support democracy. You have to show that the concept of Shura is fully in keeping with the concept of Western-style democracy. The one thing that's different and that causes me some concern, is that the overarching thing is Shariah is the word of God. There is something that has to be the structure and that structure here is the word of God, for an Islamic society based on Shura. In Western society, it seems to me that there isn't that. The overarching structure here is really the will of the people. So that the will of the people is that if they vote for oppressing a group of people, as they did with slavery, then so be it. There's no overarching principle, except what the people want–what the majority of the people want. That's the difference. But what you need to show them is that perhaps this overarching concept of Islamic law and of the word of God, is not a horror, is not necessarily going to mean the end of the universe for the United States.

Ali Ramadan Abuza`kuk: When you spoke about your reaction to Mr. Turabi's idea of the dynamists, were you thinking about what is the difference between the religiously committed people here and the religiously committed people in the Muslim environment? I think you need to study also the concept of salvation. You know the concept of salvation in Christianity and all its denominations is that, you believe in Jesus and you are saved. In Islam, you have to have faith and good deeds. The concept of salvation—believe in Jesus and you are saved—gives some kind of a passivity. The Islamic one has to be active role. You have to do it; you have to do what you believe in. The other point which I'd like to also call your attention to is that the interest of the West, which is mostly the economic interest, is now being secured by the ruling cliques in the Muslim and Arab countries, by repression or by suppression or by whatever means. If national governments Muslim governments that are representative of their communities and people come to power, the interests will not be as they are now. It is internal suppression, external exploitation. There will be no more acceptance of any kind of exploitation.

I like the way you have spoken about the coming out of Muslim women and also the Shura and democracy. My view is, even though I'm very interested in the human rights issue, that as long as there is a respect and dignity for the human being, in this society, according to which cultural background, there, I think, is the crux of the situation. Call it moral democracy, call it Shura whatever it is, but the basic fundamental issue is the respect for the dignity of the human being. Even in Western democracies, we can see there is an element of exploitation. In a Muslim society, if it is run by Islam, so to speak, you'll not accept the existence of three million homeless. You will not accept the existence of so many problems in the medical field while spending so many millions and billions for either space exploration or economic research. So there is a kind of balance in the Islamic concept of responsibility to the society. And also, you'll not accept exploitation in any capitalist society. It is true that there is free-market trade, but there is a limit for that.

Davis: I can't argue with the issue of exploitation. One of the things, for example, I told the students at Howard University, is that when I go into the Muslim world, I go as an American and I take with me some of the responsibility for what the American system and the American people are doing in other parts of the world. That's a difficult burden for me to bear, but the truth is, I am a part of that system. Now they were in an uproar. Why should we have responsibility for this? The truth is that as long as we consider ourselves Americans and we reap the benefits, we're causing some of what you described. I don't know what to do about it. In some cases, Western interests will not be served by having Islamic parties in power, especially people who are committed to the things that you've talked about. I think we can still work out a way that we can have a cordial relationship. But, the fact of the matter is, I think you're right. If indeed it means cutting off space exploration so that we don't have people starving in our streets, that seems to me to be only fair and right. But, you will find many people arguing that's stupid. Space exploration keeps the economy alive and it's continuation will help people. I mean, there are lots of arguments for why this is. They all have to do, I think, finally with the pocketbook. But, you know, that's my point of view. It is the point of view of someone coming from a different stratum of society. If I were extremely wealthy, who knows? You see part of what I say is you can't judge people. Also, I try not to judge. I guess that comes from the Bible. "Judge not" was impressed upon me. So rather than say, you're a horrible person, I try to see a way that I can show you another point of view. And, I think hearing people like you, frankly, in a tolerant way, say that there is something wrong with the system, that you would do this because you have this problem, should open some peoples eyes. Maybe it won't, because some people can't be helped.

The question of salvation and action, that's a very interesting one. There are Christian denominations that do indeed call for good works, but your point is well taken. This is something that I've thought about. For example, one of the main differences that I have been able to see between Islam and Christianity has to do also with defense and with protecting those who are wronged and your response to aggression. Christians are supposed to not respond. That's right, you turn the other cheek, and you're supposed to be passive. Islam says you have a right to defend yourself and more than that, you have a right to prevent people from hurting the innocent. Those two things seem to be incompatible and yet, in practice, what is it that Christian nations do? What is it that Christians do? They get guns and put them in their house and they point them at the door and whoever comes, they shoot. They're defending themselves. They are acting out the principles of Islam whether or not they are accepting in principle the principles of Islam. This is something else that Dr. Turabi and others have pointed out to me, repeatedly. You have the system in Islam that tolerates polygamy. It doesn't encourage it, but tolerates it. On the other hand, you have a system in the United States that does not tolerate polygamy or says it doesn't, but in practice, this is part of the problem of American society. If one people are practicing what the other people are preaching, then somewhere they ought to be able to see eye to eye on something.

Abdullah Shaikh: Do you really think that [self-]interest is the only determining factor of the United States' relations with the Islamists? Do they think that the gain of the Islamist is the loss of the United States? Or is there something more than that? I think the West thinks Islam is expansionist. They go to the work of Bernard Lewis and they also go to the practice of historical Islam when it expanded in the Balkans and [into] Western Europe. I think that is a very important factor. Number two, I think that the [policymakers] in the West [are] now ... listening to the secular people, ... [to] regimes that really [have] served the Western interest, and they don't think that in any case any other regime will come to serve the West's interest like [these regimes] have done. When you look at oil, for instance, many experts in economics and technology say the Western civilization is based on the oil of the Arab world, of the land of Islam. So no one ever suggests that Muslims will come and give the West this opportunity of taking oil at discount prices. So I think the West will still rely on the secular people and they will not tolerate the Islamists.

You said we have to educate the West about Islam. One of the Muslim leaders came here, Dr. Hassan Turabi. He presented a good message of tolerance. First of all, in Islam the economic interests, he told them, have no political partners. You don't have customs or even security checks. Islam is totally compatible with classical economics. In terms of oil and all these things, he told them clearly that our interest coincides with the U.S. interest. You need the oil, we need your technology. But he just left, and many, many articles came telling the people that this is not the type of people whom you want to deal with. These were just covering themselves with moderation, but they have another message of *jihâd,* and so on and so on.

There is another question in this relationship between Islamists and the West. As far as Jewish people in closed policy-making circles, it will be very, very difficult for Islamists to tell all our heart and find sympathy with the policymakers here because, wherever you look, these people are really distorting things. [Jewish advisors] are telling [policymakers] those are the people who are against you, they are going to destroy you, you cannot have any common interest with them, and so on and so forth. So I think it is a problem for the Islamists to [come between] the Jewish advisors and the United States policymakers.

Davis: I'll take the most difficult one this time. I'm going to say that I think your last statement is doing a disservice. For example, many Americans would do a disservice to Muslims and lump them all in one category as one kind of person. I think that's what you are doing with the Jewish issue. Clearly, there are some Jews–many Jews–who only care about Israel, and that's primary. But, you know, there are many Jews that I have met who are very sympathetic toward Islam. In fact, one of my reporters, a reporter I had stationed in Cairo until now, was one of the most knowledgeable and open people to the whole question of Islamic movements. Some of the reports that she did on the activities of Jihad and on the Brotherhood were extremely enlightening. I know, I edited those stories. We worked together on them. So, when she submitted something that raised hairs on the back of my neck, I said, "Wait a minute. You know you can't say this; you can't do this," and we'd go back and forth on it. She was very open to this. It was a learning process as it has been for me–for both of us. I resist lumping all people together. But, basically, I understand your point. Your bottom line point is that there are people, whoever they be, who are standing between perhaps the truth of what this religion is about and the people that could be your friends. That is true.

On the expansionist threats to the homeland, I just wanted to say that I think Islam is expansionist. I mean, anybody who feels that they have a message to bring tries to expand. Christianity does. You don't hold on to something as important as you know what God has to say. You don't hide it. You tell other people about it and if those people accept what you have to say, then they become part of your community. So in that regard Islam is expanding in this country and everything I see says it's the fastest growing religion in the United States. The head of the group from the Moore College commented when I addressed them at the Institute, "But it's growing in this country and that means they could vote an Islamic Party in this country." Well, yes, that's what it means. But the foreign military stuff, I think, is just ridiculous. If you really stop to examine this, as I point out, even in the Middle East region, it is not really the military threat that matters. The military threat is result of the larger threat that the majority of the people may want the Islamists in power. They wouldn't be fighting like this if they could go to the ballot box.

Stability and Political Reform
In North Africa: The Islamic Dimension

Louis Cantori: I'm very pleased and honored to be with you this afternoon. I wanted to talk about the subject of Islam in North Africa from a political point of view. To what extent and in what way is Islam in contest within each of the major North African countries? I'm going to talk primarily about Morocco, Algeria, and Tunisia. I know less about Mauritania and Libya, although we can talk about them.

I want to talk about the contesting of Islam along the two dimensions of culture and structure. By culture is meant whose version of Islam among different groups and different movements will prevail? Also related to that is the question of to what extent in the contesting of Islam does a dominant version of Islam become part of the political culture of the country? Does it become institutionalized, accepted, etc.? And one of the generalizations regarding North Africa is that this still remains to be done, with the exception of Morocco. But there's another meaning of contestation. This more structured meaning has to do with the degree of acceptance of Islam as an organized group into the political system. To some extent this is exactly what is going on in Tunisia and Algeria at the present time. There the Muslim group wants to be part of the political system, but the states or the regimes want to exclude them.

For the last few years, I've been working with the political philosophy of George Friedrich Hegel, the German philosopher, and I'm very indebted to him for some of the concepts that I've been using. So for example, as I go on to talk about religion, what I have in mind is Hegel's own sympathy for religion and the importance that he feels for religion. Hegel, when he was writing these things, was writing against the European Enlightenment. So this is an intellectual tradition in the West which is not secularist. It's religious. And the things that I've been noting is that increasingly, Arab and Muslim intellectuals are being attracted to Hegel. And I think this is the reason: Hegel's ideas seem to have a relevance to the culture of the Middle East. I personally am very excited about that because of the cross-cultural dimension. We tend nowadays not to think this way because we think that Islamic culture differs significantly from that of the West, but I'm suggesting that there is a theoretical way in which the West and Islam in fact may have something very much in common in the non-Enlightenment philosophy of Hegel.

Turning back to this question of contestation and Hegel, I would argue that a Middle East state is a "corporatist state" in Hegel's definition. That is, there exists an autonomous state, a state that exists independent of political groups and leadership. For example, there is a Moroccan state; there is a Tunisian state. There probably is not an Algerian state because there is little in the way of indigenous centralized authority. In other words, the state's institutions are independent from the politics of the moment and what people have in mind is a state that they can give loyalty to and feel comfortable with. Gramsci refers to this as "hegemony". In Algeria, this loyalty is not present. The second element of a corporate state is the existence of a political class, in which typically worldwide, the top 20% of the population receives 50% or more of the income of the country, and political power, social status, etc., follow from that. The third element is that the society is divided into "corporatist groups," meaning that groups exist in part because of the division of labor of society: bar associations, medical associations, military, etc.–all of which have a task to perform in order to maintain the society. Now, the political relationship here is one of licensing. The state gives these groups permission to exist. In exchange for that, the group has a monopoly over their activities. I think this is remarkably the case in the Middle East. At the head of a trade union federation in Egypt, in Tunisia, or to some extent but in more fragmented way in Morocco are people who have latitude of action and freedom of decision-making to a remarkable degree in sometimes what are otherwise called authoritarian systems. And the reason is this licensing process. So when I talk about contestation of Islam, I mean that there are organized religions groups (FIS for example) which want to be part of the political system, that want to be licensed by the state but the state refuses to license them. I'm thinking about Tunisia and Algeria as I say this.

And there's a further element which must also be brought in–and that is the relationship of the political class to the contesting group, in this case, to the Islamic groups. Is the political class sympathetic to these groups to some degree or not, and in what way? And I think that when we begin to think that way, we discover interesting varieties in North Africa. Having said this, now let me turn to make some remarks about Morocco, Tunisia, and Algeria. And then, I'll come to some conclusions.

I begin with Morocco, because I think that in Morocco, Islam is least contested in North Africa. By that, I mean Islam is deeply imbedded in the state. In other words, Islam in Morocco is deeply steeped in a widely shared culture. Islam in Morocco seldom is rejected, seldom is resisted. What Moroccans tend to do is take differing degrees of commitment to the religion, but they are all committed to the religion. Probably the most basic way, the most striking way, is ritualistically. One can talk to the most skeptical person imaginable from the religious point of view, and the sheep will still be slaughtered, the correct things will be done, and so on. When a person is criticized in Morocco for a religious lapse, the response can be: "'indî Islâm fî qalbî" (I have Islam in my heart)," and this can quiet a critic. There's a language there; there's a ritual there, there's a kind of universal commitment to Islam–but as I said, in varying degrees.

What is important about this is that in Morocco it doesn't appear that Islam has to be contested on a group basis, because Islam in Morocco has already won. Now of course they haven't won; the religion was always there. I mean, it is part of the long, continuous history of the country. Abd as-Salam Yasin and some of the smaller opposition groups exist, but they are small, and they don't have much of a base in the society itself. And I think the reason for that begins, with the understanding of what I just said. Then you add to this some of the very well known aspects of society in terms of the role of the king as "*amir-ul-mu'minin*," the king as Imam and so forth. King Hassan works hard as a political leader. Every night during Ramadan, he's on the floor with his legs crossed, reciting verses from the Qur'an and so forth, night after night. He's getting old and is not always in the best of health; and this must be physically demanding for him. I'm not talking about sincerity. That's another question. I am saying that he works hard, and I think that what you see in him is a very shrewd understanding of this ritualistic and universalistic nature of Islam within his own kingdom. He simply works at it just as any clever politician works at anything.

I would say therefore that the role of Islam in Morocco is imbedded in the state; it's imbedded in the political culture. It is less in need of licensing by the state, except in certain ways. For example, Shaikh Abd as-Salam Yasin has had his house-arrest lifted recently. In 1996, the authorities lightened it by allowing people to visit him even though he was under house arrest. In that sense, he is in a licensing process, i.e. he is achieving a degree of freedom.

These remarks are not to be understood as idealizing Morocco. Islam in Morocco is necessarily the ideal way in which Islam might express itself in the political system. It may be a unique expression; that is, the combination of the monarchy and the deep internalization of religion.

There is a further point to be made theoretically in reference to Morocco: If Islam is embedded the state in the way I described, what about the relationship of Islam to the political class? The acceptance or the non-acceptance of Islam by the political class nearly everywhere else in North Africa and the Middle East, can provide an understanding of the political dynamics of a particular situation. Here, I would suggest that we find further evidence on how embedded Islam is in the political culture of the country. After all, it's not simply the monarchy that has a monopoly on Islam. So when we look at the political class, it's not only a matter of the political class having internalized the norms or the values of the society. Some elements of that political class have a claim for the interpretation of Islam them-selves, e.g. the 'ulamâ', the Istiqlal Party, and the people of the city of Fez. They are always to some extent challenging the monarchy on this question, but quietly and discreetly. And therefore no member of the political class, no group within the political class, is going to challenge Islam or be indifferent to Islam. And part of the reason is that the authority of Islam and the history of Islam is in fact dispersed into the population more widely. Islam is also reinforced from below via the Zawiyyas and the Sufi brotherhoods (*turuq*).

Tunisia on the other hand, is quite different. Islam in Tunisia is not ingrained in the political culture of the country; it is not part of the automatic responses of all Tunisians in the way that they relate to their country and so on. And in fact, there's a long history of an effort to try to separate *dîn* from *dawla* and to modernize the country in a secularist direction, separate from religion. Although a reading of Habib Bourguiba is a little bit complicated, he always claimed-and you could make a case for it–that he himself was reforming Islam. In fact what he was trying to do was de-license the 'ulamâ'. He was trying to neutralize the 'ulamâ' as an opposition factor to his efforts at reforming the religion from his point of view. He was an apparent secularist, but what did he actually do? He was in fact an Islamic reformist. He never repudiated Islam. He managed to bring religious practices and values to some degree or other into his regime. He wanted to shift theology to the university, but he didn't do away with theology. When we look at the contestation of Islam in Tunisia from a political cultural point of view, the process is quite dialectical.

One doesn't find the Tunisian regime particularly excluding Islam, polarizing itself away from Islam. Instead, what the regime does is try to adapt selectively some aspects of Islam in order to legitimize itself. When we look at the Ben Ali regime at the present time, it's clear that in direct proportion to the extent to which an-Nahda is repressed, the regime then tries to make positive steps in the direction of religion in terms of mosque construction, in terms of relative autonomy of religious decision groups, etc. So the regime selectively licenses certain groups, and then refuses to license the most important, i.e. an-Nahda.

This brings one to an observation and a generalization about Islam in North Africa, and that is that the groups that are engaged in political struggles are themselves mass-based, and are themselves reflective of mainstream centrist sentiment. It need not be that way. There could be three or four such groups fighting with one another for their version of Islam. But one of the things that's striking about North Africa is the extent to which that's not the case. In fact, you could say about FIS in Algeria and an-Nahda in Tunisia are mainstream, that they are moderate in their own way, that they are centrist, etc. There is a diversity of opinion, but that diversity is within these groups, not between these groups and other groups. I think especially this is the case in Tunisia. So the regime in effect, by refusing to license and recognize an-Nahda, is repudiating its own people and its own mainstream sentiment within its own society.

Now having said this about the cultural point of view about contestation, I will now turn to the political side and look at the question of the political class. Here, we find a profoundly secularized, Francophonic political class, which however is more than that. To some extent, it has became Arabicized, and in a very important way, it is also Islamized. And what reference is made here to something that we perhaps need to know more about, and that's the role of the *turuq* or Sufism in Tunisia and in North Africa in general. Tunisians and possibly Algerians, but I think it's less the case there, also belong to *tariqa*s and because they do, they're doing something that's similar to what's going on in Morocco. In other words, as a matter of personal practice, personal values and so on, they are sincere Muslims, and I don't intend to entirely understand this as a sociological and political phenomenon, but I don think it's a conditioning factor. It makes the political class not secularized, not in a polar opposition to its own society, but somewhere in between in a complex way.

As far as an-Nahda is concerned and it's opposition, it is fair to say that it is an extraordinarily liberal party. Rashid al-Ghannouchi is a remarkable man, and his ideas about modern Islam and the role of Islam in a future Algeria and Tunisia are truly noteworthy. He himself opens the door for alternative Islamic groups. It makes his distance from the regime and the inability and the failure of the regime to deal with him constructively all the more amazing. It's just an extraordinary kind of self-destructive act on the part of the Tunisian leadership–that an-Nahda is not licensed and not allowed to participate in parliamentary politics.

Turning to the subject of Algeria: Algeria is a country in which not only is Islam not embedded in the state in the way that I've been talking about is the case in Morocco and to a degree, in Tunisia, but there's a question about the definition of the Algerian state itself, which in turn has a great deal to do of course with its political history. It was not an independent, coherent political unit before the imposition of French colonialism. And of course French policy worked pathologically to destroy and disrupt Algerian society for the 100 years or more leading into the 1954 uprising and that tremendous bloody struggle which also was destructive of the society. As a consequence, Algeria is a weak state.

In that weak state, Islam has had only a marginal role to play in the past. There are obviously some exceptions, but even then it was on the fringe. This is an instance of Islam yet to arrive. It has yet to establish itself, yet to make its full societal impact. Reinforcing this, is the question of the political class in Algeria, which is profoundly Francophonic and French-oriented in its culture. In the contestation of FIS versus the government from 1989 to the present, the political class's instinctive reaction has been to rally to the state and to the government in the name of secularization and in the name of trying to frustrate the development of a religious-based movement and the participation of an organized religious group. You can see a similar process, I think at work in Egypt. The problem with this is that many of the Algerian intellectuals, who are themselves admirable people in strictly personal terms, intellectual brilliant, etc., find themselves as members of the political class in the position of having to condone or be silent about massive atrocities and human rights violations. And that's all part of the pain that's going on in Algeria at the present. If the state itself is not very well institutionalized and very well established, and if the political class itself is isolated from the mainstream of its own society, then I think that we could also say that FIS, as a political enterprise, also is not very well institutionalized because of the recency of its creation. And almost at the time it was created, all of a sudden, it had an electoral success, and it would have been wonderful and amazing to have been able to watch it take the success, go with it, and make the decisions for themselves and for their country. But they weren't allowed to do that. So it seems that FIS, for example, has not had the time nor the opportunity for institutionalizing itself. Therefore, there is a great deal of divisiveness within the group.

There is a further element to all of this, which is a further matter interpretation. What is the relationship of the GIA, for example, to FIS? There's a definite kind of contestation going on there in a rare instance for North Africa, for one Islamic group being in tension with another. And of course that presents a problem in resolving the conflict and finding a political solution.

However, having said all of this, it is amazing that the presidential elections just concluded in Algeria were pretty fairly conducted, with a high degree of electoral turnout. The evidence, first of all, is in the figures. Then there's the electoral performance of the moderate Islamic grouping which received 25% of votes cast in that election.   Most commentators point to that and say that is the evidence of continued, moderate sentiment in the Islamic trend in Algeria.

So I think what we see in Algeria right now is a political opportunity that needs to be seized and a political opportunity that needs to be taken advantage of. Now whether this occurs or not is part of the totality of politics of the country in general. As usual, French language has the correct word: *eradicateur*, in other words, the eradicators ithin he tate nd ithin he slamic pposition. he word absolutely describes the ruthless and bloody nature of the people who are cohabiting with the leadership of the country and in the opposition. Clearly, a subgroup of the state is at one end and the GIA is at the other FIS is probably in the middle of all this. We don't know what s going to happen, but this is where we seem to be right now.

Let me conclude with some observations about this pattern of Islam and contestation in North Africa. I think on the whole, what I've been describing has some definitely ositive imensions o t. n fact, as I think about it, certainly Tunisia and Morocco, for example, may be in better shape on this issue of contestation than Egypt is at the present time.   I think the reason is that as one analyzes this as I have just tried to do, there seems to be a trend going n ere f centrism and potential for political and non-conflictual or negotiated outcomes.   At least that's what one might say of Tunisia. Now what the formula would be, what the occasion would be for a solution of the exile of Rashid al-Ghannouchi and the repression of an-Nahda is another question. But there is something intrinsic o the situation that seems to be positive. On the subject of Morocco: I think the problems of Morocco are not so much in the religious realm, but more in the realm of politics, political participation, and economic performance– which constitute some big question marks as far as Morocco is concerned. I've just suggested that even as we look at Algeria as of this moment, it still dismays us and makes us feel more negative, but there's something potential n he ituation hat ooks ositive, because FIS remains desirous of playing the game by parliamentary rules.

Finally, and this goes back to my interest in Hegel and the subject of corporatism, I and others have been forming a lot of questions about economic development and productivity. One economist has raised the question of "Why not the Middle East and North Africa?" When he says that, he means the following: In the 1960's, per capita, gross domestic product in the Middle East and in many of the Asian countries were the same. The objective economic situations in the 1960's was very much the same in both regions of the world. Yet, here we are now in the 1990's and Asia is light-years ahead. How can one try to understand the inability of the Middle East and North Africa to develop themselves in the way that Asians have? The reason that I'm asking this has again to do with this concept of corporatism which can be applied as well to the Asian countries as it can to the Middle East and North Africa.

Now there are a number of specific reasons one can cite as to why Asia and not the Middle East and North Africa. They have to do with some specific things, for example, first, the failure to invest in education in the Middle East and North Africa, second, the failure to develop competent and expert bureaucracies, civil servants who can be truly technocrats and work for the development of their countries. A third element would be an absence of a higher degree of social consultation and/or participation. We have *shûra*, and that's a very important element of the Middle East, but it doesn't compare with the combination of democratic participation and consultation in Germany (which I left out before) and the Asian countries. Finally, I see one major difference between Asia and the Middle East and North African countries and that is that in Asia and Germany, when a policy makers makes a decision, they may make the decision for their own profit– that's capitalism and they're all capitalist systems–but they also in effect ask a question: Is it good for Taiwan? Is it good for Germany? Is it good for the Taiwanese people? Is it good for the German people? Those questions are always asked there. Those questions are never asked in the Middle East.

What I'm suggesting is that one of the positive consequences of the Islamic revival and of the greater participation of Islam in politics is to introduce a sense of mutual responsibility within the

Middle Eastern and North African Islamic societies that they do not presently have. In other words, the masses have a responsibility to the few; and the few have a responsibility to the masses. It may be as Islam goes through the next 5-10 years of the inevitability of coming to power and the inevitability of taking part in policy and so forth, that this can be expressed in the way that Islam, as a religion, on a communal basis, on a family basis, on a neighborhood basis, operates with a sense of social justice. The problem that eludes us is the question of mutual regard and responsibility at the national level which, however, might come from the social responsibility that has made Islamism popular until now. The present trend is clearly for increased Islamic participation, for Islamic input, and for Islamic initiatives. This is a very dramatic and exciting story that's being played out right now in a remarkable way. It's very hard for a social scientist to stop the camera, freeze the frame, and say, "This is where we are right now." We can always comment about the past, and we can speculate with authority about the future. But what I'm trying to suggest from my points is that we are right now at a possible watershed for a more socially just and therefore more economically productive future.

DISCUSSION

Ali Ramadan Abuza`kuk: I have a question on the definitions ... of religion, of culture, etc. I have difficulties in grasping what exactly you mean between Hegel's concept or definition of religion and mine. ... I, as a Muslim believe that religion is a way of life that overreaches everything. It is the umbrella, or the source out of which comes politics, society, culture, everything. So I have some difficulties in connecting to some of your ideas. Maybe I will have to ask you to define your concepts so that it becomes easier to then accept them or challenge them in that sense.

The second point [touches] your last point of Middle East and North Africa vis-à-vis the Asian countries (though not all of Asia because we have Pakistan, Bangladesh, and a lot in the middle). They are worse than the Middle East. I think there is a hidden dimension, especially when you spoke about the failure to invest in education. There is the hidden dimension of Israel, which has changed the dimension of all the investment and development of the area. More than 40-50% of the respective GNPs have been wasted in these countries just to face Israel or at least to claim to face Israel. That is the hidden dimension that the Asian countries did not have.

The other point is referring to [your comments] about the elections. 75% of the Algerian people did participate. But as political scientists, as observers here, we have to realize that those elections, from the very start, were not democratic, because there ... [in] the 1991 elections more than 95% of the ... [voters participated].   The [recent] elections were [conducted] in a state of fear. The government even made sure that the elections would go their way by starting the army first–and you realize how many votes they had already before the popular votes even started. I lived in Algeria; I lived in Morocco even though I am Libyan, but the concept of civil society as an Islamic concept I do not see much in those countries. In Morocco, when the people are kneeling down to His Majesty, *Amîr-ul-Mu'minîn Bihî*, the leader of those who believe in him, but not *Amîr-ul-Mu'minîn in God*, I am shocked because I am seeing people kneeling to another human being. And for me as a Muslim, that was eradicated 1400 years ago. It is an oligarchy there, one that refuses to elect a peaceful Muslim thinker like Abdus Salam Yasin. Once in Rabat, one of the newspapers said *"Al-'Adil wal-Ihsân* (Justice, Benevolence) Imprisoned." The journalist meant that the group Al-'Adil wal-Ihsan is in prison. But he made it so that it translated as justice and benevolence are in prison in the society of Morocco, which it is in reality. With the concept of civil society, I think there is a hidden dimension when we speak of those three countries in the former North Africa. That is the French dimension. I cannot think of these countries being left alone developing themselves without the French factor. I need you to elaborate on that because even if you speak of the Francophonic society or group, they had nothing in the popular vote in Algeria. But in reality, they are the power-holders in Algeria, now called the "eradicateurs" or eradicators.

Cantori: As far as the definition of culture is concerned and the way that you expressed it, I would say that Hegel's definition of culture from a religious point of view is religion as a way of life, conditioned however by the role of philosophy and art. He himself sees religion as of primary importance in society and he says the state has an obligation to propagate religion. So his definition is very sympathetic I think to your own point of view.

About Israel, I don't disagree with you. You're saying that Israel and fighting and security concerns, etc. distracted budgets and I agree. But, there is a great deal that Middle Eastern countries could have been doing within their own budget. An example would be Jordan. Jordan is one of the poorest countries. And yet Jordan is the one that has done the most per dollar of expenditure in terms of *quality* of education, and I'm thinking particularly about technical education. They really have achieved something. The question is one of educational priorities. Does Egypt in fact *need* all of these college graduates? No. What it needs is high-quality primary and secondary education. It has never even occurred to them to do this. I think a similar thing could be said about at least Morocco and perhaps also Algeria.

On the elections taking place in an atmosphere of fear, I don't disagree. I'm just pointing out the remarkable nature of the size of their turnout when the GIA and others were saying, "If you vote, we'll kill you." Yet, they voted anyway. So it was kind of like counter-veiling fear somehow that worked there.

The civil society question is a point about which you and I are probably going to disagree. I don't think that the civil society in the John Locke competitive sense of groups is in fact either characteristic of the Middle East or likely to occur. What is more likely to occur is the Hegelian notion of civil society which is where these groups are licensed by the state,. are consulted with by the state, but what they don't do is compete with each other. So, Middle Eastern society in the Hegelian idea is that groups are organized vertically and not horizontally. But that's a difference of opinion I guess.

As far as Morocco is concerned and the politics of the country, I don't disagree. We're at a moment right now of remarkable liberalization by the King. There was a general amnesty last year and it's almost real; he let almost everybody free. (He really hasn't, but he says he has.) And now we have the lifting of restrictions on Shaikh Yasin and so forth. Yet behind that is Idris Basri, the minister of interior, torture, imprisonment, etc.

Abdurrahman Alamoudi: My question is regarding U.S. policy vis-à-vis Morocco, Algeria, and Tunisia, if you can comment on that. And what will be the impact of FIS's experience on Algeria and Tunisia? Did the leadership of Muslims, whether it was in Tunisia or Algeria, fail their people through lack of vision and insight?

Cantori: On the first question of US policy, as far as Morocco is concerned, the Moroccan government probably can't do anything wrong. That's the way it has been and will probably remain that way. It's pretty remarkable. The American government over the years has been uncritical and blindly supportive–almost to the point of personalization of the relationship.

The second country is Algeria. And this is quite interesting. Initially, in 1992, the American government went with the French government in supporting the military regime. But several months later, American policy came out as that the government in Algeria and the government in Egypt ought to be communicating with their religious opposition. I've been asking about this question in Washington, and it's one reason that it's interesting for me to live in this area–because you can see real people and ask them, "So if that was the policy, what happened?" The answer is nothing. But it was said, and it took me by surprise. I thought it was one of the most unlikely things that I had heard in a long time. I guess it was so unlikely that they decided to forget it. I think presently, American policy is benign or wants to see a negotiated settlement in Algeria. I'm thinking about the American ambassador to Algeria, who I know, and who's a very skilled Arabist.

On the subject of Tunisia, I think it is, along with Morocco, from an American policy point of view, looked upon as a kind of economic success story, in terms of economic reform and privatization. I don't think there's really reason for the American government to feel that way, but that's the way they see it. Furthermore, because they are supportive of the Tunisian government, they are explicitly supportive of the exclusion of Ghannouchi and [an-Nahda]. I was part of a group trying to invite him to this country but there were all kinds of problems trying to get a visa for him.

On the ramifications of FIS: I don't think that this is the fear of American policy. The fear of the Egyptians and therefore of American policy is that if FIS was to have taken power and were to have made a success of it, that it would have a demonstrable effect on Egypt. In reality, I would guess that effect would be marginal. One of the things that we've learned as analysts and as people who have tried to understand these things is that there isn't that much in the way of political interconnectedness. Egypt and Algeria are interconnected in the mind of the American State Department, but not in reality.

Did the Muslim leadership fail their people? That's a wonderful question coming from you in that I admire the element of self-criticism, but I don't know how to respond to that. Were there decisions made or not made at one time or another that could have benefited their followers? I just can't respond to that right now.

Sami al-Arian: Please comment on [the issue of the power-holder's legitimacy, ... going back to Ali Ramadan Abuza`kuk's question on the definition of religion.]

Cantori: On the subject of legitimacy ... I was simply trying to assess the relative importance or unimportance of religion within the political culture of a country. The concept of legitimacy is complex. It's not just simply religion. It has to be religion *and something else*, otherwise the system won't work. You don't eat religion. You don't clothe your children with religion. There are economics involved, and resources involved, etc. So I think the question of state performance is definitely part of that. But then I would raise the question from whom are that the State and the ruling class asking for support in order to stabilize and maintain themselves in power? Until the 1970's, that support was always restricted to the members of the political class itself, who made their appeal on the basis of Arabism. The Islamic revival and the political organizational expressions of this now is a mobilization process in which the support of the masses by the instrument of Islam is being sought, or is being denied.

We have been talking about Morocco and bribery and corruption and so on. The religious appeal is also there, and so is corruption. There's no mutual regard or social responsibility from that class. ... [W]e know from our studies of this subject that we're talking about the new business class–the new business groups as opposed to the old. The old made their deals with public sector companies. And they were all part of the system that allowed them to exploit the other 80% for profit. And now there's the possibility that the new class, in privatization and benefiting from economic reform, might be able to act as a liberalizing factor within the political system. But we don't have much evidence for this because it is still weighted so much towards business as usual. It's one of my conclusions from my research on Morocco–that the reason that privatization is not developing with much volume and energy in Morocco is the fact that the old patron-client relationships remain in place and these have to be fed. So tax revenues and so forth have to find their way as finance and capital into existing ventures and not the new ventures and not the new economic direction.

Imad-ad-Dean Ahmad: One comment I have concerns the Hegelian definition of religion versus what Ali Ramadan Abuza`kouk identified as his definition of religion–which I think is our definition as Muslims. I don't think that the centralized concept that Hegel looks at is the Islamic concept, historically. The conception of Islam as a way of life, to Muslims, *means* that it does include those other aspects that you think have to be taken into account–state performance, economics, etc. To the Muslim, that's *part* of religion. It's not religion *plus* that, it's religion *including* that.

Osman Shinaishin: Why do you say that states (in the Middle East) are in a position to "license" Islamic political expression? And if you insist on "licensing" human political expression, could it be that the only way or option left for Islamic political expression is revolution?

If not, then what other method is available for self-determining Muslims?

Cantori: All groups in the Middle Eastern states are generally in a functional relationship (i.e., provide a service) to the state and society. Medical societies, trade unions, etc., are examples of such functional groups. Islamic service organizations, mosque organizations, political groupings, etc., function to provide services to meet the spiritual needs of society. In more democratic systems (such as in Jordan) Islamic political groupings and parties are also licensed to provide opportunities for Islamic expression. In such systems, it is a democratic state that is doing the licensing. When the state is less democratic (such as Egypt), Islamic groups are repressed and, as with the moderate Ikhwan in Egypt, forced into the margin, or as with Gemaa al-Islamiyya and its violent opposition, they are bloodily repressed. The question of Islamic political expression is thus a complex one which depends on the attitude of a democratic state or an authoritarian one (such as Saudi Arabia). It also depends on the program of the Islamic group itself. Will it pursue reformism from within the system, as do the Ikhwan in Jordan, or reformism from without, as does an-Nahda in Tunisia or the committee for the Defense of Legitimate Rights in Saudi Arabia? Or will the Islamic groups seek the overturning of the regime as a revolutionary program, as does F.I.S. in Algeria or Islamic Jihad in Palestine? Therefore, licensing is a process that occurs within a system of agreed upon rules.

Where there is only a partial acceptance of the rules, an Islamic expression may seek change through reformism, and where the rules are not accepted, violence may become the adopted means. Finally, licensing is a reciprocal relationship in which the group that is licensed may agree not to oppose the state, but, in exchange, is given a monopoly of activities, such as Islamic medical and social services in Egypt, such that it has a semi-autonomous existence.

Ahmed Yousef: What kind of political accommodation between the North African governments and the Islamists there would be in the best interests of the United States? If the Islamists come to power through democratic procedures, should they therefore have the right to introduce legislation consistent with their interpretation of Islam, or do you think the West will interfere and block any change?

Cantori: American interest in North Africa is in political stability in general and specifically in creating a secure environment for United States commercial investment. Therefore, the United States could be interested in a democratic and reformist Islam that chose to compete electorally and gained power constitutionally. They might be permitted to seek parliamentary support for whatever program they put forward. This can be stated in light of, for example, the changed electoral circumstances of Algeria. In 1991, the Islamist electoral success was an isolated moment in time. The more recent elections in that country seem to suggest 25% support or perhaps more. That is the rudiments of a multi-party system that would give the Islamic expression the opportunity to democratically seek its program. United States policy could probably come to accept this.

Salem Abdallah: What is the relationship between the declining popularity of the North African governments in the late 1970's and early 1980's and the growing strength of the Islamist political movement during this period?

Cantori: The decline in popularity of the governments of Algeria, Tunisia, Libya, and Egypt (but not Morocco) in the 1970's and 1980's is primarily due to economic and governmental nonperformance. Corruption (except perhaps in Libya), administrative incompetence, and the exhaustion of ideas has created objective social and economic complaints. In addition, there is a weakening of political legitimacy as Arabism has declined and has been replaced by the centrist, moderate appeal of the Islamic revival.

Yousef: How do you see the future of Egypt? Do you think that the Islamists represent any threat to Mubarak's regime, and if yes, in what direction?

Cantori: Egypt's future is likely to remain politically stable if Mubarak remains in office or if he departs. The reason is that the combination of the mass centrist appeal of the Islamic revival and of the regime's Islamic identity politics against Gemaa al-Islamiyya extremists has created a conservative and somewhat legitimate environment. Mubarak's regime may be moribund and incompetent in policy terms, but it is likely to continue in power as long as the foreign economic assistance upon which it is dependent continues at present levels.

The Challenge to Liberal Modernity: Christianity, Islam, and the Future

Antony T. Sullivan: As one of the final speakers in this important program, it might be well to talk today in terms of beginnings, of development, and especially in terms of the future, rather than in the context of "endings" or "conclusions." And the future, indeed, is precisely my concern this afternoon. In particular, I wish to focus on how the vitally important dialogue between "Islam and the West," so usefully organized by Ahmed Yousef and UASR, might be encouraged, and expanded to include a variety of new participants.

As should be amply evident from the distinguished speakers who have preceded me, there is no shortage of intellectuals of influence in the West who share my commitment to searching for common ground between, and common objectives for, Christians and Muslims, and who are willing to labor towards these ends.

But there are many other important American commentators, in circles with which to my knowledge Muslim intellectuals have to date had limited or no contact, who might also be most usefully engaged in this discussion. It is on these other circles in the United States that I wish to concentrate today, giving particular attention to individuals, to key intellectual institutions, journals and newspapers, and above all to the political philosophy–the ideological inclinations–of each of the subject categories discussed.

Now, in regard to all this, permit me to make one foray into the past, and summarize some comments I made not long ago at a conference on Islam and the West, sponsored by the International Institute of Islamic Thought.

These remarks of mine at IIIT focused on three "tribes" of what is very loosely denominated as American "conservatism," a word which today is perhaps almost as meaningless—or invested with as many meanings—as the term "fundamentalism." Portions of two of these so-called American "conservative" groupings share many of the concerns of those of us in this room today, and offer potentially fertile ground for advancing the dialogue in which we are currently involved.

The three tribes are the neoconservatives, the paleo-conservatives, and the classical liberals. The latter two are potentially friendly to Muslims and to the contemporary Islamic revival. Before discussing the ethos out of which each of these last two groupings has evolved and their essential character, allow me to make a few remarks about the term "conservatism" itself. That word is perhaps even more widely misunderstood today than it has been in the past.

In this regard, I wish only to suggest that anyone believing that there is any cohesive, homogeneous "conservatism" in contemporary, post Cold-War America is making a serious mistake. There are in fact several, different *competing* conservatisms, sections of two of which, I believe, should be of interest to leaders of the Muslim revival. Above all, one should keep constantly in mind that this new pluralism characteristic of American traditionalism and putative "conservatism" is a development of only the past few years. The potential of this new pluralism in allowing ideological and political space for American cultural traditionalists and supporters of market economics based on private property to participate in dialogue with like-minded Muslims has perhaps been one of the best-kept secrets of the post Cold War world.

Of course, during almost half a century of Soviet-American confrontation, during the Cold War, conservatives *did* constitute a more or less cohesive community, with a clear agenda. That agenda—which often led to spectacular mistakes when applied to the Third World—was designed to contain or counter Soviet expansion wherever it was perceived to occur. Differences among conservatives were all put aside to focus on neutralizing the Soviet threat. Today,

Communism is no more, but many of the disagreements which agitated American conservatives in the 1930's and 1940's are back, some in perhaps more acute form.

Let me turn, then, to the so-called "paleoconservatives," the first conservative grouping of which I wish to speak. Paleoconservatives (in using this term, I share some in-house terminology) are conservatives of culturally traditionalist orientation who are committed to what the poet T.S. Eliot and the historian Russell Kirk have designated as the "permanent things." Trained largely in history and *belles lettres*, such conservatives dislike the Enlightenment, distrust the modern secular project, and believe that civilization itself ultimately depends on religious belief. For paleoconservatives, culture proceeds from the cult, or from religious faith, and civilization cannot endure without religious commitment. In a sense, paleoconservatives have *always* been "post-modernists," as that term has come to be used today. The roots of Western traditionalism stretch back to Edmund Burke in England and de Maistre and de Bonald in France. Many contemporary traditionalists, it should be emphasized, are Roman Catholic.

The second important component in the conservative network of which I am speaking consists of classical liberals, or what might be called conservative libertarians. More often educated in economics or in the law than in the humanities, these classical or "European" liberals are inspired especially by the work of Adam Smith, Ludwig von Mises, and Nobel Laureate Friedrich von Hayek. Not surprisingly, classical liberals give greater emphasis to issues of political economy than do paleoconservatives, focused as the paleoconservatives primarily are on the necessary relationship between cultural conservation and religious faith.

Here, let me *emphasize* that the term "classical liberal" means exactly the *opposite* of the word "liberal" in its contemporary *American* usage. Liberalism in America denotes statism, bureaucracy, and collectivism. *Classical* liberalism aims at limited government, constitutionalism, and the maximum of individual liberty that is consonant with the rule of law and a maintenance of social order.

To speak bluntly, paleoconservatives and classical liberals constitute the "good guys" on the conservative side of the intellectual spectrum, especially as far as the attitude of many of them is concerned on topics of principal interest to those in this room. In passing, I might note that paleoconservatives and conservative libertarians (or classical liberals) were perhaps the most outspoken opponents in the West of the Gulf War, and certainly the only Western critics of that conflict who spoke from the political right. Many of them are sympathetic to Islam as a faith, tradition, and culture, and constitute a community of intellectuals that might prove of major significance to Muslim-Christian interaction.

Who, then, are the specific paleoconservatives and classical liberals whom I have in mind, and with what institutions and publications do they tend to be associated? Prominent among them are Annette Kirk (widow of the late, distinguished intellectual historian Russell Kirk), journalist Jon B. Utley, historian Ralph Raico, syndicated columnist Joseph Sobran, public policy analyst Sheldon Richman, *litterateurs* George Panichas and Marion Montgomery, and Presidential candidate Patrick Buchanan. Many tend to cluster around such organizations as the Atlas Economic Research Foundation and the Cato Institute, and to publish in such journals as *Modern Age, The University Bookman,* and *The Intercollegiate Review.* Tying this entire community together is my good friend and co-conspirator, Dr. Leonard Liggio, Executive Vice-President of the Atlas Foundation, former President of the Philadelphia Society, and distinguished senior scholar at George Mason University.

If, then, paleoconservatism and classical liberalism provide potentially fruitful venues for Christian-Muslim interaction, what might be the specific subjects of conversation with which to begin and on which there is already some measure of agreement? One obvious topic is economics, especially given the traditional Islamic predisposition in favor of the market system, free trade and private property. Of that predisposition, I am sure that I do not have to convince anyone in this audience. It is unfortunate that in recent decades secular, quasi-socialist Arab nationalism has obfuscated the traditional Islamic orientation toward a price system and entrepreneurship.

On matters economic, I believe that Muslims will find conversation more productive with American classical liberals than with paleoconservatives, given the professional training of classical liberals to which I have already alluded. In initiating a dialogue on political economy with classical liberals, it would, I think, be helpful if Muslim intellectuals were to emphasize that the Holy Qur'an is highly supportive of private property, commerce, and the matrix of values which necessarily undergird a market system. At the same time, it would always be well to keep in mind that many American classical liberals will have no detailed knowledge of Islam. Therefore (and especially during the early stages of any dialogue), particular attention should be given to the proper explication of Islam as a faith and as a tradition.

In this regard, some quotations from the Holy Qur'an and Hadith may be useful to demonstrate to the non-Muslim community of classical liberals how favorable Islam is to a political economy of judicious liberty. In fact, such citations may also serve to remind Muslims themselves of an important and frequently overlooked element in their own tradition.

Concerning the sanctity of property, one might cite the Qur'anic verse, "Men shall have the benefit of what they earn, and women shall have the benefit of what they earn" (Qur'an 4:32). Concerning the importance of trade and commercial exchange, one might cite such a verse from the Qur'an as "And when prayer has ended, disperse abroad in the land and seek of Allah's bounty" (Qur'an 62:10). On the matrix of values which necessarily underlies a market system (particularly trust and mutuality), the following Qur'anic verse is certainly apropos: "Give a full measure when you measure out, and weigh with a fair balance" (Qur'an 17:35).

In addition to citations from the Qur'an, Muslims might quote from the Hadith to make these and similar points. For example, an endorsement of both commerce and the values necessary for its efflorescence certainly is patent in the following Hadith reported to us by Tirmidhi: "Abu Sayeed reported the Prophet (the peace and blessings of Allah be upon him) said: 'The truthful, honest merchant is with the Prophet and the truthful ones and the martyrs'" (Tirmidhi 12:4). The Prophet's support of economic liberty, and his opposition to monopoly and price-fixing, is clearly suggested in the following Hadith reported by Muslim: "Ma'mar said, the Messenger of Allah (the peace and blessings of Allah be upon him) said: 'Whoever with-holds cereals that they may become scarce and dear is a sinner'" (Mishkat 12:8).

In addition to such references to the Holy Qur'an and the Hadith, Muslims might draw on the vast body of contemporary "Islamic economics" to drive these points home to the classical liberal community. On this score, one would do well to take cognizance of the observation of the distinguished Pakistani economist, Khurshid Ahmad (in *Islamic Resurgence: Challenges, Directions, and Future Perspectives*, Ibrahim Abu Rabi', *ed.*, Tampa, Florida: World and Islam Studies Enterprise, 1994, p.73): "... Islam provides for freedom of enterprise, private ownership, and a market mechanism as the main mechanisms for economic decision-making." For his part, Hasan Turabi endorses this observation. "The Islamic economic system," Turabi (in *Islam, Democracy, the State and the West*, Arthur Lowrie, ed., Tampa, Florida: World and Islam Studies Enterprise, 1993, pp.50-51) argues, "is one of freedom. Society is autonomous when it comes to production and when it comes to ownership and property... Individuals have to own and relate to property directly, not through the government... The optimum (Islamic) model is one where most activities are privatized." In his identification of what an Islamic regime should truly be, Turabi leaves no doubt that he believes that such a state will be one whose minimal government will be fully congruent with the Western liberal tradition. "I have absolutely no doubt in my mind," Turabi (p. 52) remarks, "that when the Islamic state finally takes its shape, it will be a smaller state than the average state... It will be more true to the liberal tradition of minimum government than any present-day government in Western Europe."

Or one might turn for counsel to Rashid Ghannouchi, the distinguished Tunisian Islamist now living in exile in England. He, too, believes that an Islamic regime must oppose socialism and support a system of limited government and economic liberty. "We must...realize that the state is under no obligation to provide jobs for its citizens in an Islamic State," Ghannouchi writes. He continues: "It is reported that one of the companions of the Prophet (the peace and blessings of Allah be upon him) went to him with two of his cousins and both said to him: 'Apostle of God, secure me a paid position of public service in the administration that is now under your domain.'" Ghannouchi reports that the Prophet's reply was: "We do not give paid positions of public service to those who covet them or to those who are desirous of their privileges. Our major criteria are efficiency and trustworthiness and integrity." Ghannouchi writes that the Prophet then quoted the Qur'an: "Truly the best of men for you to employ is the man who is strong and trusty" (Qur'an 28:26). Honesty, industriousness, and liberty: It would seem to me that Muslims are ideally placed to draw upon their own ethical and entrepreneurial tradition to make powerfully persuasive arguments to American classical liberals.

Enough, then, on Islam and economics, and the potential for similar views on matters economic for bringing Muslim thinkers together with intellectuals in the conservative and especially classical liberal community. Before proceeding to other matters, however, let me suggest American institutions which might be good initial contacts for any Muslims wishing to initiate conversation with classical liberals. I have already mentioned the name of one of them.

The first is the Atlas Foundation. There, Professor Leonard Liggio is the person to contact. The second is the Minaret of Freedom Institute, founded by our moderator, Imad-ad-Dean. Imad knows well many of those associated with the Atlas Foundation as well as the Cato Institute. He will certainly be able to provide good counsel.

Now, what are the other subjects on which Islamists and selected American conservatives—especially paleoconservatives—might most usefully converse? The primary issues with which traditionalist American conservatives are concerned, I would suggest, are precisely the ones that are of major concern to the majority of those involved in the Islamic revival. For paleoconservatives and Islamists, I believe, the possibilities for cooperation may be even greater than that with classical liberals.

Specifically, I have in mind the whole problem of the nature and importance of tradition, the integrity of the family, the sanctity of life, and the requirement of morality as the basis for all beneficent social action. Most broadly, I would argue that the serious religious commitment that characterizes both paleoconservatives and Islamists is a glue which ought to unite the paleoconservative and Islamist resistance to the downside of modernity.

In particular, I cannot emphasize too strongly that American paleoconservatives share with contemporary Islamists a rejection of the reification of secular, utilitarian, and materialistic modernity, that very modernity which seems to be fading ever more quickly as each day passes. Together, I think that paleoconservatives and Muslim traditionalists are well-positioned to contest modernity's deification of human will and implicit rejection of any transcendental order. The gnosticism inherent in modernity's attempt to create a new earth and a "new man," which stems directly from the European Enlightenment, deserves the unremitting opposition of paleoconservatives and Islamists alike.

In this regard, let me suggest that consideration be given by paleoconservatives and Islamists to the opening of a dialogue with the American conservative Roman Catholic newspaper, *The Wanderer*, a paleoconservative publication *par excellence*.

A newspaper which has now been published for some 125 years, *The Wanderer* has long since institutionalized itself through such activities as major annual conferences on such subjects as "natural law and contemporary culture." Natural law, as you might expect, *The Wanderer* reveres, and contemporary Western and American culture it scorns.

At the 28th National Wanderer Forum, held in Washington, D.C., 27-29 October 1995, distinguished paleoconservative or traditionalist speakers included Professor Charles Rice (Notre Dame University Law School), Ronald MacArthur, President Emeritus, Thomas Aquinas College, Thomas Pauken, distinguished political theorist, and Presidential candidate Patrick Buchanan.

The Wanderer–both the newspaper and its conferences–has always been closely allied with the Vatican.   Specifically, *The Wanderer* has assumed the role of perhaps the most outspoken forum in the West supportive of the philosophy and policies of Pope John Paul II. For all those who are advocates of secular and materialistic modernity, for all who revel in the culture of the fading modern age, *The Wanderer*'s sins are many indeed!

It is *The Wanderer*'s radical critique of the modern age that I believe might provide a platform for conversation between Christian paleoconservatives and Islamist thinkers.

Today, I need remind no one in this room of the close alliance concluded by the Vatican with certain Muslim countries at the time of the 1994 Cairo conference on population. In particular, the Vatican consulted closely with Iran and Saudi Arabia concerning that meeting and sent a delegation to discuss the conference with Iran. Similar consultations were organized in Rome with representatives of the Muslim World League.

This Catholic-Islamist alliance begun before the Cairo conference continued at the United Nation's Fourth World Conference on Women held in Beijing in September 1995. That conference *The Wanderer* (Sep. 21, 1995, p. 8) has bluntly described as a "disaster."

And why–for *The Wanderer*–was the Beijing conference a "disaster"? The following developments were particularly important in leading it to this conclusion:

1) The word "mother" was deleted from the Platform for Action and replaced by the word "woman;"

2) Wording to encourage "(sexual) abstinence until marriage as responsible behavior" was similarly deleted;

3) The distribution of condoms was approved;

4) Abortion was recognized as a "health right;" and

5) Religion was comprehensively subjected to the ideology of gender feminism.

All of us might do well to consider how what began in Cairo and Beijing might be institutionalized.

But there is more.

Let me share with you an article published on page 8 in *The Wanderer* on 21 September 1995 entitled "Arabs Don't Mince Words in Describing U.N. Agenda." This article is so sympathetic to and supportive of the major point that I am making that it deserves to be quoted in full. The article reads as follows:

> As he prepared to board his plane for Beijing, the first deputy minister of Islamic Culture and Guidance, Hojatoleslam Mohammed Ali Taskiri, was asked by a reporter for the English-language *Iran News* how Iran viewed the Fourth Conference on Women.
>
> "How can we tolerate young boys and girls being allowed to have sex without being married?" he responded. "We as Muslims will resist anti-Islamic and anti-human measures adopted by the pro-Zionist elements at the women's conference." Mohammed Taskiri's answer was diplomatic in comparison to other comments made by Arab leaders and delegates. Before the conference began, Saudi Arabia's leading cleric called on Muslim nations to boycott the meeting, because it promoted obscenity and was contrary to Islamic principles.
>
> The *Gulf News Agency* quoted Abdul-Aziz bin Baz, Saudi Arabia's highest religious figure, as saying that the purpose of the conferences was to "eliminate laws that differentiate

between men and women... and (it) calls for obscenity through practicing safe sex, extramarital sex, and educating young men and women about sexual issues." The greatest contrast among participants at the Beijing conference was among the thousands of lesbians from the West and the veiled women from Arab countries.

On numerous occasions, the lesbians taunted their Arab sisters, aggressively seeking confrontations whenever news cameras were present–which was often, because some reporters when not shopping were in the company of their lesbian friends.

Early in the first week of the conference, a group of 400 lesbians practiced flirting in front of Muslim women. Chanting slogans, banging drums, hooting, and behaving obscenely, the lesbians insulted the Muslims for their decency and dignity, daring them to put a stop to the nonsense.

But the Arab women only felt pity for their Western sisters.

"They are sick," Sudanese Afaf Ahmad told Reuters. "We are not animals put on earth just to enjoy ourselves and go. If they think this is the way for living, humanity will stop."

The delegates sent by Iran and Sudan were among the most effective in Beijing, led the opposition to the European Union, and were determined to protect parental rights, oppose sex education, preserve the traditional definition of 'family,' and resist the concept of 'sexual orientation.'

If the final U.N. document does not recognize 'sexual rights' as a human right, which the European Union went to Beijing to obtain, it will be because the Iranian delegation fought it successfully.

"It was Iran that caused the deletion of the phrase 'sexual rights' from the document, and the European Union was very much against the deletion," said Shahla Habibi, Iranian Vice-

President for Women's Affairs. "They are going home empty-handed because of this deletion."

Also, it was Iran, aided by the Holy See and other Catholic and Muslim countries, which continued to fight to maintain the traditional definition of family in the Beijing Platform document after E.U. delegates made it clear that they thought the traditional definition was obsolete."

Truly, we live in a new age, when a Christian American paleoconservative newspaper with its intimate links to the Vatican speaks of Islam and Muslim values in such glowing terms.

This newness of our age is a theme that I simply cannot overemphasize. The fact is that without the collapse of the USSR and the existence of the Israeli-Palestinian peace process (of whose shortcomings we are all well aware), no such reconstruction of permissible contours of discourse in the West would ever have occurred. Certainly, without these two momentous changes in international affairs, I personally would probably not have been in a position to speak to you this afternoon, and you might well not have been in a position to invite me. Together, these two spectacular changes on the international stage have unfrozen the Western and especially the American intellectual landscape, and opened up possibilities for Christian-Muslim conversation that would have been unimaginable only a few years ago. What *The Wanderer* has to say on the culture of radical secular modernity, and on the developing inter-religious and international alliance to combat this modernity, certainly could not have been said before these dramatic changes occurred.

Turning specifically to the future, my personal hope would be that at last all of us can begin to surmount stereotypes pitting Islam against Christianity, and the West against Islam, and begin to work together as children of Abraham to win a better future for our joint posterity. We do now have the potential, Christian and Muslim conservatives and traditionalists, together to facilitate the emancipa-tion of humankind from the cultural corruption of liberal modernity that continues to bedevil us all.

If we can truly begin to work toward achieving that emancipation–despite all the prejudices, hatreds and mis-understandings, West and East, which would seek to prevent us from so doing–I have no doubt that it is we, Muslims and Christians linked in common cause, who shall together redeem the new century.

DISCUSSION

Charles Butterworth: People like myself are often accused of being Orientalists ... that we essentialize the Orient, that we try to deal with the Orient, or with Islam as a monolith. It now occurs to me ... [that] we here must be wary of treating the West as a monolith or of treating ... groups within the West as [a monolith], trying to essentialize them. What I'd like to challenge you on is that you thought that the paleoconservatives would be postmodernists, and that anybody since Burke was postmodernist. I think that's wrong because, for me, being postmodernist means being historicist–historicist to the point of being relativist. I'd rather have you think about calling them anti-modernist.

Sullivan: You have a very good point. The difficulty is that in different disciplines modernism and post-modernism are used in very different ways. In English literature the discourse is different from what I'm talking about here. "Anti-modernism" has an excessively dogmatic flavor to it. It suggests that paleoconservatives are rejecting all aspects of something called modernity, loosely considered, and that certainly is not true. Neither paleoconservatives nor Islamists are "reactionary" in that sense. In the West, the Islamic movement is very commonly accused of being nothing but a kind of primitive throwback, an example of a knee-jerk rejection of everything "good" and "modern." The interesting thing to me about the Islamic movement is that most of its leaders have studied in the West and admire aspects of Western civilization. Their thought has been profoundly influenced by Western ideas. Some of my criticism of contemporary Islamists is that they are not "fundamentalist" enough. They go back to *fiqh* and they go back to the jurists, but sometimes they don't go back beyond the jurists to the Holy Qur'an itself. A new and more nuanced focus on the Qur'an as a religious text may be among the most important tasks to be undertaken by contemporary Islamists.

Imad-ad-Dean Ahmad: Paleoconservatives share some criticisms of modernism with the post-modernists, but they are not the same. Some paleoconservatives have criticized some post-modernists as relativists, charging them with rejecting all absolutes.

Changing the subject, I'd like to comment on the third tribe of American conservatives, which Dr. Sullivan mentioned only in passing. The neoconservatives are among the most strident opponents in the West today of Islam and Islamic values, and are ardent Zionists. The neo-conservatives are advocates of the "clash of civilizations" concept. Thirty years ago, they were Henry Jackson Democrats who believed that modern history began with the New Deal and went astray with the student uprisings of the 1960s. In simplistic terms, one can say that they were part of the Democratic party until the McGovern campaign, when they broke with the more liberal element of the Democratic party over two issues: Vietnam and Israel. One should remember that in the late sixties the New Left, which was united in its opposition to the intervention in Vietnam, also split over the issue of Israel. The common cause that the neoconservatives made with other conservatives opposing the Soviet Union during the Cold War allowed them to develop great influence in the conservative movement.

Ahmed Yousef (United Association for Studies and Research): What major themes would serve as a common and mutually agreeable basis for the meeting of minds and the development of strategies between Islamists and American paleoconservatives?

Sullivan: Keep in mind that for the most part American paleoconservatives have refrained from taking part in the debate concerning civilizational conflict, which of course primarily targets Islam. Most commentators who entered this fray have been at least loosely aligned with the neoconservatives. As I have argued, at least some paleoconservatives already have a sympathetic understanding of Islam as a civilization, admire the seriousness of Muslim religious belief, and disagree with important aspects of American foreign policy especially as it pertains to the Arab and Islamic world. In other words, the inclinations of a number of prominent paleoconservative intellectuals are already potentially congruent with those of Islamists in both the cultural/religious and geostrategic areas.

As far as cultural matters are concerned, I believe that the fundamental importance assigned by both Islamists and paleoconservatives to faith, family, and tradition constitutes a solid basis on which to develop a consensus on a variety of matters both theoretical and practical. Both American paleoconservatives and Islamists believe that the fundamental purpose of society is to make men and women good. Reviving an important element of a classical Greek political philosophy, Islamists and paleoconservatives agree that political power cannot and should not be divorced from the word of God as articulated in the three Abrahamic revelations. This being the case, a host of cultural issues including secularism, promiscuity, abortion and the collapse of the family suggest themselves as subjects for sympathetic discussion between American paleoconservatives and Islamists.   On the geostrategic level, Islamists and American paleoconservatives ought to be able to find common ground on what American foreign policy might most appropriately be, now that the Cold War is over and a new century approaches.   Specifically, Islamists and paleoconservatives might agree that American foreign policy, both generally and specifically in regard to the Arab World, ought to be based on the principle of non-interventionism. From an American standpoint, non-interventionism means that the United States would intervene militarily only in those highly unusual circumstances in which American national security is put directly at risk. As regards the Arab and Islamic world, this would mean that the United States would undertake no future adventures such as that in Kuwait, and would eschew any campaign to keep the Arab world frozen in any particular political configuration.

A clear distinction should be made between non-interventionism and isolationism.   No paleoconservative is an "isolationist" in the hermetic sense in which that term was used in the United States during the 1930's. I make this distinction because the many and powerful enemies of the paleoconservative vision of appropriate foreign policy insist on confusing the concepts. Clearly, the United States is and will remain a great power, enmeshed in a global economy that will permit no simple retreat into the past. What paleoconservatives advocate is a prudent American foreign policy, neither interventionist nor "isolationist" (in the old, classic sense).

Finally, Islamists and paleoconservatives should have little difficulty agreeing on the geostrategic level that uncritical American support for Israel should be terminated. All paleoconservatives believe that American foreign aid should be dramatically reduced, and several have identified Israel as worthy of the largest reductions. A number of paleoconservatives have risked their careers to argue publicly that Israel has been an aggressor, and has compiled a lamentable record of repression of the Palestinians. At least some paleoconservatives support the establishment of an independent Palestinian state, adjacent to Israel. This, too, should facilitate conversation between Islamists and paleoconservatives.

Such a dialog would have enormous international political implications. Were Americans who dissent from contemporary American foreign policy able to find responsible Muslim interlocutors who agree with them on important matters both philosophic and pragmatic, not only American foreign policy but relations among states and peoples might be put on a new course. Moreover, the development of a dialog between Western and Muslim conservatives would make it far more difficult for Professor Samuel Huntington and others to argue that Islam has replaced the USSR as Western Public Enemy Number One, and that civilizational conflict pitting the West against a Muslim-Confucian coalition is inevitable. In turn, such a dialog would provide American paleoconservatives and Western cultural conservatives more ideological "space" to contest the accepted parameters of legitimate discussion in the United States concerning both Islam and American foreign policy.

It is true that many of those marginalized by the New World Order both in the United States and the Muslim World are parochial. Even the leaders of such marginalized people are often parochial.

Through no particular fault of their own, the dispossessed in both the West and the Islamic world tend to be less educated, culturally disoriented, and understandably angry at the dismal future which confronts them. Given this reality, it is all too easy for such marginalized masses to adopt simplistic and exclusionist positions on complex issues. What we require are authentic conservative leaders, Muslim and Christian, who comprehend the potential of dialog and are in a position to speak persuasively to the public in their own societies.

Ahmed Yousef: Under what conditions do you foresee a future of cooperation between Islam and the West?

Sullivan: Fundamentally, the world is governed by ideas, historical and political change being primarily shaped by the regnant ideas of an age. As the distinguished American *literateur* Richard M. Weaver so aptly phrased it, "Ideas have consequences." Therefore, I find it difficult to imagine any rapprochement between Islam and the West unless intellectuals from both traditions begin to talk seriously with one another, and begin more critically to analyze their own traditions to identify what I believe are the many commonalities that do exist and which an unkind history (particularly in the past few decades) has too often obscured. In this fashion, I am convinced that over time we can not only change many of the stereotypes that each civilization presently holds of the other, but begin to alter the course of history.

Yousef: You noted that Muslims could find common ground with classical liberals on the topic of free market economics. Could you identify spiritual issues that could expand that common ground?

Sullivan: It will be easier for Muslims to identify spiritual commonalities with Western cultural and traditionalist conservatives than it will be with many libertarians or classical liberals. The fact is that a significant number of classical liberals are agnostic. Obviously, this creates some problem in advancing the larger agenda with which we are concerned. Catholics, Protestants, and even Jews are found among classical liberals. What counts is which classical liberals are engaged by Muslims and on what subjects. By engaging even libertarian agnostics in conversations concerning how political and economic affairs might most appropriately be ordered, Muslims may at least hope that, over time, a door may be opened to greater religious sensibility.   Possibly such engagements would help libertarians to acquire at least some appreciation of transcendence.

What Westerners committed to dialog can accomplish within their own societies is directly dependent upon the support and encouragement they receive from their Muslim counterparts. Perhaps moderate Islamists are similarly dependent upon assistance from the West.

Omar Abraham al-Haddad: [There has been discussion as to how to engage in dialog with paleoconservatives and libertarians.] How does all this apply to the popular media, if it does at all?

Sullivan: In some ways I think there is a lot of potential openness on the popular level which you do not find in the elite media.

Imad-ad-Dean Ahmad: I would consider the New York Times, the Washington Post, the Wall Street Journal, ABC, NBC, and CBS as the elite media.

Ali Ramadan Abuza`kouk: The absence of Muslim reporters on reporting teams is related to the lack of sensitivity to Muslim concerns.

Antony Sullivan: The Muslim community could set up a professional institution to train journalists.

Ahmed Yousef: Given the fact that the Enlightenment forms the basis for Western civilization and liberal theory as we know it, which elements of the Enlightenment might Islamists feel most comfortable with? Economic considerations aside, which elements of the Enlightenment are most compatible with Muslim teachings? Which of these elements could form a partial basis for cooperation?

Sullivan: What is perhaps most noteworthy today is the discussion of democratic principles and political pluralism by Muslim intellectuals (*pace* Martin Kramer). Rashid Ghannouchi, Adil Hussain, Abdul-Salam Yassin, and Fahmy Huweidi are only a few of the Muslim intellectuals who, during the past two decades, have been urging upon highly unreceptive regimes the principles of *demokratiyya, ta-*

'addudiyya (pluralism), and dialog as a way of solving problems. A new organization founded by distinguished Muslim and Christian personalities, The Circle of Tradition and Progress, is attempting to build on their accomplishments, while firmly opposing the damages caused by secular Enlightenment radicalism. One should always keep in mind that the Prophet ruled through consultation and consensus, and that each of the first four Caliphs were chosen either by election or consultation among the leaders of the Muslim community. In other words, I would suggest that the positive legacy of the Enlightenment is consistent not only with the burden of Qur'anic revelation but with the actual practice of Muhammad and the *rashidûn* Caliphs.

A Quest for a Model
for Conflict Resolution/Management
in the Relations Between the States
and the Islamic Movements

I. William Zartman: *Bismallah ar-Rahmân ar-Rahîm.* Let me identify myself a little more in regard to this topic, which was suggested to me, "A Quest for a Model for Conflict Resolution/Management in the Relations Between the States and the Islamic Movements." I'll be talking tonight as somebody who does a good deal of work on conflict management in addition to the work I've done on Africa and the Middle East. I was asked to address this; I didn't do that on my own. The latest book I have edited is *Elusive Peace: Negotiating an End to Civil Wars*, published by Brookings. I also talk as a religious person, although I am not a Muslim, and what I am discussing really has to do with religious movements, dissident movements, movements of protest, rather than something that is specifically Muslim. I will not be using the word Islam and Muslim; I will let you do that. You are far better placed to see what fits in and what doesn't and how one can make it fit. I do this on purpose, because I think that there is a lot, at least in the discussion with non-Muslims, that is attributed to Islam or to Muslims as if that were something special and has nothing to do with the way other people act. I think that the protest movements are protest movements and religious movements are religious movements and the content certainly is going to vary slightly, but as social movements and then as conflict resolution, there is a basic similarity.

Happily the title of my talk is a quest, rather than the finding of models, because I'm not sure we'll find one. Let's begin with an ideal model I think that we would all share of politics–one that I would call normal politics. Normal politics is a situation where people can bring their grievances to a government, a government that they feel is their own, but is also everybody else's. Those grievances are brought upward and handled, and decisions are made and translated downward to be enjoyed by the population. In this kind of situation, groups come together to make demands. They frequently preexist on the basis of a number of different categories–social-political categories, or regional or ethnic categories, or even age, or ideology–and they cohere or hang together in support of the demands they make. They may or may not last. They may be as long lasting as the demand itself, and then they may disappear after that, as issues arise and the agenda changes and other groups come up. Or they may in fact be permanent such as labor unions, or religious pressure groups, or ethnic or cultural associations or something of that kind. This is a happy picture of politics and even if the petitions of these groups are not answered immediately, the groups continue to exist in this model of normal politics until finally the pressure becomes great enough or the new government after an election turns their attention to their grievances. Unfortunately, this is an ideal picture. We may see it taking place in any number of countries at any number of times, but it probably does not characterize a given system of politics, even the American one, that we think we like to enjoy, forever or even for long periods of time in all places.

What frequently happens is that the group's demands become ignored and in fact the group, either passively by ignoring or actively, become repressed in its demands. People don't pay attention to it, people close their doors to it, and we move on to the next stage, and away from normal politics. The group feels it is repressed because of what it is. The demand it makes becomes an expression of its identity and so we have administrations that are known as anti-labor, for example, not paying attention, not only to labor demands, but then to labor itself; let's say to people for what they are. Again, on the margins of a normal system, we would find these ignored, even repressed groups, coming together in the next election, making common cause with other groups, shifting the majority, and getting attention the next time. But if these grievances continue to be ignored, and this ignoring moves from a passive to a more active phase, and then the groups actually become actively repressed, then we can say that the beginning of a protest movement is at hand, and the groups starts to organize and increase pressure on the government to get recognition. Now, it's not simply that it wants grievances handled, but it wants to overcome the discrimination that is exerted against it that keeps it out of politics, keeps people from paying attention to it. Before one enters into this phase, the additional activity of the group brings it into a position of exerting greater pressure on the government, on a government it calls its own and from which it wants an appropriate response. But as one moves into this next phase, the group is no longer interested simply in a redress of grievances. In fact, it's not even interested anymore in an answer from the government. What it does is move into a phase of consolidation. That is, it comes together, builds its identity, builds its strength, builds its political organization, perhaps there are a number of groups so they seek to unite, to increase their strength, and during this period, during this second phase of protest, the phase of consolidation, efforts to manage conflict, to negotiate, to deal with the initial grievances are simply too little too late.

Groups aren't interested in redress anymore. Now paying attention to one's problems is a distraction. It moves the group away from the task at hand, which is to come together, to unite, to build up a solidarity, to consolidate one's movement, in order to prepare for a more important confrontation. And that confrontation then becomes the third phase of social group protest. That's when the group now comes back and feels itself strong enough to take on the government in some way or other, often by very concentrated political pressure, but often as well, by moving into violence. Frequently at this stage, and as one gets more and more into the confrontation stage, social protest movements no longer consider the government theirs. They are no longer interested, at all, in the redress of their grievances, they are not interested in substantive demands that they place on the government. They're interested in procedural grievances, that is, the fact that they are not participating in the government. They no longer feel that they can get a fair deal from this government; they have to be in the government, take it over, or pull away from it. At this point, protest movements of various kinds, either take the path of contesting the governmental leadership in general or turning into a secessionist movement if they have a regional base or some kind of ethnic or identity base.

This pattern, this general model, with a lot of greater detail added to it, can be applied to all kinds of social movements over rather long periods of time. It is the anti-colonialist movement, the black liberation movement in the United States and lots of other countries, and lots of other protest movements, at various steps along the way. I am not suggesting that all of them go all the way to the end, but that there is a succession of phases. In the first phase the solution involves paying attention to the grievances, the substantive attention to the demands of the group. In the third phase, the solution involves attention to the procedural demands. That is, not only making sure now that the group participates in some way in politics, but in fact, by the time of the full confrontation, there is a struggle for full control of the system. In between, as I have said, is a time that is not propitious to resolving the conflict, because the government tries to keep pushing the group back, away from consolidation. The group itself tries to consolidate and move ahead to a position where it is ready for confrontation, pushing back and forward, rather then negotiating or discussing on various types of issues and grievances.

In the third phase, there are two different kinds of possible solutions. One is victory for one side or the other. In an internal protest, most of the protests, the confrontations that go to this third phase, end in victory for one side or the other. Either the protest movement is crushed and goes back to scratch or the government is overthrown and the protest movement then takes over or, in some cases, secedes, as I've mentioned if it's a case of a regional type of protest. Victory for one side or the other is the most common result in internal conflicts and confrontations. There is the case of Eritrea that finally after thirty years of war, and how many decades before that of building up its own identity, seceded from Ethiopia. There is the case of Iran, where the government was overthrown by a social protest movement. However, there is another possibility, and that is a possibility where the two sides get into a position where victory for neither side is possible, or is seen as unlikely by either side, and then some kind of conflict resolution can be obtained but at the price of creating a new political system. A new political system involves both of the two sides in a new type of structure, where both sides feel that they have a stake in participating in the new system. That is, neither side takes over, the state is reformed and the new group comes in to participate in power. A good example of this–and examples are not very frequent–has been in Columbia, where a number of left wing groups who spoke for an increasingly large group of the population that had been excluded from a previous solution to a conflict, a group of protest groups, increased their pressure on the government and finally the government opened up to a new constitution, new elections in which these people could present themselves as candidates, and a large part of the rebellion was resolved by the creation of a new system.

How does one find the solution, then, that is short of victory? What is necessary in order to resolve a conflict in a way that respects the rights and dignity of all? Even when one gets to a situation of confrontation that goes on for a long time, and typically these do, the way out of that confrontation is not obvious. We enjoy our fights as human beings. If you really get into a fight, unless you are just mad at the moment, or something went wrong, you feel it's a good cause. And the person who opposes you generally feels it's a good cause as well, even though we on our side don't feel that he has a good cause, and he on his side doesn't feel that we have a good cause. This engagement in a conflict prevents parties from seeing a way out of that conflict, because people get so caught up in the conflict that they don't have an eye open for a solution other thn victory.

There are three different keys to resolving this difficult problem: What to do when victory is unlikely on either side, or for that matter, what do I do if victory seems to be impending on the other side? One key is substantive, one procedural and the third one, something else. In substantive terms, we usually think that the way to get oneself into a good outcome faced with an adversary is to think of a mutually attractive solution, one that will get the attention of both parties and will be susceptible to pulling them away from the conflict. For a long time, we have thought of negotiation, of this kind of solution, as a division of the goods. We are fighting over a stake, we are fighting over peace, we are fighting over government, something of that kind, and if we divide it up in some way, maybe that should bring the end to a conflict. This is known frequently as a zero sum or a fixed sum solution. That is, I get the majority in parliament, you get the minority, or you get the majority of ministries, I get the rest. And any gain I make is at your expense and the reverse as well. A fixed sum solution may be better than continuing conflict, and, even when the stake is continuing conflict, it is not simply division of the spoils but also the fact of peace that makes it a little larger than a zero sum.

The problem with fixed sum solutions is that there is not much in it for the other side, in fact for either side. The moment that the balance of forces change, there is a temptation to try to get out of this solution, because one might get a better outcome. We have no incentive to keep it, because we think we might do better next time. So people have been talking about a different type of solution, a positive sum solution—or an integrative solution, or what some people call a win-win solution. That is, something in which we both get something out of the solution, and therefore we both have some reason to hold to the agreement. This is the new political system mentioned above. Negotiators often forget the importance of a positive sum solution, that each side gets something out of the solution in order that each side has an incentive to keep the agreement. If the other side doesn't get something, he doesn't have any incentive, and that of course applies to me. If I don't get something out of the solution, then I have no incentive to keep it. Therefore, I want to overthrow it at the first occasion possible.

So how do you turn a zero sum type of situation into a positive sum type of situation? How do you turn a win-lose type of an attempt to manage conflict into a win-win attempt. There are only three different ways of doing this. One is through what we call technically differential values. That is the fact that for one party some things are more important than the other, and for the other party, some things are more important than for the first. If we divide the outcome in such a way so that each one gets what is important to them, then one can get a type of a solution in which both sides are satisfied. Or, second is through side payments, or sweeteners, that is, additional elements that one brings in, such as peace itself in my first example. Or, third is in what is called re-framing or finding a formula for a solution, that is, finding some over-arching principles, some sense of justice that we can both subscribe to and that will re-govern, re-cast, re-define the solution in such a way that we both come out happy. Therefore, if we are looking for a solution, particularly at the third stage of a conflict, we have to remember that we do this best by making sure that both sides have some reason to buy into the outcome, and that the parties are able to trade off what is valuable to them in order to find an agreeable solution for both sides. This is the most common way. In an internal conflict, and in a conflict over social or ideological, including religious values, that is not always easy.

There is another key to finding a solution, and that is a procedural key, having to do with timing. Much of the discussion about conflict resolution suggests that one can find an agreement any old time if one just comes up with an attractive solution. In fact, as we've seen in the model I've pointed out of the three phases, in the middle phase it's very hard to find a solution at all. People aren't interested in a solution to the conflict. Each one wants to strengthen its own side and push the other back to an earlier stage of the protest. Instead, one has to find moments in a conflict that are particularly propitious to finding a solution: ripe moments. There are such moments; diplomats sense it; a lot of people understand it. There are moments that are more propitious to finding a solution and there are times when it's just not worth trying, when the situation is not ready for a negotiations or resolution.

Unfortunately, ripeness of a moment depends on perceptoins, usually of hurt, of mutually felt hurt in a stalemate in a conflict between parties. The fact is that in this world we only do what we have to do; if the conflict between us is bearable, then we have no incentive to make peace, to come to some kind of a resolution. Only when both of us feel that things can't go on like this are we ready to forget or turn away from those perceptions of conflict and look for some kind of outcome. We wish it were different, and theoretically, conceptually, we would think that there might be a positive alternative to this mutually hurting stalemate, something like a mutually enticing opportunity when there is a chance, a moment that makes things better for us if we both come to an agreement.

Unfortunately, not only are negotiated solutions in internal disputes relatively rare, but positive impetus for negotiated solutions is even rarer. I can give many examples of mutually hurting stalemates. I can give very, very few examples of mutually enticing opportunities–that is, people who turn to make a peace, resolve their conflict, because they thought they suddenly saw a moment when things could get better rather than see a moment ahead of them, or a present situation, where things were getting worse and worse. You say, well, worse, better, it's all the same thing isn't it? But it depends on what you focus on, and whether you are attracted or pressed; whether there is push or pull that leads you to a solution, and that makes a mighty difference. Relying on the pressure of conflict and violence gives the protest movement a costly and debilitating struggle and bloody repression. Finding the positive pull is the challenge of protest movements.

We have to remember in this situation too, that protest movements, including religious protest movements, are the protesters against the government, by definition. They are in negotiation parlance, the demandeur, the ones who want something. They want, initially, attention to their grievances, or they want "in" into the system. And that means that they are the ones who either have to pro-duce the stalemate or produce the opportunity. The monkey is on their back. That explains, I think, a lot why protest movements, in many cases, including Islamic movements, turn to violence. What have they to offer otherwise to a government that is locked into power? The best thing they can offer is letting up on violence and a carrot is simply the reverse of a stick. A reward is to stop beating on somebody, just as a threat is to start beating on somebody. The trouble is that violence, once begun, runs away with the movement and takes over, robbing it of its original purpose. In this way violence has taken over the Islamic protest movement in Algeria and emptied it of all its religious content. What is it that movements can offer, then, in order to make either the mutually hurting stalemate, or what is it that a protest movement can offer in order to make the situation more attractive to the government, to entice them into an agreement? Because this is a difficult question and empirically, factually, it's a difficult situation; the examples are rare in the universe of internal conflicts.

There is a third key, happily, again, for resolving internal conflicts and that is neither procedural nor substantive within the conflict itself, but external, namely, a mediator. In an internal conflict, the mediator has a much tougher job than in interstate conflicts. In interstate conflicts the two sovereign parties who are fighting together, and if you have a third party, who is also a sovereign state who comes in, are equals and they talk together about international, interstate relations. A mediator, who comes into an internal conflict, however, is an illegitimate meddler. He's sticking his fingers into the affairs of a state, and the state is sovereign, and here comes this guy who comes from the outside who says, "Let me help you out of your internal difficulties," and the government's response is to tell him to go away. He also, particularly if he's a state, comes into the affairs of the protest movement and the movement regards him with a good deal of suspicion, because after all the mediator, if it's a state, is a state and therefore shares the same nature with the government.

Part of the success of the mediator in this kind of situation, contrary to what we might think, is to be a biased mediator. We usually think of mediators as being absolutely neutral and it's true in some sense. The mediator has to be trustworthy, has to be a trustable carrier of messages and a party that makes honest suggestions. But the mediator can very well have a bias toward one party, that is, have preferential ties to one party as opposed to another one. That actually gives it an entry into the situation, into the conflict, but under one condition: that the biased mediator in the end deliver the party that it is biased towards. If a biased mediator comes in and then tries to deliver a solution in favor of the party that it is in favor of, then it loses all credibility. But a biased mediator is frequently invited in in order to be able to bring along the party that it favors. As I said, there is much more we can talk about in mediation, but there are some possibilities of mediation in internal conflict to be able to find a solution that takes the parties out of the stalemate, either by simply ending that stalemate or by providing an attractive opportunity that deals with the protest against the political system.

We can't talk much more–or even as much as I've talked– about conflict management in this type of situation between religious protest movements and the state without defining what the nature of the conflict is. There are two different natures of the conflict that complicate things mightily. First of all, the conflict might be over access to the political system, that is, relations within the state. As I've said, groups turn into protest groups because they feel they are locked out. Either their grievances aren't handled or they aren't allowed to participate within the system. And once they have undergone some kind of lock out or inattention or discrimination they have to convince the government in practical politics to pay attention to them. How do they do that? What trade-offs can they provide if the government itself wants to turn its back to them? Oddly enough, the most frequently used tradeoff is simply to appeal to the nature of government. You are a government of all the people of this country; you should be paying attention to us and along with this comes political pressure as may or may not be available within the country. I haven't talked about whether there is a democratic government, or an authoritarian government, and obviously lots of things are very different according to the type of government. But the point is that in trying to get entry and participation within the political system from which one is excluded, one has to make some kind of a convincing argument to the side that is excluding. I am not saying whether they are right in exclusion or not; I'm saying if a decision has been made, then the party who's excluding has to be convinced to act or think in a different way.

The other side of that trade off is that entry into the political system means accepting the rules of the political system, that is, participating according to whatever the established rules are. If we are talking about an open political system, we are probably talking about rules of democracy: rules of majority winning and succession of majorities, rules that exclude violence.

There is at least one more question. How does one guarantee the continuation of adherence to these rules? If one demands entry into the political system and then accepts the openness of a democratic system, how does one guarantee that this openness will be adhered to once entry has been achieved? This was a problem the West had for a long time in regard to Communist parties. Is it possible for a democracy to let in the participation of groups that are openly dedicated to the termination of democracy? It was a serious debate that went on for a long time. Happily, in this country, we could finesse the argument. We had a Communist party here that was particularly ineffective, and it could participate in elections because we knew it wasn't effective, because we knew it wasn't a real threat. But there were much more serious and un-finesseable debates in other countries, France and Italy, for example, in the late 40's, where the Communist party was a threat to the system and carried a threat of carrying out what it said it would do.

My topic is called relations *between* the state and the Islamist movements, suggesting not relations within the state, but questions of transfer of power, victory of one over the other, a re-writing of the rules; relations between the state and the movement–a confrontation between the two. If that is the level on which the confrontation is placed, then it is a non-negotiable confrontation because the rules held to by the two systems have essentially different validation. In a democratic state system–and now here I use a democratic system as an example– the validation is that of experience, of accountability, of a renewable return to a population. Democracy is not just the ability to be voted in, but also the ability to be voted out, and these are the rules to which the participants have to subscribe. A religious movement that contests the state rather than simply seeking entry into the political participation in the state operates under a different kind of validation, the validation of revelation. In political terms, a validation of revelation is a hoax, because it cannot be verified. No one else can verify what the receiver of the revelation has heard. And as we know, in any religion one can interpret the revealed word in lots of different ways. Witness the fact that there are democratic Islamic groups and then groups that contest the state itself, just as there are groups that have very rigid notions of government on a Biblical basis and other that simply seek personal inspiration from their religion and take part in politics as Christians. Revelation is a valid personal motivation, but as a social motivation it can never be verified and, therefore, it runs up against the verification process that is constituted by democratic elections and re-elections.

So, what is the basis of a model of conflict management and resolution between religious protest groups and the state or of religious protest groups within the state? It depends very much what the goal is of such groups. There are plenty of models for conflict management and conflict resolution, but they begin with a respect for the interests and the power of trade-offs of both sides. If we are talking about bringing issues on the political table, about different ways of answering political, social, economic, intellectual, or cultural questions, these are debatable and resolvable issues. If we are talking about the nature of the state, this is a non-negotiable, or zero sum, confrontation.

DISCUSSION

Imad-ad-Dean Ahmad: Your theory sheds some extremely interesting light on why it was the Oslo negotiations and not the Madrid negotiations that led to the current situation in the Middle East. Applying your model, the purpose of the Madrid negotiations would have had to have been for the United States, as a biased mediator, to deliver Israel to the Palestinians–something that it was incapable or unwilling to do. On the other hand, the purpose of the Oslo negotiations was for the Labor Party in Norway to deliver the Palestinians to the Israelis, which, I think, most of the people in this room would consider to be the current situation.

Ahmed Yousef: Please, address the issue of conflict resolution among Muslim groups in the United States

Zartman: This a natural and unfortunate situation that arises when a lot of people, a lot of different people in the modern world, and in a country like the United States mix together. As we were coming over we were talking about relations between two congregations that use the church where I worship. One of them is Korean and the relations between the two are relations of misunderstanding. If people were all the same together, we might have lots of other problems, but we wouldn't have relations of misunderstanding. By same I mean look the same, dress the same, that kind of thing, we wouldn't have problems of misunderstanding that we attribute to national differences. Establishing similarities with people is one of the things that we try to do everyday as we improve communications. When diplomats get together, even hostile diplomats, one of the first things that they do as soon as the formal session is broken up, is try to establish commonalities: Were you in India? Do you remember the gardens? Gee, you've been in Argentina, do you remember the pub? Oh, you have children, I have children the same age. It's a natural reaction to establish similarities, commonalties among people, which is the reverse way of saying differences are something to overcome. And I think we could all do much more. But if I am talking for minorities that feel that people look at them in funny ways, we could all do much more to try to work to overcome those differences and those perceptions of those differences. That is absolutely true and it's absolutely true in this country because it is open to so many differences, and I think one has to remember that other side of the thing.

Anwar Haddam: I am an elected member of Parliament in Algeria and President of the FIS Parliamentary delegation. I am one of those who have created the dilemma, that Islamists could come to power through the electoral process. However, the process was thwarted by the military regime, which voided the Parliamentary election and hence transgressed the Constitution and confiscated the choice of the people. Mr. Zartman was very eloquent in his lecture. From his speech one could see how the West has tried to get a way with its support for the *coup d'état* of January 11, 1992, in Algeria by creating a new problem or suggesting that the problem in Algeria is the problem of "the way out." We have never seen these questions asked concerning the existing authoritarian regimes. So my question will be related to the concerns the West is having with the ongoing revivalism within the Muslim World.

First of all, as far as the FIS is concerned, we have nothing against the State. And here, it seems to me that there is some confusion. I do not know if it is done on purpose or not, confusion between the notion of a State and that of a regime. That is what is happening in Algeria. Any opposition to a regime or to the head of state is considered to be against the security of the state and is punishable by law. I think the first problem we have to face, for those who are willing to help, is to realize the situation we inherited from the postcolonial era. There are several factors that characterize our different countries in the Muslim world in the postcolonial era. One of them is this vague notion of "state" among the ruling elite. So one has to solve this issue. And, as far as Islam is concerned, I don't know whether there is a new school of thought that I am hearing here today. Islam has no problem with the notion of a State. As a matter of fact, our scholars back home, in Algeria, expressed themselves clearly on the matter concerning the notion of political authority; the people have the right to choose freely their authority and the separation between powers. Based on this principle, we have been elected twice in Algeria, in local and national elections. So the problem is not between political Islam and the notion of State. The problem is how to get the authoritarian regimes to accept the principle of freedom of choice in the Muslim world. One has to resolve this. Of course we do need people from foreign countries who can help, to mediate, etc. But, what we need really is to do a little bit of study: what are the new concerns in international relations? It seems–and we want to take your opinion about this–it seems that after the collapse of the socialist block these notions of democracy and human rights are being left out based on certain economic interest and so forth.

We feel that there is a certain new international order being built up based on three issues that Muslims organizations should address seriously. (By the way, we at FIS do not accept being labeled as a religious movement; we are a political party.) These issues are well known. The first issue is the problem of peace in the Middle East, or exactly how much security each and every country will give to the state of Israel. Secondly, is the issue of the source of energy, or exactly how securely those sources of energy are provided to the United States and its allies by different oil and gas countries. Thirdly is the issue of the free market economy. How wide will the market be open to the United States and its allies. I think these issues should be clearly discussed by the Islamic movement, and I think it's a good opportunity to take your advice on these issues, because, as far as Algeria is concerned, we feel that the position of the West concerning Algeria is mainly based on those issues.

We in the FIS have not been that outspoken in expressing ourselves to the international community. We are trying to do so now. We hope it is not too late now, but I myself think we have always, as far as those issues are concerned, been clear. We have stated that the problem in the Middle East is not the problem of peace. It is the problem of the representation in the Arab world. On one side you have the Jewish people, who have their own elected representatives. In the Arab world we don't. So, to have a lasting peace, and [a] stable peace, you have to solve the problem of representation in the Arab world. You should not try to avoid this. The PLO in the 60's and the 70's is not the same as the PLO of the 90's–Yassir Arafat is just the chief of police in Gaza and so forth. Secondly, on the issue of the energy, we have been over exploited in Algeria, for instance, and in the Muslim world in general. But on the other side, we don't want to keep those sources of energy for ourselves. The West should not be worried about this. All that we want is to share and we would like to profit from those sources of energy that we were blessed with in having them in our own countries for our economic development. Thirdly, for this free market economy we think that no one could avoid being part of this free market economy, but we have to do it gradually. We have seen the problem in the East Bloc, so we have to do it intelligently.

There is no reason whatsoever to crack down on people because of their way of life, because of what they expect to have, as long as certain values and principles are respected, which are universal values, such as the principle that authority should be based on the popular will, the separation of powers, respect for human rights, ... [and] global security. We have to address those issues. Once they are addressed, we should open our minds to this new dimension of the respect of the plurality of cultures. We think that ... our pursuit of happiness [involves more than] just ... Western values. We do have our own values. I think that this notion ... that the problem now is how to let these Islamic movements be voted out [is just an attempt to] to justify support of the existing authoritarian regimes in the Muslim World. Algeria is a good example of this. However, we think that change is coming. It is better for the West to be prepared to accept the change, instead of calling for confrontation with the Muslim World on the eve of the new century. We in the FIS are for a peaceful cohabitation and cooperation among civilizations.

Zartman: Just three things quickly. On the question of the rules, I didn't make the Algerian move in 1992 and that's an Algerian question. Whether one subscribes to being voted out of power or not, this was a rule or a principle that was subscribed to by the other parties in the elections at that time, and the elections later that took place. It is true, I think, that one of the FIS leaders said that democracy is heresy and another leader said at another time during the campaign that "we will certainly open up the elections to any party that follows the Way." So, if you say that your position was clear, I think you are ignoring statements made by members of your own party that need to be clarified. You shake your head, but I'd be happy to hear something more about that. The three policies that you talked about are internal policies. I agree with you completely that the Middle East problem, the question of the sale of oil, and the question of an open economy, are internal policies made by individual countries. In the last, which I think is an issue rather outside the debate, we know that the state-run economies in large parts of the world were catastrophic for the countries themselves. They were living out of an empty pocket and spending it. In Algeria, as you know yourself, when para-statal industries had a deficit, the government printed up money to cover up the deficit. That kind of an economy cannot run. I can't run out of an empty pocket, and if anybody here can, I'd love to know how.

Just picking up one other point for further discussion that leaves me a little bit perplexed; you mentioned at one time you were a political movement and then you said you were an Islamic movement. I'm a little confused by that, but I'm even more confused by your reference to your values and then elsewhere to universal values. I think that we are talking about universal values when we are talking about participation and about good life, when we're talking about even relations between man and his Creator, or her Creator, and I've always been perplexed by what our different cultural values [are]....

Haddam: [We do not reject the principle of voting out as well as voting in.] One of the characteristics of the post-colonial Algeria is that the media were actually state-run, military-regime run media [to be precise], so we never had a free media. As a matter of fact, the only time people can express themselves freely is in jail. Many people have quoted Shaikh Alib El Hal as he wrote in jail, and he wrote a book concerning how to face the authoritarian regimes. He specifically stated, and I quote, that "no one has the right to decide what should be spread and taught in the Muslim world, and no one will be allowed to gain power by force, even if he would like to implement Sharia and Islamic law." As a matter of fact, in his book, he gave many examples of what is going on here in the United States. He tried to say that what made the United States strong is that they respect the freedom of choice. So, it was based on this that we were elected. How [could it be that] the Algerian people will elect a dictatorial system? They say that it may be like Hitler's time, but Hitler never spoke clearly to his people. We did, and maybe this is what made a problem for us. Because we are still considered the backyard of Paris. We want an independent economic system; this is why we have a big problem. We are the ones who have been calling for a free political system and multi-party system.... It's a problem of the definition of Islam. We consider ourselves, as I've said, as a political system, as a political party, [an] Islamic political Party. But because we don't believe in any theocratic system, like the Iranian system, we don't believe that [human beings] have any religious authority over the *ummah*. As far as the universal values the principle of political authority should be based on popular rule. It is the universal, the common ground among us. The ... criteria [upon which] I will elect my political representative is based on our own ideology. And ... [the] criteria [by which] those people [who are elected] will rule are based on their political values. Those are common ground. As a matter of fact, we claim that they can be found [in] Islam.

Saleh Saleh: [Regarding] the United States' role in the Middle East peace process, the United States is always perceived by the Arabs as a biased mediator. I want to elaborate on this and why we perceive the United States like this. Is [policy determined by] the administration that is ruling at the time of the mediation or does the State Department have its own policy regarding these things? [Then, regarding] the problem of revelation and the validation of revelation and how people interpret Islam, we know that most of the Islamic movements have at least two or three interpretations, and we have a kind of continuum to go from the far left to the far right, but in general Muslims believe that this is the source of life for them.

Zartman: The United States has had closer relations with Israel than with a certain ensemble of the Arab world, and even more so with some of the Arab countries. I think we would differ on some of the results of some of these mediations, but it is certain that successive American governments have been very interested in a peace with justice in the Middle East, understanding that this is the only solid basis of a peace. As I've said before, if there isn't anything in it for all of the sides, it's not a peace that is going to be kept. It's obvious that we could go on to a long debate about what is peace and what is justice? That opens a long window.

Anisa Abd El Fattah: I want to go back to this topic of America as a biased mediator in the Middle East. It seemed as though you were justifying the United States' right to play the role as mediator, and at the same time be very biased towards Israel. [Shouldn't the first step in] trying to seek resolution to conflict be to analyze our perception of ourselves and what we're doing in order to determine whether or not the things we believe, or the things we are trying to promote, are not things that of themselves are contributing to the conflict rather than to the solution. As you say, there is a role for a biased mediator to play, but the biased mediator has at least to be perceived as a mediator that has some level of integrity. In the Middle East and in the role that the United States is playing or trying to play, their biases have resulted in, I think, somewhat of a stigma of not having much integrity nor having much interest in seeing a win-win solution for both players in that scenario.

On this issue of revelation not being able to be verified, I am an American. I was raised here in the United States, and I watched the United States go from a country that defined itself as a country based on Christian values to a country based on Judeo-Christian values. I never really understood how that transition occurred, but being that it did occur, I am perplexed as to why a Judeo-Christian-Islamic definition of American social and cultural values seems to be something that is irreconcilable to the powers that be, so to speak, in the United States. Because all of these concepts are based on some type of assumption that the holy books that support these particular religions have somehow been validated. Israelis are in Palestine and for years they promoted their presence there as being based on divine revelation. The United States did nothing to refute their promotion of their presence in that part of the world based on this divine revelation or right. What I'm saying is this concept of a biased mediator covers up a myriad of other hypocrisies and discrepancies in our thinking and our behavior with respect to the people of the Middle Eat and Islam in particular.

Zartman: I think your last point is particularly good. It is an innovation that Islam brings by considering the People of the Book as having common Judeo-Christian-Muslim values. I am someone who has looked at Islam and has lived in the Middle East, so I would welcome this kind of recognition that these are common values and that we worship the common God. The answer to your question I think is a straight-forward answer, and it, socially, helps us understand the situation. The reason why it is a double rather than a triple basis is because until recently the Muslim population in the United States has been very small and is still very small compared to the rest. That's just a factual statement. The growth of a Muslim population in the United States is one that brings us face to face with that question, and then opens up a debate about it and helps us perhaps to better understand the commonalties of our faiths. In that discovery, there certainly going to be misunderstanding, there is going to be disagreement, but as we get off one position and then move on to the other, I hope we would go into it more.

A comment on your biased mediator: I wasn't thinking about the United States; I wasn't referring to the Middle East position. I understand how that was taken in a particular way and we can open that up to further discussion. I used the word biased–a shock word–rather than simply a mediator as favorable to one side or the other. Nonetheless, on the conceptual level, in certain situations, favorableness to one party gives the mediator leverage with that party that it would not have otherwise. Now, how this is exercised takes us back to debate on the Middle East question and it's certain that there have been times when it has been exercised and there are times when it was. In my opinion and certainly yours too, it has not been exercised enough. I would say don't overplay it. The present Israeli government is an embarrassment to the United States. The United States certainly put a lot on the line to have Peres elected and we will see some fancy dancing, if you will, having to deal with the state, but having to deal with a state, with a government, the United States finds [itself] uncomfortable with.

Ahmad: Although you are quite correct that until very recently the Muslim community in the United States was very small, the situation now is there is a dispute whether there are more Muslims or more Jews in the United States.

Akram Kharoubi: I have two small questions about Jerusalem. Sometimes the dictatorship regimes tend to push movements to the third stage where they use armed struggle, for example where they will be labeled terrorists and easier to crush in the eyes of the world. My second question is that the conflict in Palestine now, in the model you discussed, is between two parties, but now we have three parties– Israel, the Palestinian Authority, and the Islamic movement, or those who are against the Palestinian Authority and their way of solving the problem. I heard some of the analysis that the Israelis went into this agreement because their major reason was to crush the Islamic movement in coordination with the Palestinian Authority and the Israeli regime. Whether this is true or not, being a specialist in the conflict management process, what suggestions do you have for the Islamic movement there in terms of solving the problem, because they have a problem with the Palestinian Authority and they have a problem with the Israelis.

Zartman: It is not for tactical reasons that dictatorial regimes try to push movements of protest into dissidence. It's just because they are dictatorial regimes. It's their opposition to open and participatory politics. I think it is true that part of the impetus to the Oslo agreements and it's successor is the fact that both the PLO and Israel faced a threat from Hamas. What should Hamas do? That puts me in an odd position. I'm not sure I know enough about all of Hamas' beliefs to make suggestions as to what it should do.

The threat of armed struggle is important, by a lot of what I've said. By the same token if it is true that Israel and PLO had a common cause, a common impetus for agreement in Hamas, it is also true that Hamas elected Netanyahu.

Laura Drake: I want to come back to the subject of the biased mediator. When you said that it is not conducive for peace when the biased mediator, instead of delivering the side that its supporting, actually renders stronger the side it is supporting, I think that probably everybody in this room thought about the United States and Israel. I think it is very important because it goes back to the tension in your talk between the concept of the zero sum game. It seems that the whole concept of conflict mediation, maybe for you, is the idea that you can have a positive sum solution attributed to a zero sum game. So if this is a zero sum game and it is about definition, I think that what in fact happened at Oslo was we had a positive sum solution applied to a zero sum game. The only way that this could occur is when the party which is seeking to redefine the rules, as you put it, is put in a position where it no longer has access to the rules. The transformation of the conflict from a horizontal conflict into a vertical conflict is in essence what has taken place. I think this is the difference between your two types of conflict, namely, the internal state versus group in the state. This is as opposed to either interstate or a group which has developed its own identity, its own independence and has separated itself from the state: Islam versus the state not what the movement does inside the country. If in fact it has been changed from a horizontal conflict to a vertical conflict, this in itself accounts for the rise of Hamas in the latter phase. [This is precisely] because the party which is rendered at the bottom of the vertical structure, if you will, loses the credibility of the people, if you will, that have created it, or the people that it was to supposed to serve. Therefore a new independent movement comes out because really the Palestinian Authority is no longer an independent entity. So, I think these touch on all aspects of what you said.

Zartman: I don't quite understand the horizontal and the vertical conflict, but to go back to positive sum and zero sum conflict, let's remember the topic I asked to address was conflict management and conflict resolution. It's a subject I think important, but there are conflicts, or positions in conflicts, that are non-negotiable. One can have a position, and one can judge from inside or outside, and one can debate whether it is right or wrong (whatever that means), but there are situations where conflict resolution, that is, looking for some kind of agreement that allows the other side to continue to participate in the situation is not what we want, is wrong. If one makes that judgment, however, one has to take two things into account. One is the cost, and the second is the attainability of the outcome. And again, I am stating principles that then one can apply to whatever conflict one wants. That's why we take the stance that we take in this world. There are plenty of things in daily life that we'd like to stand up for, that "I'm right," and then you realize that I can't I have the right of way in traffic darn it, and then people get shot on the beltway. That's a zero sum kind of thinking. That's a stupid example, right? But it happens in this city of ours. If someone took a resolvable situation and turned it into a zero sum conflict, didn't think about the cost and he didn't think about the attainability of the outcome that he wants. Now, put this to Hamas.

Imad-ad-Dean Ahmad: Perhaps you could answer her other question if I rephrase it. Instead of horizontal and vertical, think of it as internal and external. You had said it is easier in some ways to resolve external disputes between states. If you have two states and a third state comes in to negotiate, at least they consider themselves as equals, whereas resolution of an internal conflict between the state and a non-state group under it is more difficult. Had the United States recognized Palestine, when it declared itself an independent state, it could have come in as a third state negotiating between Palestine and Israel. Instead, by having the PA, or Palestinian Authority, as a subcontractor to the Israelis to enforce the occupation, now there is a dispute between the PA and essentially, not just Hamas, but the Palestinian people. And that is an internal dispute which, according to your model, is harder to deal with.

Zartman: I think that in this, one has to base a judgment on, or take into account, the attainability of the goals. I may be wrong in this, but it is the assumption that colors my views of the Oslo and post-Madrid kind of negotiations. Once a Palestinian Authority, even that, has been established, statehood is inevitable. I think a lot of people look at the other end of that progression. That's a future bet, and people might say, "I don't agree with that." But I think there is another difference too. I think people look at a different moment in that progression and say, step one is not enough. My judgment is step one inevitably leads to step whatever. My question would be should one take step one as the end step, or is this a step, as in lots of other situations of this kind, that is certainly going to lead to an outcome that people want. I think that's the basis of a difference in the judgment of these things.

Ahmad: I think the interesting question, the important question here, is that given that it is easier to negotiate among states than it is to negotiate in a vertical direction (internally), doesn't putting off the inevitable step make the negotiation process more difficult and increase the possibility of violence? Again, using your model, if we cannot resolve things, then the Palestinian people now being repressed by the PA are going to feel themselves motivated to resort to violence because they feel they have no other alternative. Whereas if it becomes an issue of negotiation between states, the problem is approached in a different manner.

Zartman: Yes, but even if the PLO had been recognized as such, it is not yet a question of relations among states. It is relations between a state and a proto-state, exactly for the constitution of that state, that is, giving it territory and control over the territory, so that one cannot by definition, change reality. The other thing is, it's a question of a whole loaf or half a loaf? Then we go back to my question, whether the whole loaf follows the half loaf, or whether you judge that half a loaf is just a half a loaf and not enough at this time. Could one have gotten a total agreement? I don't think one could have gotten much more out of Oslo or from Madrid. You may notice we are away from our original topic somewhere. Could one have gotten more out of Oslo, whatever the position within the realistic limits of any of the parties? I don't think so.

Ahmad: Given your model and your theory, it appears that if one is trying to negotiate a settlement, the logical next step must be to establish, with all speed, a democratic Palestinian state, so that the negotiation process could conclude along the optimistic lines you described. If you said we are going to put off the formation of the democratic state until much later, then the negotiations you are trying to address are extremely difficult, if not impossible.

Zartman: Yes, and don't apologize for keeping it going, because I am very interested in your response. Let's say that the problem now is with an authoritarian Palestinian authority. With whom would one have negotiated in order to get a democratic state. Look at the history of decolonization. Look at Algeria. What France negotiated with was a body that spoke in the name of the Algerian people and brought in a single party dictatorship that was not even a single party. The FLN was a facade. And whom are you going to negotiate with? Draw me a scenario for an Oslo talk that is going to give us a democratic state; I'd love it. That's a question.

Ali Ramadan Abuza`kuk: I come from a country in North Africa, Libya, where the state has closed all doors for any kind of resolution of solving the conflict between the people and the dictatorship. We know that today there is no isolation; there is no state that can say I am an isolated island in this world. There are international powers, there are neighboring countries, there are a lot of other factors at determining a situation–even though the boycott the United Nations is making against Libya, is hurting the Libyan people, not the regime itself. And I like the [distinction] that Mr. Haddam [made] between the regime and the state. The question is how to find solutions and where is the role of the international bodies? For example we find that there is a problem of two countries in the Middle East that do not acquiescence to the superpower of the area, Israel, and the rest of the petty states, the Arab states: Iran and Libya. We find that both of them have been labeled terrorist, and both of them have been condemned by the United States. The other point is also we have a conflict between the United States as a state and the Islamic movement, [seeking] to be recognized, because the United States has labeled Hamas as terrorist to serve another country, another state, and that was subservient to the political agenda of Israel. So here we come to either accepting the facade of peace as it is, or telling the truth. Whoever reads what Israel and Egypt agreed upon will find that it was the victorious, the Israeli state, against the defeated, the Egyptian state. Or follow up the same system with Jordan and the PLO at the same time. So here we have two problems. In one area, the United States is subscribing to the Israeli agenda or the pro-Israeli lobbies and creating a conflict with the Islamic movement. Then, we find in the Middle East ... closed systems that do not open up, and the world in general, with all the leverages that are there, do not subscribe to opening up the system. What can we do, even if we are intellectuals with voices?

Zartman: If we are intellectuals with voices, we can make ourselves heard in discussions, in the public media, and so forth, about what we think is important. I don't like Qadhdhafi's regime any more than you do, but what I would like even less is if the United States government tried to overthrow it. I was once talking in a place that is now called Burkina Faso about American policy in Africa, if you can imagine having to make such a talk, and someone got up afterwards and said I tell you two things. We are tired of the United States throwing its weight around in Africa and telling little countries what to do, and second of all why don't you support us in our war against Mali? I don't like Qadhdhafi, but I haven't seen terribly much effectiveness in policies towards Iran or towards Libya, and I'm not quite sure how the United States would be able to help your cause in ways that you should like. For the other one, I disagree with you on the Camp David and Washington agreement, as you would imagine. When Egypt gets back it's territory, I don't see how you can say it was taken to the cleaners. It was taken out of the military confrontation, it's true, but you see what the military confrontation has got us so far, so, what world are you talking about? The real world, or some other one?

Abuza`kuk: We see that an the United Nations resolutions, and we know that the United States goes behind most of them, against Iraq, and they will implement them…. [Resolutions] against Israel were not implemented, against Serbia were not implemented, [and] now they are trying to implement [resolutions] against Sudan. So there is, I don't want to say bias, but there is a tendency that … resolution against [countries] the United States [opposes] will work, or at least be put into action.

Imad-ad-Dean Ahmad: I think you're talking at cross-purposes. When you say it will work you mean the United States will take a position, but when Dr. Zartman says it doesn't work, it's just that that position doesn't bring any results.

Muhammad al-Asi: If we want to figure out where Hamas or where the PA stand regarding some type of serious issues in the Middle East crisis, it behooves us to look at the population base, either the

Palestinians or the Arabs or the Muslims or the Jews, who, in the final analysis, are both sides of the conflict that we are trying to deal with. Instead of dealing with it on the basis of approaching the power of the state, we should deal with it on the basis of the population as a whole. Popular participation is ignored, although]this has to do with democracy. We always speak about whether you can vote some people in, then likewise vote them out. But we never look at our trump card over that region, and that is we veto them out, and we keep them out. This has been the policy pursued against Islamic political representation. You can take it in Algeria, in Egypt, in Palestine, wherever you go it seems to be a broken record. So the veto is another very important factor in this conflict. How do you factor into your theory of conflict management and resolution the population, instead of speaking about a segment that may or may not represent the population, an opposition?

I. William Zartman: I talked about a protest movement. I didn't talk about everything in this world, I admit. I talked about resolving conflict. I talked about a protest movement. A movement represents population. You can put in the amount of the population that you want into the thing. You talked about vetoing, taking groups out, this is what protest groups are about, people who are I protesting not being part of the system. I'm talking about exactly what you are.

Osman Shinaishin: The question that I am more familiar with relates to events that happened in Egypt. [In a previous discussion] Robert Neumann was asked what was happening in Egypt between the government of Mubarak and the Islamic Brotherhood. He commented that he believes that the U.S. government is not very happy about what is going on there, but it has no option because Mubarak is very important to the peace process. Isn't it a very short-sighted approach on the part of the US government to seek a short-term benefit at the cost of a possible catastrophe? If events change radically from what they are right now–and this is not a representation of facts, just a projection of possibilities; I hope it never happens– should the Ikhwan take arms up, as they are much, much larger than the groups that are currently fighting the government? Should they take arms and fight for their freedom? In the last few days people have been arrested and sent to prison. Some of them were members of parliament, elected during Sadat's [reign]. People who are not the Mob, but the heads of professional syndicates. Should these people give up hope and find there is no alternative but to fight to get their freedom, the United States will find itself in a much, much more regrettable situation, worse than anything that happened in Iran. [Couldn't you] and others who can advise it, show that in the long term they should stand with people who believe in rights?

Now the question of the system in Egypt, one man, one vote, one time, is utter nonsense as far as Egypt is concerned, because the Ikhwan have made it abundantly clear that they are not interested in taking power. In fact they have constantly made it clear that they are not going to run in the elections. They just want to have access to speak because their view is that if our voice is known, it doesn't have to be us that is elected, but the people will implement what they want. And the best comment that I heard about this is that we do not want to rule by Islam, and Islamic law, we want to be ruled by Islamic law, meaning that if Mubarak would, it's fine, we would be happy with it. But he is not willing to listen. And I think the U.S. government especially in the position it is in now, with tremendous authority around the world, both monetarily, economically, through the U.N., the IMF, etc. should take a more active role.

One last comment: *The Washington Post* a few days ago had a rather positive comment about the new dealings between Turkey and Iran saying we think this a step forward. Even though we don't like them getting close to Iran, this will give them access to ameliorate the behavior of Iran towards the West. But then comes *The Wall Street Journal* article two days ago. They say that the IMF is tightening the economic screws on Turkey. One line about the economic conditions that cause this and twenty lines about the fact that Turkey is coming close to Iran. You read from it that the IMF is tightening the screws not because of the economic conditions in Turkey, but because Turkey is doing this and this and that, in terms of the economic and political arena. I think if you can answer this, it would be very helpful. Most of my colleagues here would find that hard to swallow your comments about the U. S. government being embarrassed by the election of Netanyahu, given the reception that Netanyahu was given in Congress when he made a declaration about Jerusalem. It was announced that there was tremendous applause for him, and it was very irritating to others. I don't want to say that everybody supports this, but there is a pent-up support for Israel regardless of what Israel does. I hope you can answer that.

Zartman: I probably can't. I think what you said was very eloquent about Egypt. Events in Egypt are troubling and I think that there is a lot to be said for the Turkey-Iran arrangement. It certainly helps Turkey, which is an element to be taken into account as well, and gives stability to economic benefits to Turkey. Another question to be asked, and I'm not an Iran specialist, is how moderable by that kind of action is the Iranian government? But there is always a debate between exclusion and trying to moderate. I'd stick by what I said about the U.S. government and Netanyahu. I was referring to the executive. I was referring particularly to the State Department, and so on. Congress is elected by the U.S. people and acts funny on things like that. Congress has been kind of crazy on the Jerusalem issue. This is something on which I think people will agree with me here. I think from the executive side there is a different perception.

Shinaishin: It's a conceptual question.... It seemed to me [that] you closed the model itself for analytical purposes, the Islamic movement and the state, but did not take into account ... the notion of the relations of dominance in the international system itself, e.g., if we take the case of France versus FIS. France is probably much more involved and much more influential in the Algerian case itself than the regime itself. This is debatable, I'm not saying exactly that, but the relations of dominance in the international system certainly affect the internal situation at the level of both the state and the movement. Also ... we are assuming that these movements came up after the state system was created, but the fact is that the state system was superimposed on a cultural domain that was Islamic. ... These movements are interconnected because this was an Islamic domain before the creation of the modern state. [Outside intervention] precludes the notion of political change. Who can guarantee any rules or any guide?

Imad-ad-Dean Ahmad: Prof. Zartman, I think your insightful model could indeed be useful in discussing the situation in the Muslim world, but I think that some things at the end of the talk require comment. The fact that Islam includes the concept of pluralism, inherent in the status granted to the People of the Book, to a large degree responds your concern regarding the problem of validation of revelation. Nor do I think that the differences people can have on the interpretation of religion need be a problem. On both issues I am reminded of the comment that Thomas Jefferson reportedly made to the effect that the problems caused by the differences among religions would be much less significant if people would follow those principles which all religions have in common.

Conclusions

There are significant differences between culture in the Muslim world and in the West. Yet the presumption that those differences are vastly greater than the differences among varying Western ideologies or among varying understandings of Islam is refuted by the dialogs printed in this volume. The differences between the enlightenment in Britain and the French enlightenment are more significant than the difference between the natural law theory embraced by American paleoconservatives and the understanding of shari`ah advanced by moderate Muslims. The views of secularism advanced by the French and those advanced by the Turkish military have much in common, and both differ from the concept of pluralism as practiced in America or Malaysia.

None of this can erase the impression that Muslims and Westerners view one another with suspicion. On the Western side this appears to be due to the legacy of the crusades. Those who recall that the Western civilization lived in the shadow of the Islamic civilization for centuries and exploit the fear that an Islamic resurgence may once again upset the geopolitical dominance of the West. "The New World Order," a modern rendition of the old colonialist and imperialist mentality, has caused much of this suspicion to resurface and has reinforced suspicions that were remnants of the past. Muslim participants have especially been prone to note how easily Western powers overlook violations of International Law by Israel and how quickly they move to sanction and ostracize violations by indigenous states. This double standard continues at the date of publication exemplified by Western indignation over nuclear weapons testing by India and Pakistan while Israel escapes sanctions or even censure for its nuclear program or even its kidnapping and political imprisonment of Mordechai Vanunu for attempting to publicize it.

Despite all this, any claim that all Islamic and Western values inherently conflict is given the lie by the existence of Western Muslims, particularly by the comfort the American Muslims participating in these discussions exhibit with their dual identity. Given the frequency with which the term "universal values" crops up in this dialog, we must accept the importance of the question as to what degree are certain Western values derived from the Judeo-Christian-Islamic tradition and thus not secular at all, but religious values common to the Abrahamic faiths? To whatever degree this may be the case, we expect that at a fundamental level there are some values that are the same in both the Western and Muslim contexts, albeit phrased, perhaps, in a different manner of speaking.

The most provocative suggestion made in this series is that the significant struggle in the coming century will be not between the West and Islam, but between religious people of faiths united against what might be termed "secular fundamentalism." We note how in Turkey, after the military pressured the Islamists from power, moderate secularists demonstrated side-by-side with Islamists at Istanbul University against the banning of beards and headscarves.

Without doubt the overdue dialog between Islam and the West has begun. Perceived and imagined dichotomies between the two are being narrowed by shared moral and religious values, and a common prayer for a future of peace, prosperity, and justice for all the world's people. Scholars, Western and Islamic (some both), have approached one another as equals and have treated dialog as a universal good rather than a device for advocacy of special interests. In such enlightened interaction is hope for a 21st century that will be a period of Islamic and Western cooperation and not the confrontation that has dominated the past.

Capsule Biographies
of Roundtable Participants

Anisa Abd El Fattah is President of the National Organization for Muslim Women and Children and a research fellow at United Association for Studies and Research.

Dr. Salem Abdullah is a former research fellow at the United Association for Studies and Research.

Mr. Ahmad AbulJobain is Managing Editor of *Middle East Affairs Journal*.

Mr. Ali Ramadan Abuza'kuk is a former lecturer of communications at the University of Benghazi, Libya, Vice President of the Minaret of Freedom Institute, and Chairman of the Board of Directors of the United Association for Studies and Research.

Dr. Imad-ad-Dean Ahmad is the President of the Minaret of Freedom Institute. He is an adjunct professor at the University of Maryland and at the Johns Hopkins University's School for Advanced International Studies and co-author of *Islam and the Discovery of Freedom*.

Mr. Muhammad Y. Alami is an international broadcaster and translator with the Middle East Service of the Voice of America.

Mr. Abdurrahman Alamoudi is President of the American Muslim Foundation and a member of the Board of Directors of the American Muslim Council, a national Muslim advocacy group headquartered in

Washington, DC, which aims at organizing and empowering the Muslim community in America.

Dr. Sami Alarian is a professor at the University of South Florida and a well-known lecturer on the Islamic movement.

Mr. Muhammad al-Asi is a Lebanese-American community religious leader and writer on Islaic affairs who has traveled to Iran.

Mr. Nihad Awad is Executive Director of the Council on American-Islamic Relations, an organization devoted to the promoting understanding of Islam and the rights of Muslims in America.

Mr. Tariq Hamdi Al-Azami is a free-lance journalist and an independent research consultant on contemporary Islamic movements.

Dr. Charles Butterworth is a professor at the University of Maryland and an expert on Ibn Rushd and Al-Farabi. He is co-author with William Zartman of *Between the State and Islam*. He is a member of the Board of Advisors of the Minaret of Freedom Institute.

Dr. Louis Cantori is Major General Matthew C. Horner Chair of Military Theory, Marine Corps University. Quantico, Virginia for 1997-98, Professor of Political Science at the University of Maryland, Baltimore County. He is editor of *Political Inclusion and Exclusion in the Middle East and North Africa*. The views expressed here are personal and are not those of the U.S. Marine Corps.

Dr. Robert D. Crane heads the Center for Public Policy Research in Springfield, Virginia, was a policy advisor to the Nixon administration, and is the author of *Shaping the Future: Challenge and Response*.

Ms. Joyce Davis is a journalist at National Public Radio and was a fellow with the United States Institute of Peace.

Ms. Laura Drake teaches political science at American University and is a research fellow at the United Association for Studies and Research.

Dr. Michael Collins Dunn is a senior analyst at and co-founder of the International Estimate Inc. and of its biweekly newsletter, *The Estimate*. A former lecturer at Georgetown University's Center for Contemporary Arab Studies, his work appears regularly in the journal Middle East Policy.

Dr. Graham Fuller is a senior political scientist at the RAND Corporation and was a vice-chairman of the National Intelligence Council at the CIA. He has written many books about the Islamic movement and Middle East politics.

Mr. Anwar Haddam was an elected member of the Algerian Parliament and represents the Islamic Salvation Front (F.I.S.) in the United States.

Dr. Jafar Shaikh Idriss is former professor of Islamic studies at the Institute of Islamic and Arabic Science in America and chairman of the founding committee of the American Open University in Virginia.

Mr. Mehmood Kazmi is Distributing Manager for Astrolabe Pictures, a producer and distributor of Islamic videos.

Dr. Akram Kharoubi is a professor at Al-Quds University in Jerusalem.

Dr. Muhammad Mosleh is with the global Center for Democracy and Human Rights.

Dr. Mazin Muttabaqani is an assistant professor of the College of Da`wah in Madinah Munawwara.

Dr. Bashir Nafi is former associate editor of the American Journal of Islamic Social Sciences and has written extensively on the Islamic movement.

Mr. Robert G. Neumann is a senior advisor at the Center for Strategic and International Studies and a former ambassador to Afghanistan, Morocco, and Saudi Arabia. His academic career includes 19 years teaching at UCLA in foreign service and political science.

Dr. Stephen C. Pelletiere is a professor at the Strategic Studies Institute co-located with the U.S. Army War College. From 1982 until 1987 he was an intelligence officer in Washington monitoring the Iran-Iraq War. He has written three books on the Middle East, most recently one on the war in Kuwait.

Mr. Saleh Saleh is former President of the Dar-al-Hijrah Islamic Center.

Dr. Emad Shahin is a lecturer at George Washington University.

Mr. Jafar Shaib is a former Saudi Arabian human rights activist.

Dr. Abdullah Shaikh is a Sudanese Islamist and a former research fellow at the United Association for Studies and Research.

Dr. Osman Shinaishin is a prominent Islamic thinker and activist.

Dr. Antony Sullivan is an Associate at the Center for Middle Eastern and North African Studies at the University of Michigan and has published widely on the Islamic world.

Dr. Ahmed Yousef is Executive Director of the United Association for Studies and Research and Editor-in-Chief of the *Middle East Affairs Journal.* He is an experienced journalist and author of many titles including *Political Islam and Contemporary Thought.*

Dr. I. William Zartman is a professor of International Studies and Conflict Resolution and Director of African Studies at Johns Hopkins University's School for Advanced International Studies, past president of the Middle East Studies Association, and founding president of the American Institute for Maghrib Studies.

Islamic Roundtables is a serial publication of the United Association for Studies and Research (UASR). It serves to make available to the public the proceedings of the UASR Roundtables in which Muslim and non-Muslim experts on Islamic affairs meet with Muslim intellectuals and activists for an open discussion of vital issues regarding the Islamic movement and the Muslim world of interest to academics, policymakers, and journalists.

Islamic Roundtables #1 is co-published by United Association for Studies and Research (UASR), P. O. Box 1210, Annandale, VA 22003-1210 and the American Muslim Foundation (AMF), 1212 New York Avenue NW, Washington, DC 20005-6102. This inaugural issue has been edited by Imad-ad-Dean Ahmad and Ahmed Yousef.